World Cruising Survey

By the same author

WORLD CRUISING ROUTES
ISBN 0-87742-246-X

A brilliantly comprehensive guide to nearly 300 cruising routes around the world. It contains essential information on winds, currents, regional and seasonal weather as well as a great deal of first-hand advice gained during the author's six-year circumnavigation and subsequent journalistic assignments.

All the necessary information for planning an extended cruise in any of the world's oceans has been brought together for the first time in a single volume. While this book is primarily an aid to route planning, it will also be useful during a cruise to select alternative destinations if the need arises.

WORLD CRUISING SURVEY

Jimmy Cornell

INTERNATIONAL MARINE PUBLISHING COMPANY
Camden, Maine

International Marine Publishing Company
A Division of TAB BOOKS, Inc.
P.O. Box 220, Camden, Maine 04843

First published in Great Britain by Adlard Coles, 1989

ISBN: 0-87742-250-8

Printed and bound in Great Britain

International Marine Publishing Company offers software for sale. For information and a catalog, please contact TAB Software Department, Blue Ridge Summit, PA 17924-0850.

CONTENTS

For Doina and Ivan,
the best crew any father could wish for

ACKNOWLEDGEMENTS

This book is based on the contribution of so many people that it is impossible to mention them all by name. Over one thousand yachts were involved in the various surveys that form the basis of this book and listing them all would take up too much space, but my thanks go to all of them.

I am particularly indebted to the customs and port authorities in some key locations around the world who have either allowed me to sift through their records or have generously compiled themselves the statistics of yacht arrivals and departures. Unfortunately some officers who have helped me did not give their names, but I wish to thank those who have:

William Hinkle, of the Panama Canal Commission

Ian Brash, of the Whangarei Customs Office

G. N. Pathikirikorale, Counsellor at the Sri Lanka High Commission, London

J. Nuza, Customs Officer, Gibraltar

Miss Sharon Gan Chew Chee, of the Port of Singapore Authority

Fernando Fernandez Melle, Junta del Puerto de Las Palmas y La Luz

Luis Morais, of Horta Marina in the Azores

Mrs Brenda Rainer, of the Bermuda Customs Office

My work entails a lot of travelling and in many parts of the world I have been helped by tourism offices. I wish to express my belated gratitude to the following people who have supported my various projects and, often unknowingly, contributed indirectly to this book:

José Antonio Torrellas of the Canary Islands Government

Arturo Molina and José Ortega of the Patronato de Turismo de Gran Canaria

Patricia Nehaul of the Barbados Board of Tourism

Joe Viale of the Gibraltar Tourist Office

Joao Carlos Fraga of the Azores Tourist Board

My thanks also to:

Juan Francisco Martin, the Port Captain of Mogan, on Gran Canaria, for whom nothing is ever impossible.

Angel Luis Padron of Club Vela Latina Canaria, my loyal friend in Las Palmas.

Gilberto Duque Lugo, Commodore of the Yacht Club in Santa Cruz de la Palma.

Reds Packer, the sorely tried president of the Barbados Yachting Association, without whose constant struggle the ARC would have either ceased or gone to another Caribbean island.

Leo Hageman and the Antigua Yacht Club for their support with the TRANSARC.

Micko Sheppard-Capurro and Ernest Felipes of Sheppard's Marina in Gibraltar.

Alan Brunström of INMARSAT who was instrumental in getting the Communications Survey off the ground.

Ken Watson of Avon Inflatables Ltd for his support in the Liferaft Survey.

Walt Gleckler of the Orange Coast Community College who invited me to a lecture tour in California during which the idea for this book was born.

Dr Peter Noble, who scrutinized the contents of the recommended medicine chest and made some valuable suggestions of his own.

Bill Dixon, who spent countless hours trying to turn my many ideas into reality and has succeeded in designing *La Aventura*, a boat that comes closest to my own ideal of a cruising yacht.

Trevor Moulds of Perkins Engines, my constant source of reference concerning diesel engines.

Yachting World magazine for its continuing support in my various projects, from the ARC to the Pacific and Atlantic Surveys, first published in its pages. I am greatly indebted to the editor, Dick Johnson, who is always the first sounding board on which I try my various new ideas.

Across the Atlantic, I have enjoyed a long friendship over the telephone wires with Bernadette Brennan, deputy editor of *Cruising World* magazine, whose suggestions on various matters have been of great value.

My assistant, Trish Jenkins, for sifting through countless survey forms panning for tiny nuggets of wisdom.

This list would not be complete without acknowledging the contribution of my editor, Janet Murphy, whose constant encouragement, tact and flexibility have earned my unfaltering loyalty.

My deepest gratitude, however, goes to my wife Gwenda for her valiant attempts to coordinate my various activities and for her unexhausted patience in dealing with my self-imposed deadlines, which I could never meet without her help.

FOREWORD

by George Day, Editorial Director,
Cruising World and *Sailing World*

The book you are holding in your hands is unique in the forest of sailing books published each year. It is the result of years of work, more years of thinking and the vast sailing experience of the author. Behind Jimmy Cornell lies a circumnavigation aboard his first boat *Aventura*, during which he interviewed hundreds of his fellow cruising folk. Those interviews evolved into two earlier books, *Modern Ocean Cruising* and *Ocean Cruising Survey*, both published by Adlard Coles.

Also behind him lies the experience of organizing the Atlantic Rally for Cruisers (ARC), which has brought hundreds of boats and sailors across the Atlantic via the trade wind route. Naturally, during these annual events, Jimmy has taken the time to survey those sailing, and these surveys have added tremendously to the body of knowledge accumulated during his trip around the world.

Sailors who seek to set out for long cruises are information fiends. They gather information on gear, boats, engines, dinghies, gallies, self-steering gear, sails and much more. Files grow thick with brochures, magazine clippings and the notes jotted after cockpit discussions. But no matter how well sailors research the thousands of items on their lists, the real learning about what works and what doesn't happens once they've sailed out there across an ocean to some far port. Experience is what counts. And, there is a subtle but significant difference in the perceptions of those with experience at sea and those with only anticipation and thick research files.

Quite a few years ago I was lucky enough to sail into Academy Bay in the Galapagos Archipelago on my way across the Pacific. Although I had spent nearly a year in the Atlantic and Caribbean and had visited many of the favoured cruising harbours, the Academy Bay landfall struck a deep chord. We dropped the hook among approximately twenty other cruising boats and at once noticed there wasn't a clunker among them. The flags of perhaps ten nations flew from the transoms. The boats had the look of years of seafaring, years of improvement and care, and the tidy, ready look of vessels prepared for the trans-Pacific passage to French Polynesia.

During our weeks in the Galapagos we spent our time among this fraternity of offshore sailors, comparing notes on where we'd been and where we were going. We discussed gear and sails, boats and rigging, dinghies and hull paint. I was a young man, so looking back now I think of those weeks in the Galapagos as a kind of graduate seminar in offshore sailing taught by a varied and somewhat ragtag group of professors who all shared one dynamic quality: seatime.

There are several ports like Academy Bay in the circuit around the world. To name a few, you'll find the offshore fleet in harbours like Las Palmas in the Canaries; Grenada in the Caribbean; Balboa, Panama; Papeete, Tahiti; the Bay of Islands, New Zealand; Bali; Sri Lanka; and Durban, South Africa. Each of these ports offers sailors the companionship of many other like-minded souls, whose shared experience can be illuminating.

In a way, Jimmy Cornell's *World Cruising Survey* is the best cruising port available, for it brings together in one place the wisdom of hundreds of sailors who have seatime. Like my visit to the Galapagos, a passage through the pages of this book offers sailors an advanced seminar in offshore and world cruising. The opinions, the experience, the ideas gleaned from around the world, have been distilled into meaningful discussions and charts. The information has been organized far better than most of us would ever organize it for ourselves.

And, most importantly, the distilled experience in these pages has the ring of pure authority. This is the way it is out there, world cruising. All you have to do is learn from the shared experience and prepare yourself for your own seatime.

1989

INTRODUCTION

Many changes have occurred in the ten years since I carried out my first cruising survey in the South Pacific. There has been a general improvement in boat design, equipment is much more reliable and marine electronics are at long last worthy of the age we live in. In some ways the people have changed too, both those who go cruising and those whom the cruisers have to deal with in the places visited.

The advances made in communication technology particularly have made it possible for those who need to keep in touch with their business or professional life to be able to undertake lengthy cruises far away from their normal base. These jet setting sailors, however, are still in the minority and many people still go to sea in order to get away from the stresses and conventions of modern society.

Yet in spite of certain changes, whether on a technical or a human level, life afloat has remained in essence the same. The sea itself never changes and the challenge it presents to the present-day sailor is as powerful as ever. In dealing with this challenge, whether in the preparatory stage of planning a cruise or when actually cruising, many of the problems that occur have changed very little. During the last ten years I have conducted several surveys in various parts of the world, in which I tried to examine as objectively as possible every single aspect of cruising. This book attempts to concentrate the essence of all those surveys and thereby bring together the collective wisdom of hundreds of sailors whom I have interviewed in various parts of the world. My task has been helped by the fact that during the last three years I have been involved with the ARC (Atlantic Rally for Cruisers), an annual event which brings together some two hundred yachts making the transatlantic passage from the Canaries to the Caribbean. There cannot be a better cross-section of the present cruising scene than the one provided by the ARC. Talking to and observing the participants in the last three ARCs has taught me a lot about what is right and what is wrong with today's cruising boats, their equipment and often their crews and skippers too. I have taken note of these observations myself and many features of my new boat *La Aventura* are based on suggestions culled from the ARC participants and my previous surveys.

Whereas most of my earlier work took place in the Pacific, in recent years, more by force than by choice, my base of operations has moved to the Atlantic. Although the South Pacific continues to be for many sailors the most tempting cruising destination in the world, it is in the North Atlantic that most development in the yachting field is taking place. Many important yachting centres are spread around the rim of the North Atlantic and during a cruise to the Canaries, Caribbean or the Azores, one comes across anything that is new in yachting. The weather in the North Atlantic can also teach us sailors a thing or two, as it is amongst the roughest in the world, from mega-hurricane Gilbert to vicious winter gales. Therefore I feel that the lessons learnt in the North Atlantic are valid for any part of the world and although a great deal of the material which forms the basis of this book was gathered in the Atlantic, its worldwide validity cannot be doubted. The ARC itself, which is my constant source of material, attracts boats and people from all over the world. This gives me the opportunity to keep up to date on boats and equipment from many countries, not just those bordering on the Atlantic. As organizer of this event I learn about both good and bad things concerning yacht design, boatbuilding, equipment, instrumentation and a host of other matters. The principal aim of *World Cruising Survey* is to make this information available to anyone who is interesting in cruising.

The greatest satisfaction of an author is to be told by his readers that they have enjoyed his writings. In my case, the satisfaction goes further as many people have told me that my books have also been a source of practical and helpful information. There are many yachts cruising the oceans of the world whose owners were helped in preparing for their cruise by suggestions made in *Modern Ocean Cruising* and *Ocean Cruising Survey*. Much has changed since I wrote those books, so in *World Cruising Survey* I have tried to take a fresh look at the present state of ocean cruising and particularly the areas where change is continually taking place. Yet although yacht design and equipment have taken great strides forward during the last decade, many of the basic principles of offshore sailing and seamanship have remained the same.

The findings of my earlier surveys, which formed the basis of my first two books, are only used in this book as terms of comparison against which to assess the changes that have occurred in the intervening years. Many of the findings of the later surveys have not been published before.

1. *The Suva Survey.* A first cruising survey was conducted in Fiji in 1978 and dealt with various aspects of cruising boat design.
2. *The Cruising Survey.* A more extensive survey was conducted the following year in a variety of places in the South Pacific. Its findings presented a comprehensive picture of life afloat.
3. *The Seawives Survey.* Cruising women in a variety of boats sailing in the South Pacific took part in this survey which examined the role and attitudes of sailing women.
4. *The Circumnavigators.* Twelve crews from a variety of countries who had successfully completed their circumnavigation formed the basis of a comprehensive survey undertaken in 1983.
5. *The Pacific Survey.* The skippers and crew of fifty long distance cruising boats were interviewed in the South Pacific at the end of 1984 on a comprehensive range of subjects with a particular focus on equipment and instrumentation.
6. *The Atlantic Survey.* Cruising boat design, equipment as well as different aspects of life afloat were covered in a survey conducted in 1985/86 among one hundred boats on both sides of the Atlantic.
7. *The Liferaft Survey.* The skippers of one hundred boats who had recently crossed the Atlantic were interviewed in the Caribbean on the subject of liferafts and their design. The survey was conducted in association with Avon Inflatables Ltd.
8. *The Ideal Cruising Boat Survey.* Two hundred participants in the first ARC took part in this survey which attempted to see if there was a consensus on the essential features of the ideal cruising boat.
9. *The Communications Survey.* The present and future of marine communications were examined by this survey conducted among participants in ARC 86 and commissioned by INMARSAT, the international satellite communications organization.
10. *The Equipment Survey.* The quality and performance of marine equipment and instrumentation were analysed in this comprehensive survey involving almost two hundred yachts taking part in ARC 87.
11. *The Cruising Life Survey.* Participants in the ARC and TRANSARC rallies supplied the data for an assessment of the daily problems of life at sea.
12. *The World Yacht Movement Survey.* A worldwide survey of the distribution and movement of cruising yachts was carried out between 1985 and 1988. Its findings are based on personal

research, as well as on data provided by customs, immigration and port authorities in sixteen key locations throughout the world.

One of the aims of this book is to provide an answer to the questions that I am asked each year by participants joining the various events with which I am involved. As the questions are usually put at the critical preparatory stage for their forthcoming voyage, I believe that they have a relevance for anyone preparing to leave on a longer cruise. Moreover, during a lecture tour undertaken in California in 1988, I was fortunate to gain an insight into the kind of problems that preoccupy those who are preparing for a voyage. The theme of the lectures was 'Planning Your Dream' and perhaps the most successful section was the question time, which often lasted longer than the lecture itself. The questions asked by the audience enabled me to form a distinct picture of the kind of problems that matter most to people and the things they really want to know. The areas of interest sometimes took me by surprise, as I realized how much people knew about boats and equipment, yet how little about the conditions of life at sea and other aspects of cruising. Some of the questions I was asked made me realize that many people have little idea where cruising boats sail to, how they get there and when. This is the reason why I decided to include in this book a chapter on the world distribution of cruising yachts.

The ARC has been an invaluable source of inspiration and I am grateful to the participants who took the time to answer my many questions so diligently and often in great detail. From the amount of mishaps, breakages and emergencies that have been included, this book may appear at times to be a catalogue of disasters and the worst advertisement for cruising. However, I firmly believe that in sailing more than in any other field we can learn a lot from our own mistakes, which does not imply that we have to make the mistakes ourselves, just to gain the experience. The mistakes of others can be equally instructive in helping us to avoid similar problems. The mishaps and emergencies that I have included are those which I feel are relevant to other sailors.

My main objective, however, remains to present an overview of the present cruising scene, seen mostly through the eyes of those who are out there cruising, and in this way help others plan and prepare their own dream voyage.

Chapter 1

THE AGE OF REDISCOVERY

Five centuries after Columbus pushed westward the limits of the known world, hundreds of sailors set off each year in search of adventure, moved by that same urge to penetrate the unknown. In this age of space technology, mass tourism and fast communications, the sea remains a great challenge and there is little to equal the satisfaction felt by every sailor on the successful completion of an ocean passage. This challenge, coupled with the temptation of exotic destinations beckoning from beyond the horizon, acts as a magnet to which many are irresistibly drawn.

Some outstanding voyages have been accomplished in recent years and cruising yachts have reached the remotest corners of the world, from the frozen wastes of the Antarctic to the steaming upper reaches of the Amazon. These remarkable voyages completed in small boats have spurred other sailors to follow their example. It can almost be said that the hundreds of sailing yachts crossing the oceans of the world signal the dawn of a new age of discovery.

Although the number of people who undertake offshore voyages has shown a steady increase over the last ten years, it has not been quite as substantial as was predicted. The most important factor that has contributed to the recent expansion in offshore cruising has been the improvement in yacht design and construction. As a result, there is a considerable increase in the number of sailing boats which have the potential to undertake offshore voyages, even if the number of those who actually leave on cruises of long duration is still relatively small.

In parallel with the increase in the global yacht population, or as a result of it, there has also been an expansion of yachting facilities; the improvement of port facilities for yachts and the building of marinas in attractive locations have encouraged many sailors to cruise away from home. Another recent develoment has been the large number of yachts which are based abroad, especially in Europe. This particularly applies to owners from countries where, due to the climate, the sailing season is short; or those lacking a coastline, such as Switzerland and Austria. The reduction in air fares and the availability of berthing facilities in marinas developed in pleasant cruising areas have encouraged many owners to base their boats away from home. Often these owners move their base from season to season to provide a greater variety to their cruising. This applies particularly to the Mediterranean where the choice of good wintering facilities is very wide. Yet another recent phenomenon is the proliferation of yachts flying flags of convenience, the usual reason being the owner's attempt to avoid paying national taxes or import duties.

Yet in spite of the increase in the number of cruising boats that undertake offshore passages, the ocean routes show little variation and the number of yachts that stray away from them is small. Most sailors seem happy to stick to the well-tried routes, which have their origin in climatic and oceanic conditions. Like migrating birds, cruising yachts follow certain patterns and a useful factor that must be borne in mind when examining their movement is the seasonal character of most trans-ocean passages. Thus, the number of yachts undertaking winter passages in higher latitudes (e.g. Northern Europe to North America, North America to the Far East, Australia to New Zealand, and vice versa) is so small as to be almost negligible. Similarly, summer passages in tropical areas are considerably less frequent, mainly due to the danger of tropical storms, the hurricane season coinciding in most parts of the world with the summer months. These factors narrow down the existing cruising routes to well defined 'lanes' in all oceans. Sailing yachts are much more susceptible than large commercial vessels to prevailing wind and sea conditions, which govern the routes that they are able to sail. For this reason these main cruising routes are unlikely to change greatly in future years.

During the last three years I have investigated the worldwide movement of yachts to find out exactly how much of an increase there has been in the number of cruising boats in the years since I undertook my own circumnavigation. Although statistics rarely make exciting reading, this chapter attempts to show where the cruising boats go and when they go, and perhaps just as important for those who are looking for solitude, what places to avoid and at what times.

In an earlier survey on seamanship I drew the conclusion that one of the most important attributes of good seamanship is a strong dose of common sense. This is what most cruising people are guided by, so that when one discovers that perhaps only a dozen cruising boats cross the Atlantic from east to west on the northern routes in any one year, while one thousand take the more southerly route, it must mean that the vast majority know something that one ought to know too. By saying this, I do not aim to discourage anyone from attempting less frequented routes; on the contrary, after reading these statistics some people might be tempted to choose one of the less frequented routes or ports of call. I hope the information in this chapter will cater both for those who wish to know where most cruisers go and for those who want to find out how to avoid the crowds.

Both when collecting this data and in my various surveys I have been interested primarily in the long distance cruising boats, that is those who have been away from home base for at least one year and are undertaking a long ocean voyage. In order to understand the present yachting scene better and particularly to gain an overview of the most popular cruising destinations, the movement of yachts will be examined in a number of key locations along the principal world cruising circuit, which is depicted on Map 1 (see over). Any ocean voyaging yacht must pass through some of these ports during a longer cruise, and during 1987 and 1988 I visited many of these ports myself and so could both gather statistics and talk to many of the men and women behind the figures. In this way I obtained exact figures concerning yacht arrivals from port and customs authorities throughout the world. In order to present a clearer picture, the results have been processed on a regional basis by dividing the world into six areas coinciding with the two hemispheres of the three great oceans.

North Atlantic

The northern half of what was known in Columbus's time as the Ocean Sea is where most exploration started and its two shores still have the largest concentration of sailing vessels in the world. Although the northern routes were plied by the Vikings long before Columbus, modern sailors prefer warmer weather, so that the tropical and subtropical routes continue to be the most popular.

Northern routes

The transatlantic routes of higher latitudes are used only in the summer months by a handful of cruising boats sailing from Northern Europe to North America and vice versa, their number being augmented by yachts taking part in events such as the Carlsberg Singlehanded Transatlantic Race. Most westbound passages along this northern route are made between 1 June and 15 September, but

Map 1 Principal Passage Routes

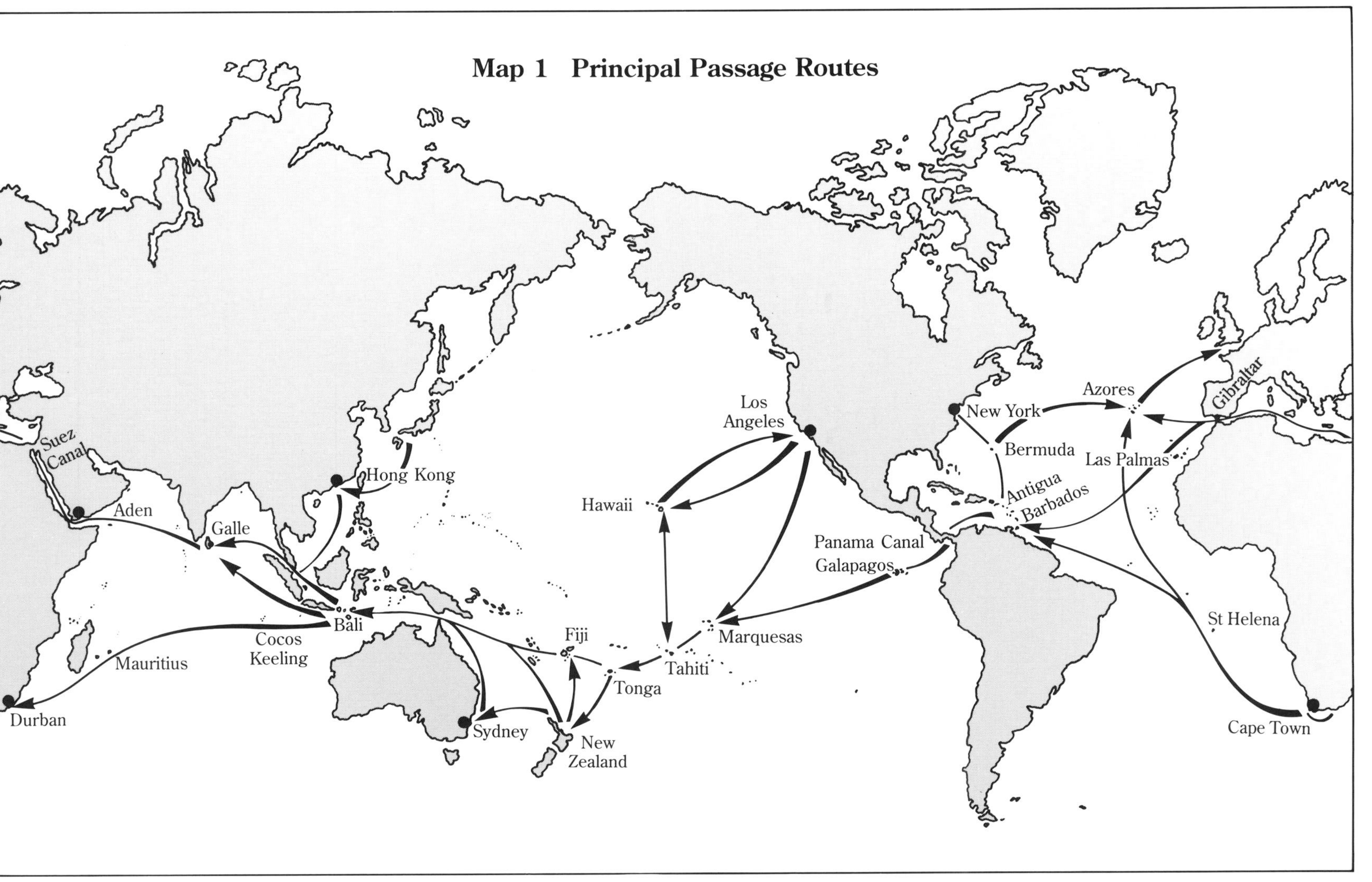

Table 1. YACHT ARRIVALS IN HORTA 1985–87

Flag	*1985*	*1986*	*1987*
Argentina	1	–	3
Australia	–	–	3
Austria	7	7	9
Bahamas	–	1	1
Belgium	9	13	8
Bermuda	–	1	–
Brazil	1	4	1
Bulgaria	1	1	1
Canada	23	21	27
Cayman Islands	–	1	–
Chile	–	–	1
Denmark	12	19	16
Finland	2	6	14
France	218	246	187
Gabon	1	–	–
Germany	30	37	54
Ireland	1	4	2
Israel	–	1	–
Italy	16	19	20
Japan	–	1	1
Liberia	–	1	–
Malta	–	–	3
Netherlands	16	51	28
Norway	12	11	17
New Zealand	–	2	4
Panama	3	3	3
Poland	2	3	1
Portugal	6	7	10
S. Africa	8	10	4
Saudi Arabia	2	–	–
Spain	8	6	5
Sweden	12	17	20
Switzerland	16	20	12
United Kingdom	168	139	168
USA	123	106	100
Vanuatu	–	–	1
Venezuela	–	1	1
W. Indies	–	–	2
Zimbabwe	–	–	1
Total	**698**	**759**	**728**

because of the prevailing westerly winds and generally inclement weather, this direct route is not very popular with cruising boats.

The majority of boats making the east to west crossing starting from Northern Europe go south from the English Channel in search of warmer weather, either sailing direct to their destination or via the Azores. Only a few boats, usually those starting from Scandinavia or more northern ports, make a detour to the north, following a track close to the great circle route. As the northerly route passes through an area with a high incidence of fog and ice, it is usually undertaken later in the summer, when much of the ice has melted. Because of this problem, and for other reasons, a detour is often made to include the Azores – although longer, it has the advantage of warmer weather and a mid-Atlantic stop for reprovisioning.

The west to east crossing of the North Atlantic is undoubtedly easier and can also be made either direct or via Bermuda and/or the Azores. Most yachts bound for Northern Europe from ports NE of New York sail across direct. The great circle route from North America passes south of Nova Scotia and Newfoundland from where it splits into a northern branch, going round the north of Scotland towards Scandinavia, and a southern branch to the English Channel. The danger of encountering ice deters most yachtsmen from choosing this route, and the number of cruising boats attempting to sail direct to Northern Europe is very small. Those leaving from more southern ports on the Atlantic seaboard of the United States usually call at Bermuda. Virtually all the yachts heading for the Mediterranean choose to sail there by way of the Azores.

Situated in the centre of the North Atlantic, the Azores are a most convenient springboard for a number of routes. The new marina at Horta on the island of Faial is a hive of activity between the middle of May and the middle of June when hundreds of cruising boats call there on their way from North America and the Caribbean to Europe or the Mediterranean. More than three quarters of all the boats that call at Horta in a year pass through during those two busy months. Table 1 shows the number and flag of the yachts that called there between 1985 and 1987. The figures do not show a great variation, although two races from France in 1986 brought more yachts to the Azores that summer than is normally the case.

Early summer is the time when most cruising yachts pass through the Azores and by looking closer at their movement on a monthly basis, the last port of call as well as the destination after the Azores, some interesting conclusions can be drawn (see Table 2). One significant change in recent years is the larger number of boats arriving in the Azores directly from the Caribbean and not via Bermuda as used to be the accepted procedure. This trend was started by delivery skippers on charter boats, always in a hurry to reach the Mediterranean. Bermuda is also bypassed by a number of US boats who sail direct from more northerly ports to the Azores in mid-summer, their example being followed in August by yachts from Canada who obviously have to wait for warmer weather before crossing the waters near Newfoundland (where ice lingers on until well into summer). Arrivals from the Caribbean peter out after July and none were recorded between September and January. Yachts crossing from Bermuda also seem to avoid the hurricane season with a total of only eight yachts arriving from Bermuda between September and the following March.

The destinations after the Azores are split almost equally between yachts bound for Northern Europe and those heading for

Table 2. YACHT MOVEMENT TO AND FROM HORTA 1987

	Jan	*Feb*	*Mar*	*Apr*	*May*	*June*	*July*	*Aug*	*Sep*	*Oct*	*Nov*	*Dec*	**Total**
Arrivals from													
Caribbean	–	3	4	43	89	91	19	7	–	–	–	–	**256**
Bermuda	–	–	1	9	51	103	51	7	4	2	1	–	**229**
USA/Canada	–	–	–	2	2	14	20	18	1	–	–	–	**57**
Cape Verde/ W. Africa	–	–	1	–	1	1	1	2	–	–	–	–	**6**
Brazil	–	–	–	–	2	4	3	–	–	1	–	–	**10**
St Helena/S. Africa	–	–	–	–	3	1	2	–	–	–	–	–	**6**
N. Europe	–	–	–	2	7	4	10	5	4	–	1	–	**33**
Spain/Portugal/ Gibraltar	–	–	–	–	–	2	3	1	–	1	–	–	**7**
Canaries/Madeira	–	–	–	2	1	2	1	–	–	–	–	–	**6**
Other Azores	1	–	1	1	12	23	49	27	4	–	1	–	**119**
Destination													
Caribbean	–	–	–	–	2	–	–	–	1	–	–	–	**3**
Bermuda	–	–	–	–	2	2	1	3	1	1	–	–	**10**
USA/Canada	–	–	–	–	2	2	6	2	1	–	–	–	**13**
N. Europe	1	1	5	17	71	81	52	16	1	1	–	–	**246**
Spain/Portugal	–	2	–	6	12	33	14	13	2	1	–	–	**83**
Med/Gibraltar	–	–	1	30	62	72	28	9	4	–	1	–	**207**
Canaries/Madeira	–	–	–	1	–	5	1	3	1	1	–	–	**12**
Other Azores	–	–	–	5	17	50	57	21	1	–	2	–	**153**

ports on the Iberian peninsula or in the Mediterranean. The number of yachts making east to west passages and stopping in the Azores is insignificant and in 1987 only 13 yachts went from the Azores to the USA or Canada, all of them in summer with an additional three heading for the Caribbean. There were more yachts using the Azores as an intermediate point on the way from the Mediterranean to Northern Europe. The same also happens in the opposite direction, with yachts calling in the Azores between ports in Northern Europe or Ireland and the Mediterranean.

Southern routes

The vast majority of cruising sailors do not like cold weather and this is the main reason why the most frequented routes coincide with the warmer parts of the world. The North Atlantic is no exception and this is why its southern part attracts more cruising boats. The majority of east to west transatlantic routes have their starting point in the Canary Islands, with only a small number of yachts setting off from Madeira or directly from continental Europe. Most passages are undertaken between 15 November and 31 December, with only a few boats making the crossing later in winter, although the winds continue to be favourable. As the sailing seasons in the Caribbean and Europe, particularly the Mediterranean, are so finely matched, both cruising and charter boats plan their transatlantic passage for the interim period. There are other considerations too, such as the wish to spend Christmas in a Caribbean island and the necessity of avoiding passages during the hurricane season. Therefore passages are rarely undertaken after 1 June or before 1 November because of the danger of hurricanes in the western part of the ocean.

The number of yachts crossing the Atlantic from the Canaries has been increasing steadily over the years and has now reached an annual figure of approximately 1000. This increase is due not only to the larger number of European sailors tempted by the Caribbean, but also to the number of charter boats. Because of the high investment involved in charter boats and the limited season in the Mediterranean, many charter operators move their boats every year from the Mediterranean to the Caribbean in October/November and back again in April/May.

Although a few boats start their Atlantic crossing in Madeira, the vast majority carry on to the Canaries before taking the trade wind route across. Las Palmas de Gran Canaria is by far the most popular Canarian port, mainly because of its excellent shops. The small boat harbour, which has been greatly improved in recent years, is bursting at the seams in the second half of November with some 300 yachts getting ready to leave across the 'pond'. Most of them are participants in the annual Atlantic Rally for Cruisers (ARC), which starts from Las Palmas on the last Saturday in

Flag	*1986*	*1987*
France	287	318
United Kingdom	123	157
Spain	32	124
Germany	71	110
USA	75	74
Switzerland	31	39
Netherlands	26	37
Canada	21	31
Sweden	22	27
Norway	17	24
Italy	28	23
Denmark	14	23
Australia	8	11
Austria	11	9
Finland	12	8
Belgium	17	7
Brazil	3	4
Poland	2	4
Honduras	–	3
New Zealand	2	3
Yugoslavia	–	3
Korea	–	3
Bulgaria	–	2
Greece	3	2
Ireland	–	2
Israel	–	2
Portugal	2	1
Venezuela	2	1
Argentina	3	1
Others	3	9
Total	**815**	**1062**

Table 3.
YACHT ARRIVALS IN LAS PALMAS 1986–87

November and finishes the 2700-mile passage in Barbados. Many of the yachts not taking part in the ARC stop at one of the other Canary Islands before setting off across the Atlantic. However, the figures in Table 3 showing the number and flag of the yachts that called at Las Palmas in 1987 are representative of the entire archipelago. The figures show an increase of almost 20 per cent over those for 1986.

About 90 per cent of the yachts stopping in the Canaries are on their way to a transatlantic destination. A survey conducted among participants in the ARC showed that the average time spent by the boats in the Canaries was only 13 days. Relatively few boats spend any length of time cruising the seven islands of the archipelago, usually because they arrive too late and are not prepared to waste any time before leaving for the Caribbean. However, the situation is rapidly changing as the Canary Islands government positively encourages cruising, and yachting facilities are being built or improved in all the islands.

Although most boats leaving the Canaries are bound for the Caribbean, two other destinations which are becoming increasingly popular are West Africa and Brazil. The former is primarily the haunt of French boats, who were the first to sail in large numbers to Senegal and its southern neighbours. Most continue their voyage across the Atlantic later in the season. Brazil is also included by more cruising sailors on their itinerary, most of whom restrict their forays to the north eastern part of this vast country, with only a few continuing towards Rio de Janeiro.

A compromise solution for those who do not wish to make a detour to the African mainland, but prefer to break the passage to the Caribbean, is a stop in the Cape Verde Islands, which are conveniently situated close to the recommended trade wind route. There appears to be a definite pattern in the choice of Caribbean destination, with North European and American yachts making their landfall in English speaking Barbados, St Lucia or Antigua, while French yachts and some other Europeans prefer the French speaking islands of Martinique or Guadeloupe.

Approximately 40 per cent of the boats reaching the Caribbean by the trade wind route make their landfall in Barbados. Table 4 shows the flags and last port of call of the yachts that arrived in Barbados from July 1986 to June 1987, which gives a good indication of the kind of ocean voyaging yachts that reach the Caribbean during the course of a year. The figures in the right-hand column show the figures for the previous season, the considerable increase being

Table 4.
YACHT ARRIVALS IN BARBADOS 1986/87 SEASON

July 1986–June 1987 Arrival from:

Flag	*Canaries*	*Cape Verde*	*W. Africa*	*Madeira*	*Gibraltar*	*French Guyana*	*Brazil*	*Uruguay*	*St Helena*	*S. Africa*	*USA*	*Bermuda*	*Other Caribbean*	**Total**	*1985–86 season*
United Kingdom	101	7	1	1	3	3	3						27	**148**	52
USA	49	7				2	2		1			1	12	**74**	56
Canada	8	2					1		1	1		1	1	**15**	11
France	9	9	4	1		4	1						7	**35**	25
Norway	15	1											4	**20**	10
Sweden	19												1	**20**	16
Italy	4												2	**6**	5
Netherlands	17	3	1			1							3	**25**	13
Cayman Islands	3												1	**4**	–
Denmark	10	1											2	**13**	8
Finland	6			1									1	**8**	6
Germany	24	1		1			3				1			**30**	11
Spain	4	1												**5**	–
St Lucia													8	**8**	–
Belgium	2	1												**3**	2
Bermuda													1	**1**	–
Australia	7					1	2							**10**	4
Austria	6												1	**7**	4
Ireland	2													**2**	2
Trinidad													2	**2**	–
New Zealand	1						1		1					**3**	3
Venezuela	1												1	**2**	–
St Vincent													1	**1**	–
Switzerland	4	1					1							**6**	10
Gibraltar	1	1												**2**	–
Yugoslavia	2													**2**	–
Hong Kong	1													**1**	1
India	1													**1**	–
Poland	1													**1**	2
Greece	1	1											1	**3**	–
Solomons	1													**1**	–
Israel	2													**2**	–
Argentina								1						**1**	–
Panama													2	**2**	–
Others															8
Total	**302**	**36**	**6**	**4**	**3**	**11**	**14**	**1**	**3**	**1**	**1**	**2**	**78**	**462**	**249**

entirely due to the ARC, which finished in Barbados and brought approximately 200 yachts to the island.

Three quarters of the yachts which arrived in Barbados in 1987 came from a transatlantic destination. The monthly arrival figures highlight the seasonal character of the transatlantic yacht movement with virtually no ocean crossings during the hurricane-prone months from July to October. The peak arrival time is December, as most cruising boats try to reach the Caribbean before Christmas.

The majority of boats sailing back to Europe from the Caribbean leave at the end of April or beginning of May. Antigua Sailing Week, which attracts racing, cruising and charter boats for a week of racing and festivities, signals the end of the safe season in the Caribbean after which most boats take their leave. From a total of 2348 yachts that cleared into English Harbour in 1987, only 7 per cent arrived from an overseas port, the rest all being local Caribbean traffic, implying that the foreign yachts had made their transatlantic landfall elsewhere. Even among the 167 yachts that arrived from overseas, only 111 came from across the Atlantic, most of the others coming from Bermuda (38) or direct from the USA (12). One interesting observation is that although the largest number of transatlantic yachts came from the Canaries, almost one third had left from a more northerly port, such as Madeira or Gibraltar, and there were even a few who had come direct from Northern Europe. Yacht movement in English Harbour was also broken down on a monthly basis, the busiest month (of 436 arrivals) being April, when traditionally yachts congregate in this famous harbour regarded as the premier yachting destination in the Caribbean.

A favourite stop for cruising boats, whether *en route* to North America or Europe, is the island of Bermuda, which welcomed

Table 5. YACHT MOVEMENT FROM BERMUDA 1987

	Jan	*Feb*	*Mar*	*Apr*	*May*	*June*	*July*	*Aug*	*Sep*	*Oct*	*Nov*	*Dec*	**Total**
Destination													
USA/Canada	–	–	1	31	162	155	42	12	6	8	3	1	**421**
Azores	–	1	2	32	124	61	19	5	1	2	–	–	**247**
Caribbean/Bahamas	2	–	–	2	4	5	9	3	18	112	99	13	**267**
Europe Direct	–	–	2	5	7	3	4	1	–	–	–	–	**22**
Local	–	–	–	–	–	6	4	–	–	6	1	1	**18**
Other	–	–	–	–	1	10	5	3	1	2	–	1	**23**
Total	**2**	**1**	**2**	**70**	**298**	**240**	**83**	**24**	**26**	**130**	**103**	**16**	**998**

almost 1000 yachts in 1987. Virtually all transatlantic departures were made from Bermuda in the first half of the year, being predominantly European boats returning home from the Caribbean. The second half of the year, from July to December, is dominated by US boats. Most yacht traffic in July is taken up by US boats returning home from the Caribbean or those making a short summer cruise to Bermuda. The other busy time is October and November when US boats head for the Caribbean via Bermuda, 95 per cent bound for the Virgin Islands.

Yacht movement in the first half of the year is extremely seasonal, half the number of boats that call at Bermuda in any one year arriving in the island between the middle of May and the middle of June, whether destined for the USA or Europe. The number of boats heading east across the Atlantic after the end of June is very small, only 27 boats sailing from Bermuda to the Azores in 1987 and 11 more taking a northerly route to Europe.

The worldwide movement of cruising yachts is dictated by the trade winds and is therefore predominantly east to west. Just as the sailors on the square riggers of yesteryear, modern sailors prefer to sail before the wind and this is why most circumnavigations are made in an east to west direction, very few yachts circling the globe from west to east. In the North Atlantic, the yachts on east to west routes include Europeans bound for the Caribbean or continuing to the Panama Canal as well as North Americans returning home. In recent years a considerable number of Americans have purchased their yachts in Europe and sailed them home instead of having them shipped, another factor which has contributed to the westward flow of yachts.

This east to west flow is nowhere more obvious than in Panama, where the number of Pacific bound yachts is always larger than that of yachts heading for the Atlantic. Table 6 shows the figures for 1987 and as the Panama Canal is such an important transit point for any boat undertaking a world voyage, the figures are a good indication of their approximate number. From the 362 boats that transited into the Pacific in 1987, approximately 300 carried on towards the South Pacific and most of those yachts will eventually complete a circumnavigation. The remaining boats were mostly Americans and Canadians returning to their home ports on the West Coast, often at the end of their own circumnavigations. The figures for 1985 are included only to show that in spite of the persistent rumours about impending troubles in Panama, the number of sailors who have tried to avoid the Canal has been insignificant. The only alternative to

Table 6. YACHT MOVEMENT THROUGH THE PANAMA CANAL 1985 & 87

	Total	Pacific–Atlantic	Atlantic–Pacific	1985
Austria	2	–	2	3
Australia	17	1	16	12
Belgium	4	1	3	3
Brazil	1	–	1	–
Canada	22	9	13	17
Colombia	10	5	5	9
Czechoslovakia	1	–	1	–
Denmark	6	–	6	3
Ecuador	2	–	2	1
Finland	2	–	2	3
France	63	6	57	73
Honduras	2	2	–	–
Iceland	1	–	1	–
Italy	1	–	1	4
Japan	3	–	3	4
Mexico	1	–	1	1
Malta	1	1	–	1
New Zealand	8	2	6	10
Norway	3	–	3	1
Netherlands	9	–	9	5
Panama	39	29	10	51
Poland	4	–	4	1
South Africa	2	–	2	4
Spain	1	–	1	–
Sri Lanka	1	–	1	–
Sweden	13	2	11	7
Switzerland	6	1	5	9
United Kingdom	61	15	46	42
USA	266	132	134	242
Virgin Islands	1	–	1	–
Venezuela	1	–	1	1
West Germany	14	–	14	15
Others	–	–	–	9
Total	**568**	**206**	**362**	**531**

Panama for anyone trying to reach the South Pacific is via Cape Horn, although a few sailors returning from the Atlantic to the Pacific coast of the USA have their boats trucked across the continent.

MEDITERRANEAN SEA

The number of foreign boats cruising in the Mediterranean has shown a remarkable increase in recent years. An estimated 2000 yachts are now cruising at any one time during the sailing season. This figure includes both people on longer cruises and North Europeans who keep their yachts in one of the Mediterranean countries. An even greater number of North European yachts are permanently based in the Mediterranean, but only a small proportion are actually cruised for any length of time. The main contributing factor in this development has been the steady improvement in yachting facilities, primarily the building of marinas.

No other region in the world has witnessed such an explosion in yachting as the Mediterranean and this expansion shows no sign of slowing down. To cope with the influx of yachts, both visiting and local, marinas have been built in all countries bordering on the Mediterranean, particularly in the most popular cruising areas. One of the busiest among these is Spain's Costa del Sol, mainly the stretch between Gibraltar and Malaga, although marinas can now be found along the entire Spanish coast. The Balearic Islands are another busy yachting centre with Palma de Mallorca as its nerve centre. How-

Aerial view of Gibraltar's two marinas, with the anchorage visible north of the runway.

ever, the largest number of yachts, mostly engaged in coastal cruising, is found along the French coast. To cope with the insatiable demand, many beautiful new marinas have been created to compete with the older fashionable ports of the Riviera. A favourite offshore destination for French based yachts is Corsica, as well as neighbouring Sardinia, which has also developed into a thriving yachting centre.

The Mediterranean has been described as the cradle of Western civilisation and for anyone even slightly interested in history there is probably no other area in the world to offer such a variety of interesting places to visit. Top of my own list is the Aegean, where many ancient monuments seem to have been created for the benefit of seafarers. Many ancient sites are easily reached from the sea, both in mainland Greece and its myriad islands, and along the Turkish coast. Not surprisingly, the Aegean has also seen a vast expansion in yachting in recent years, the number of cruising yachts being overshadowed by countless charter boats, both bareboat and crewed, as well as the ubiquitous swarms of sailing flotillas. In spite of the never ending animosity between the two countries bordering the Aegean, there is a steady flow of yachts between the Turkish ports of Asia Minor and the Greek islands. Yet another corner which is attracting an increasing number of foreign yachts is the Adriatic, particularly the Yugoslav coast and its offlying islands.

Although the Mediterranean enjoys good sailing weather from April to November and even in winter is never too cold, most cruising is restricted to the summer holiday season. For those who do not like crowds, the time to go is spring and autumn, when the weather can be perfect and the ports are not overflowing with visitors. Although most cruising in the Mediterranean is coastal, there are a few well defined offshore routes, used mainly by boats moving from one cruising area to another. There is also a certain migration of yachts from west to east in the spring, followed by a westerly migration in the autumn.

The two points of access into the Mediterranean from the west are Gibraltar and the Canal du Midi, although the latter is used mostly by smaller vessels of shallow draft. Gibraltar is undoubtedly the most important transit point for yachts in the world, which is demonstrated by the fact that over five thousand yachts flying the flags of 45 nations called at the Rock in 1987. The busiest time is during the summer months when yachts move in both directions through the Strait, the peak being reached in August of that year when a record number of 800 yachts cleared into Gibraltar. Their movement becomes increasingly unidirectional at other times, as the spring is the time when yachts call at Gibraltar on their way to the Mediterranean, while the autumn sees a migration in the opposite direction as yachts stop in Gibraltar on their way to the Canaries and the Caribbean.

South Atlantic

Compared with the North Atlantic, the South Atlantic is crossed by only a few routes and the number of cruising yachts is very small. Most yachts used to arrive in the South Atlantic via the Cape of Good Hope as part of a longer voyage, but the number of yachts sailing from the Indian Ocean by way of South Africa has shown a substantial decrease in recent years. However, there has been an increase in the number of cruising boats sailing from the North Atlantic to South America, particularly Brazil.

According to South African Customs, a total of 71 foreign yachts called at Cape Town during 1987, the majority coming from the Indian Ocean, most having made their first South African landfall at Durban. As there are no details available concerning the flag of the yachts which arrived in Cape Town in 1987, Table 12 on page 32 gives an indication of the national makeup of the yachts that arrived in the South Atlantic by rounding the Cape of Good Hope. Practically all westbound yachts that stop in Durban also call at Cape Town and the figures for both ports show a considerable drop compared to the 1970s. There are two reasons for this decline, the first being the present tendency among most circumnavigators to reach Europe via the Red Sea and Suez Canal rather than by the roundabout way calling at South Africa. The difficulties which have been encountered by many boats on the passage from Mauritius to South Africa have deterred many from that traditional route. A variety of factors have combined to make the Red Sea more attractive to the long distance sailor with a resulting drop in those willing to face the risks of a rough passage around the tip of Africa.

The other reason why less people are inclined to visit South Africa is its increasing isolation caused by the policy of apartheid pursued by the government. Even the Whitbread Round the World Race is now bypassing South Africa by having a nonstop leg from Punta del Este in Uruguay to Fremantle in Western Australia. Cruising boats would find this long route quite demanding, so that while eastbound yachts still call at Cape Town, most westbound yachts go via the Red Sea instead.

However, a number of yachts still do round the Cape of Good Hope on their way to the North Atlantic and most northbound passages are made between November and January when conditions for rounding Africa are best. There are hardly any yachts sailing the South Atlantic during the southern hemisphere winter from May to October. Apart from ocean races such as the Whitbread Round the World Race, only a handful of cruising yachts take the southbound route from Europe or North America to the Cape of Good Hope, again during the southern summer. The reciprocal route is more frequented and direct, the northbound route passing close to both St Helena and Ascension Islands. However, judging from the few boats that called in the Azores during the last two years on their way from South Africa to Europe, it would appear that a substantial decline has occurred on that route too. This traditional route, made famous by early circumnavigators, is now almost deserted and it is significant that among all the boats that arrived in Horta, Barbados, Antigua or Bermuda during 1987, there were only four boats that had come directly from Cape Town with an additional three who had stopped at St Helena.

Another northbound route enters the South Atlantic via Cape Horn from where it heads in a north-easterly direction before it crosses the equator, but this route is rarely used by cruising boats and mostly by round the world races. However, with an increase in the number of people attracted to cruise in Patagonia and even Antarctica, more boats are heading for the South Atlantic every year, some sailing down along the eastern coast of South America, others coming from the South Pacific through the Magellan Straits.

North Pacific

Sailors on the Pacific coast of the United States are less fortunate in their choice of cruising destinations compared to their east coast brethren. Although there are a large number of boats on America's western seaboard, particularly in California, most of the sailing is coastal and the only foreign destination within a reasonable distance is Mexico's Baja California. Canadian sailors have been blessed with a much more interesting coastline but even they have little choice when it comes to ocean cruising.

The offshore passage which is undertaken by the largest number of yachts in the North Pacific is to and from the Hawaiian Islands. Because of the prevailing NW winds in the immediate vicinity of the continental landmass, which gave way to steady NE trade winds further offshore, the passage to Hawaii can be sailed direct from any port on the North American coast. The same prevailing NE winds that blow consistently between Hawaii and the continental landmass make a return voyage to the west coast along a direct route almost impossible. For this reason, on leaving Hawaii most sailing boats bound for the USA or Canada follow a northerly course that takes them into the area of prevailing westerly winds before setting a course for the coast. Similar to the North Atlantic, fewer yachts are found on the return routes, as a proportion of yachts continue their voyages westward from Hawaii, usually into the South Pacific.

According to US Customs, approximately one thousand US yachts based on the mainland visit Hawaii every year. This is an estimated figure as the authorities do not log the movement of US yachts arriving from the mainland. However, accurate figures are available concerning the movement of foreign yachts as well as that of US boats arriving from foreign destinations. Altogether 176 yachts arrived in the Hawaiian Islands from a foreign port during 1987 and Table 7 gives a breakdown of the various ports that the yachts had cleared prior to arriving in Hawaii.

	Foreign Flag	*US Flag*
Line Islands	5	11
French Polynesia	15	38
American Samoa	1	16
Western Samoa	2	4
Marshall Islands	2	6
Cook Islands	3	3
Tonga	1	2
Galapagos	–	1
Japan	5	–
Philippines	–	1
Australia/New Zealand	4	1
Canada	4	–
Central America	16	21
USA	14	–

Table 7.
YACHT ARRIVALS IN HAWAII 1987

As a matter of interest, the majority of these yachts arriving in Hawaii from a foreign destination were North American (104 US, 22 Canadian). The rest were as follows: New Zealand (10), French (9), Great Britain (8), Japan (8), Australia (4), Switzerland (3), Germany (2), Mexico (2) and one each from Bermuda, Belgium, Netherlands and Hong Kong.

Compared to the large number of yachts returning to the mainland, a much smaller number of yachts undertake passages to Japan or the Far East, using Hawaii as an intermediate port. A trans-ocean route that has been increasing in traffic is that from Hawaii to Alaska. This route is very seasonal and is used almost exclusively between 15 June and 15 August. Hawaii is also the starting point for routes taken by yachts heading for either Micronesia or Tahiti and the South Pacific.

Only a small number of yachts undertake west to east passages across the North Pacific. Boats setting off from the Far East normally use Japan as a starting point in order to make the voyage in the belt of prevailing westerly winds. Such passages are usually made during the summer months.

Far East

The Far East has yet to become popular as a cruising destination and although some boats cruise the Philippines or Japan, their number is small. The main reasons for this are that the area is off the beaten track and the weather unpredictable. While the former reason should encourage rather than deter people from sailing to the Far East, the second reason is what really concerns most sailors. Even if not in practice, in theory typhoons can occur in some areas at any time of the year and because of this there is no absolutely 'safe' season. This means that cruising plans have to be tailored very carefully to suit local conditions, which is not always easy. The western part of the North Pacific does not lie near any of the major cruising routes and to include the countries of the Far East in a world cruise necessitates a lengthy detour, which few people are prepared to do.

In spite of the favourable NE trade winds that blow across the North Pacific ensuring fast passages from North America to the Far East, the number of yachts that embark on such a transpacific voyage continues to be insignificant. Even Hong Kong, which has an increasing yacht population itself, attracts only a handful of foreign cruising boats each year and the number of visiting yachts is so small that the authorities do not consider it worth keeping statistics on them. According to the Aberdeen Boat Club, about six to eight foreign cruising boats call there every year, most of them flying the US flag. Most sailing boats that do venture into the North West Pacific do so at a later stage in their voyage, usually arriving in the Far East from Papua New Guinea at the end of a cruise among the islands of the South Pacific. Another route that used to bring cruising boats to the Philippines and Hong Kong in the past was the route from Singapore. The reported cases of piracy in the South China Sea have made most people avoid this route, while the difficulty in obtaining a cruising permit deters many from making a detour through the Indonesian archipelago.

South Pacific

Robert Louis Stevenson was neither the first nor the last to praise the South Seas, but few other writers have managed to describe the seductive beauty of the islands and their charming people better. Like Stevenson, I became hopelessly addicted to the Pacific islands and still suffer from withdrawal symptoms when I write about that area. The three years spent sailing the South Pacific was the apogee of *Aventura*'s voyage around the world. Not only for

The waterfront in Papeete, Tahiti, is a favourite gathering point for long distance voyagers.

myself, but for countless others, the South Pacific remains the ultimate destination of which dreams are made.

The main cruising route links the Panama Canal in the east with the Torres Strait in the west and most boats undertaking a world voyage rarely stray more than a few hundred miles from it. There are many variations to this trunk route, with secondary routes branching off and rejoining it along its entire length. Approximately 250 boats take the route from the Panama Canal to French Polynesia every year and the westward flow is also fed by a substantial influx of American and Canadian boats, most arriving directly in the Marquesas from the Pacific Coast of the USA or Canada, others coming via Hawaii. At the western end the main route is joined by boats coming from New Zealand or Australia.

Having passed through the Cook, Tonga or Samoa Islands, this main route reaches Fiji, which is at the centre of a number of routes. As the central part of the route from Tahiti to Vanuatu and on to the Solomon Islands is liable to hurricanes between November and April, there is virtually no yacht movement between island groups during that period. Yachts that choose to remain in this area during the tropical summer invariably stay close to a protected port or 'hurricane hole'.

Flag	*1985*	*1987*
USA	89	88
France	32	19
New Zealand	58	67
Australia	45	40
United Kingdom	40	34
Canada	20	23
Scandinavia	14	17
Other European	19	17
Germany	5	11
Japan	3	–
Hong Kong	3	–
Western Samoa	1	–
Fiji	–	1
Norfolk	–	1
South Africa	–	1
Argentina	–	1
	329	**320**

Table 8.
YACHT ARRIVALS IN SUVA, 1985 AND 1987

Approximately one thousand cruising yachts are to be found spread out among the islands of the South Pacific at any one time, most of them taking two or even three seasons to cross the Pacific. Few yachts undertaking a world voyage miss Fiji, with the exception of some French yachts who prefer to bypass the Fijian archipelago and sail direct to French speaking New Caledonia. The position of the Fijian capital, Suva, astride the main east–west trade wind route makes it a perfect spot to assess the movement of cruising yachts.

Fortunately, I have been able to obtain precise figures concerning the movement of every yacht that called in Fiji in 1987, including its nationality, length of stay and onward destination. These figures could be compared with similar statistics from 1985 and the first conclusion that could be drawn was that, in spite of the political troubles that had befallen Fiji between those two dates, the actual number of yachts that called there has not been affected at all. Looking at the figures for 1987, if one subtracts the considerable number of New Zealand yachts which can be regarded as involved in short term cruising, particularly those taking part in the Auckland to Suva Race, the number of long-distance cruising yachts that pass through Fiji in any one year is about 300. This figure tallies with the statistics concerning yachts that transit the Panama Canal from the Atlantic to the Pacific Ocean and shows that the total number of circumnavigating yachts is not much higher than it was ten years ago. If these figures are compared with the staggering total of 5000 yachts that passed through Gibraltar in 1987, one can easily deduce where the real concentration of cruising yachts is and that, compared to the North Atlantic and Mediterranean, the South Pacific continues to be a cruising backwater.

Although the total number of yachts that passed through Fiji has not been affected by the recent political upheavals, the number of those cruising in the outer islands is very small as this is only allowed with the permission of the central authorities, which is not easily granted. Yacht movement through Fiji is very seasonal, as can be seen from Table 9 which shows that most sailors try to avoid the area during the cyclone season.

A popular destination in the SW Pacific continues to be New Zealand, where a large number of cruising boats spend the cyclone season from November to April before returning to the tropics. Approximately 250 foreign yachts arrive in New Zealand at the start of every cyclone season and over the last few years this number has been fairly constant, with a slight decline shown in the latest available figures. Most yachts arrive in the Bay of Islands or Whangarei

Table 9.
YACHT MOVEMENT FROM FIJI 1987

Destination	Jan	Feb	Mar	Apr	May	June	July	Aug	Sep	Oct	Nov	Dec	**Total**
Samoa	1	–	–	1	2	2	2	2	3	1	1	–	**15**
Tonga	–	–	–	1	1	5	3	–	5	–	1	–	**16**
New Zealand	2	–	–	–	16	2	1	3	12	42	19	–	**97**
Vanuatu	–	–	1	1	1	13	10	14	39	5	3	–	**87**
New South Wales	–	–	–	–	–	–	2	1	1	8	4	–	**16**
Queensland	–	–	–	–	–	1	–	2	3	6	4	–	**16**
New Caledonia	–	–	–	–	–	1	2	–	9	17	7	–	**36**
Norfolk	–	–	–	–	–	1	–	–	–	–	–	–	**1**
Hawaii/USA West Coast	–	–	–	–	1	1	–	–	–	–	–	–	**2**
Tuvalu	–	–	–	–	1	–	1	–	–	1	1	–	**4**
Solomons	–	–	–	–	–	–	–	–	–	1	–	–	**1**
Marshalls	–	–	–	–	–	–	–	–	1	–	–	–	**1**
Futuna	–	–	1	–	–	–	–	–	–	–	1	–	**2**
													294

Table 10.
YACHT ARRIVALS IN OPUA AND WHANGAREI 1986–87

	1986	*1987*
USA	95	75
Australia	39	30
United Kingdom	32	25
Canada	23	21
France	18	19
Germany	14	13
Scandinavia	8	9
South Africa	7	1
Belgium	5	2
Other European	13	7
Others	6	5
Total	**260**	**207**

area and as the vast majority of yachts clearing into New Zealand make their landfall in these areas, their breakdown by flag may be significant and is shown in Table 10.

There has been a 20 per cent reduction in the number of arrivals from one year to the next, the biggest drop being among American, British and Australian boats, for which there is no obvious explanation.

The busiest time for arrivals is November, when almost half the boats arrived in the Bay of Islands, most of them from the tropics. The end of November is regarded as the start of the cyclone season and by this time most cruising boats try and be out of the dangerous

Table 11. YACHT MOVEMENT TO AND FROM WHANGAREI DISTRICT 1987

	Jan	Feb	Mar	Apr	May	June	July	Aug	Sep	Oct	Nov	Dec	**Total**
Arrivals from													
Fiji	4	–	–	–	1	3	1	1	5	16	39	4	**74**
Tonga	2	–	–	–	1	1	2	2	–	9	40	35	**92**
Cook Is.	–	1	–	–	–	–	–	–	–	–	3	3	**7**
Tahiti	–	–	–	1	–	1	–	–	–	–	–	1	**3**
Samoa	–	–	–	–	–	–	–	–	–	–	–	1	**1**
Vanuatu	–	–	–	–	–	–	–	–	–	1	3	1	**5**
New Caledonia	–	2	–	–	–	–	1	–	–	4	3	6	**16**
Queensland	1	–	–	–	–	1	–	–	–	5	4	2	**14**
New South Wales	4	6	7	11	4	1	–	–	1	1	8	10	**53**
Norfolk Is.	–	–	–	–	–	–	–	–	1	–	–	2	**3**
Destination													
Fiji	–	–	–	8	16	2	–	1	1	–	–	–	**28**
Tonga	–	–	–	16	25	10	3	1	2	1	1	–	**59**
Tahiti	–	1	1	5	6	–	–	–	–	–	1	–	**14**
Samoa	–	–	–	1	–	–	–	–	–	1	–	–	**2**
Vanuatu	–	–	–	3	1	1	1	1	–	–	–	–	**7**
New Caledonia	–	–	1	3	3	4	4	3	–	–	1	–	**19**
Queensland	1	–	4	5	3	2	1	–	1	–	–	–	**17**
New South Wales	4	6	5	4	1	–	–	–	2	–	4	2	**28**
Victoria	–	–	–	–	–	–	–	–	–	–	2	–	**2**
Mauritius	–	–	–	–	1	–	–	–	–	–	–	–	**1**
Alaska	–	–	–	–	1	–	–	–	–	–	–	–	**1**
Hawaii	–	–	–	–	–	–	–	–	–	1	–	–	**1**
Falkland Is.	–	–	–	–	–	–	–	–	–	–	1	–	**1**
Chile	–	–	–	–	–	–	–	–	–	–	–	1	**1**

areas. In the past the gathering point for the passage to New Zealand was the Fijian capital Suva but, because of political unrest in that country, in 1987 almost half the skippers left from Tonga instead. Tonga has always been the starting point for those who had dawdled on their way from Tahiti and were in a hurry to leave the cyclone area behind.

The summer is also the time when yachts arrive in New Zealand from Australia, the busiest month being December, although yachts do cross the Tasman Sea in both directions throughout the year, even if the number who do so between June and September is extremely small. Most yachts coming from or going to ports in New South Wales break their passage at Lord Howe Island, the conveniently placed Australian outpost in the Tasman Sea.

New Zealand is at the centre of a number of routes and most of the yachts spending the summer there return to the tropics in April and May when winter begins in the southern hemisphere. The previous year's movement is now reversed, with the majority returning to Tonga and some to Fiji to resume their interrupted cruise, while those who are in a hurry head for the Torres Strait, either via New Caledonia, Vanuatu or Australia. The majority of those crossing the Tasman Sea continue inside the Great Barrier Reef towards the Torres Strait and beyond.

A southerly route links New Zealand with Tahiti, which turns north in the vicinity of the Austral Islands. Passages along this route are made between March and May mostly by New Zealanders, Australians or North Americans returning home. An even more southerly route from New Zealand heads east for Cape Horn, but this is taken mostly by racing yachts taing part in round the world races and only rarely by cruising boats.

Indian Ocean

There is little doubt that the next ocean to be discovered by cruising boats in larger numbers will be the Indian Ocean. For the time being, the number of cruising boats is still small and most people only pass through as part of a world voyage. The best thing about the Indian Ocean is its weather, which is more predictable than anywhere else, the seasons being much more definite than in other parts of the world. This applies both to the northern half of the ocean, which is dominated by the NE and SW monsoons, and to its southern half which is under the influence of the SE trade winds.

There are two major routes crossing the Indian Ocean, both starting at the Torres Strait. For those who wish to cruise in the Mediterranean or intend to reach southern Europe by the shortest route, the logical way leads through the North Indian Ocean and Red Sea. In the case of those who wish to reach the Atlantic by way of the Cape of Good Hope the route leads across the South Indian Ocean to South Africa. Political considerations have often had their effect on the choice of route, such as during the closure of the Suez Canal and more recently the situation in Sri Lanka or South Africa.

North Indian Ocean

Yacht traffic along the main route crossing the northern half of the Indian Ocean is dictated by the two monsoons. As most cruising boats undertaking a world voyage do this in an east to west direction, the majority of boats cross the Indian Ocean during the NE monsoon, which lasts approximately from December to March, although most passages towards the Red Sea are made in January and early February. Among the 302 yachts that called at Singapore in 1987 a large number were westbound, most intending to reach Europe via the Red Sea. Yacht traffic in the opposite direction is very limited, not just in Singapore, but throughout the North Indian Ocean as very few passages are undertaken during the SW monsoon. An increasing proportion of yacht movement is regional as more sailors from Australasia undertake longer cruises (see Table 12).

On leaving Singapore through the Malacca Straits, the main route heads west towards Sri Lanka, where the protected port of Galle used to be a popular stop until political violence erupted in the north of the island. About half the yachts crossing the North Indian Ocean now avoid Sri Lanka, which in 1987 was visited by 84 boats on their way to the Red Sea, over 85 per cent of these between the months of October and March. Among those who called at Galle, most did not seem too concerned about the troubles which had affected the northern part of the island, although they rarely ventured outside of Galle itself. The total number of yachts crossing the North Indian Ocean has remained stationary compared with the 1970s and early 1980s, the number of boats that cleared into Galle in 1987 being almost equal to the previous year.

From Sri Lanka the westbound route continues towards Bab-el-Mandeb at the entrance to the Red Sea. Although facilities for visiting yachts in Aden are minimal, more than half the yachts heading for the Red Sea stop there. The rest, mainly French-speaking crews, make for Djibouti instead.

Eastbound passages across the North Indian Ocean are made during the SW monsoon (May to September), which is the season of extremely high temperatures in the Red Sea and Gulf of Aden and also of very strong winds east of Socotra, where the frequency of gales is one of the highest in the world. It is therefore perhaps not surprising that the number of boats undertaking eastbound voyages is very small. In 1987 only four yachts stopped in Sri Lanka on their way east compared to 84 sailing in the opposite direction.

Table 12. YACHT ARRIVALS IN SINGAPORE AND GALLE 1987

	Singapore	*Galle*
Australia	60	19
United Kingdom	50	14
USA	47	19
Hong Kong	19	–
Panama	16	–
France	14	6
Germany	12	5
Indonesia	11	–
New Zealand	10	2
Malaysia	7	–
Singapore	6	–
Canada	5	2
Thailand	4	–
Cayman Islands	3	–
Denmark	3	2
Norway	3	4
Sweden	3	3
Switzerland	3	5
Gibraltar	2	–
Austria	1	–
Belgium	1	–
Italy	1	1
Netherlands	1	4
Poland	1	1
St Vincent	1	–
Unregistered	18	1
Total	**302**	**88**

Transequatorial routes

Most yacht traffic in the Indian Ocean keeps to one or other of the hemispheres, with only a few routes crossing the equator. The most frequented of these is the route from Bali which bypasses the Straits of Malacca by staying south of Sumatra and joins the main transindian route in the vicinity of Sri Lanka. This transequatorial route is a continuation of the trunk route which reaches the Indian Ocean through the Torres Strait. It is used by boats that have either stopped in Bali, but do not wish to carry on towards Singapore, or are coming directly from the South Pacific or Australia. Approximately half the yachts crossing the North Indian Ocean towards the Red Sea use one of the transequatorial routes instead of sailing via Singapore and the Malacca Straits.

South Indian Ocean

The traditional route from the Torres Strait to the Cape of Good Hope touches the islands of Christmas, Cocos Keeling and Mauritius, where most voyagers call at least briefly before heading for Durban. An alternative route takes in the Chagos Archipelago and possibly the Seychelles before turning south and rejoining the main route. Because of the difficult weather conditions encountered by vessels rounding the Cape of Good Hope, few boats go nonstop from Durban to Cape Town but break the voyage into shorter legs.

Approximately 120 cruising yachts used to call in South African ports every year on their way from the Indian to the Atlantic Ocean, but their number has declined steadily over the last few years until it has almost halved. 1987 saw a slight increase in the number of foreign cruising boats that called at Durban as can be seen in Table 13.

The island groups scattered across the centre of the Indian Ocean are attracting more cruising boats every year, either arriving from the east (South Pacific or Australia) or the north from the Red Sea. More of these yachts are also visiting the east cost of Africa, particularly Kenya, cruising boats now being welcomed in most East African countries bordering on the Indian Ocean.

Red Sea

After years of conflict and uncertainty, the Red Sea is no longer perceived as such a dangerous area by cruising sailors and the countries bordering it have gradually adopted a more tolerant attitude to yachts. Political hazards were not the only obstacles that kept yachts away from the Red Sea as the navigational dangers were regarded equally with awe by many sailors. Its reef strewn waters and paucity of aids to navigation as well as the difficulty of obtaining reliable sunsights were a navigational nightmare, which now can be avoided with the help of satellite navigation.

Although the majority of boats sail through the Red Sea as part of a longer voyage, there are an increasing number of people who make the Red Sea their cruising destination, particularly during winter, moving down from the Mediterranean when the weather there starts deteriorating. Traffic through the Red Sea has shown a slight increase, as more sailors who are undertaking world cruises route their voyages through the Mediterranean.

As the countries bordering on the Red Sea do not permit cruising in their waters, with the exception of Sudan and Egypt, the extent of sailing routes is very limited. The main route both for north and southbound vessels follows closely the axis of the Red Sea. Very few people, however, are prepared to make the entire 1200

	1986	*1987*
USA	17	15
United Kingdom	9	17
Australia	8	9
Germany	7	6
Canada	5	2
France	3	4
Denmark	1	1
Netherlands	1	5
New Zealand	1	2
Poland	1	1
Sweden	1	1
Switzerland	1	5
Belgium	–	2
Finland	2	–
West Indies	2	–
South America	2	–
Hong Kong	1	–
Ireland	1	–
Total	**63**	**70**

Table 13.
YACHT ARRIVALS IN DURBAN 1986–87

mile voyage from one end of the Red Sea to the other without stopping and branch off into Sudanese or Egyptian coastal waters. The main movement of the northbound yachts is during the winter months from January to March, when winds are likely to be favourable for at least the first part of the passage.

The predominantly northbound traffic in the Red Sea is shown by the larger number of yachts passing through the Suez Canal from south to north than in the opposite direction. As in most other parts of the world, the most commonly seen flags are from USA, France and UK, with a substantial increase in the number of Australian boats heading for Europe. According to the figures for 1986 and 1987 compiled by Fathi Soukar, a Suez based shipping agent, more commonly known as the Prince of the Red Sea, whose services are used by most yachts heading for the Mediterranean, the busiest month for northbound yachts is April. Almost 50 per cent of the annual number of yachts passing through the Canal from Suez to Port Said do so during April, the second busiest month being May. There is virtually no northbound traffic between August and January. Southbound traffic is spread out more evenly through the year, although the overall number of southbound boats is smaller and will not increase significantly until the Red Sea itself starts attracting more Mediterranean based yachts looking for an alternative cruising area for the winter.

Current and Future Trends

This assessment of the cruising routes and the distribution of yachts along them has concentrated on those who are cruising away from their home base. Two areas with a high concentration of cruising yachts are the Mediterranean and the Caribbean, as well as the trans-ocean routes that connect these two areas, which are so conveniently matched that their best sailing seasons complement each other.

The highest concentration of cruising yachts worldwide is found on the routes going in a general east to west direction, namely the more southerly route in the North Atlantic, as well as the main cruising routes across the South Pacific and North Indian Oceans. Seasonal and climatic factors are unlikely to change in future years, although the attitude of yachtsmen to them may. Following several benign cyclone seasons in Tahiti, an increasing number of yachts took the risk of staying and even cruising the Society Islands during the cyclone season. The severe cyclones which occurred in 1983 caused the loss of several boats and very few people chose to remain in this area during the following summers. A more recent example occurred in the Caribbean, where there has been an increasing amount of cruising during the hurricane season, primarily due to the false impression given in some publications that hurricanes are rare and when they do occur, there is sufficient warning to get to good shelter. Hurricane Gilbert has blown asunder that assumption and devastated a large area in September 1988. The previous September hurricane Emily tore through Bermuda, giving ample indication that West Indian hurricanes should be treated with the utmost respect.

Apart from the weather, political factors can also change cruising patterns in certain areas, as countries make yachts more or less welcome, impose permit restrictions or even close certain areas to cruising yachts. On the other hand, some areas, which were long closed, have opened up and more may do so in the future, for example a few yachts now cruise in China. On the other hand, reported cases of piracy in the South China Sea, Colombian waters and the Bahamas have deterred many people from cruising in those areas.

While certain areas might gain or lose popularity with cruising yachts, overall there has been an increase in the total world cruising population in the last ten years, a trend which is likely to continue. The nations with a tradition of ocean voyaging such as the United States, Britain and France still dominate the world cruising population, with a higher proportion of Australian and New Zealand boats in the Pacific and Asian regions. The comparatively large number of French yachts is due not only to tradition, but also to the convenient location of French Overseas Departments and Territories, such as Guadeloupe and Martinique in the Caribbean, Tahiti and New Caledonia in the Pacific or Réunion in the Indian Ocean, where French citizens can stop and work for a period of time before continuing their voyage. Sailors from Germany and Scandinavia can also be seen in increasing numbers and the general rise in the cruising population has been accompanied by a striking change in the national origins as yachts from countries such as Switzerland, Finland or Italy, who are relative newcomers to the world cruising scene, are to be seen in greater numbers.

However, although there has been an increase in the overall number of people cruising, this has been mostly on a regional basis and the annual number of boats completing a circumnavigation has not changed significantly over the last few years. This can be seen from the number of boats passing through major transit ports, some of which have seen an increase while others have recorded a decline in the number of visitors. One area which has seen a steady increase in the number of voyagers over the last decade is the North Atlantic, which is perhaps as it should be as we approach the quincentenary of the opening up of the routes linking the Old and New Worlds.

Looking at the cruising scene on a worldwide basis, the increase in the number of people undertaking offshore voyages has been brought about by three main factors; improved yacht design and construction methods, which have resulted in more comfortable and seaworthy yachts, greatly improved aids to navigation, which have given a greater sense of security to those cruising, and thirdly, the greater prosperity enjoyed by the developed nations, which has changed yachting from a hobby of the rich to a leisure activity accessible to all. More people are financially able to take early retirement and for many sailors this provides the ideal opportunity to embark on a longer cruise. Those who are tempted to make a longer cruise while still young, but who do not wish to abandon their careers,

English Harbour, Antigua, is one of the most picturesque anchorages in the world.

sometimes prefer to take the option of a sabbatical leave. With plentiful and reasonable flights to all parts of the world, people with restricted time schedules often plan their cruises in stages, returning when necessary to their business or professional commitments. This trend is becoming widespread among professional people and several ARC participants are doctors, architects or businessmen taking off a few months to undertake a voyage which could not be fitted into the normal annual leave. This kind of attitude is contributing more than anything else to an opening up of the oceans to more cruising boats. However, this does not mean that the oceans are getting as crowded as a motorway on a holiday weekend. There are certain people, usually indefatigable writers of letters to yachting magazines, who deplore the expansion in offshore yachting, as if the oceans should belong only to an elite which includes themselves. Fortunately for those who are prepared to make a detour off the beaten track there are still plenty of unspoilt places and as the statistics quoted on the foregoing pages have shown, there are certain places where the number of cruising boats has in fact gone down. It is a phenomenon that nobody could have predicted ten years ago.

It has been said that the definition of a pessimist is a well informed optimist. I hope that the above findings will make both optimists and pessimists happy.

A FRIEND IN EVERY OCEAN

Along the well-beaten tracks that yachts have sailed over the years, there are certain key points where a welcome has been provided by very special people, who for one reason or another have taken on the role of friend to visiting yachtsmen. Libby and Chris Bonnet in Durban, the Azevedo family in the Azores, the late Tom Neale in Suvorov, and Don Windsor in Galle are but a few of the names that spring to mind.

Open house in Galle

Don Windsor's house on Closenberg Road close by Galle harbour is the hub of yachting activity in Sri Lanka. As well as acting as a mail drop, Don keeps an open house and his large verandah is a meeting place for visiting sailors. Don sells cool drinks, provides meals or showers and acts as a genial host, always prepared to listen to people's problems and to try and find solutions for them. From providing watchmen for boats, arranging tours to visit the antiquities of Sri Lanka or renting bicycles, almost anything can be arranged through Don. His courtyard is always busy with people coming and going, as members of his family assist in the numerous activities generated by the international cruising fraternity. As well as listening to the tales of others, Don has many a story to relate about the characters who have passed through Sri Lanka in the last twenty years. Whether returning from sightseeing or with a load of shopping, there are few sailors that pass Don Windsor's verandah by.

Azorean amity

At any time of day and long into the night the Café Sport overlooking the port of Horta on the island of Faial is full of local fishermen, boatbuilders and dockworkers. However, during the summer months, Peter Azevedo's blue fronted café is just as popular with sailors from overseas as witnessed by the autographed ensigns, pennants and club burgees which are displayed three and four deep on the walls or pinned to the wooden ceiling. Interspersed with the countless flags are various gifts received by Peter from visiting yachtsmen: T-shirts inscribed with affectionate dedications, posters, drawings, rag dolls, even a miniature foul-weather gear suit donated by the crew of *Berge Viking*. They are tokens of gratitude from the many sailors who over the years have been welcomed to Horta by this warm-hearted Azorean.

According to family lore, the tradition was started by Peter's grandfather who greeted Joshua Slocum during the solo navigator's visit to Horta in 1896. Unfortunately that historic encounter is not documented, but this is more than made up by the detailed recording of the many yachts that followed in the famous singlehander's wake. The next known yacht to make a landfall in Horta was also from the USA, *Sea Bird*, which passed through in 1921. During the 1920s and early 1930s the number of yachts stopping in Horta increased to two or three a year, then their number doubled and after the Second World War the trickle became a flood, with now over seven hundred yachts calling at Horta every year.

Peter Azevedo's establishment has been described an institution and rightly so as Café Sport is much more than a waterside bar. It provides such essential services to the peripatetic yachtsman as a mail drop, long distance telephone, money exchange at any hour, weather forecasts and expert advice on any local matters. Occasionally it has also acted as a credit bank and the generous Azevedos have bailed out several yachtsmen over the years.

In 1966 Peter started his first guest book of which there are now

Peter Azevedo's working corner in Café Sport where everything is available, from scrimshaw to money exchange.

over sixty. Looking through his early books feels like reading a history of modern yachting with all the famous names cropping up again and again. The first book was started in March 1966 and the first visitor to sign it was Bill Greenhalph of the Canadian yacht *Ariadne.* The third signature belongs to Eric Tabarly who passed through Horta in his first *Pen Duick.* Humphrey Barton came next during one of several visits on *Rose Rambler*, then Julian Roosevelt on *Warlock* and Mike Richey on *Jester.* Eric and Susan Hiscock stopped by in *Wanderer III*, homebound at the end of a two year voyage to the USA. It was already the Hiscocks' second visit to Faial, like that of the most assiduous transatlantic migrator, Frank Casper, who during the next two decades took his *Elsie* to and fro across the Atlantic more often than anyone else. David Lewis also called at the Café Sport at the end of *Rehu Moana*'s circumnavigation. Soon he was back again on *Isbjørn* bound for the Pacific to study traditional methods of navigation.

The first book also bears the signature of Bill Howell on *Golden Cockerel* as well as the particulars of *Kialoa II*, John Kilroy's 73 ft aluminium yawl built in Los Angeles in 1962. Francis Chichester and his *Gipsy Moth* only made it into the second book, after which the number of entries accelerated and include *Half Safe*, the record of Ben Carlin's successful crossing of the Atlantic in an amphibious jeep.

'I try to do my best for everyone, not just for famous people or old friends. Everyone is welcome here.' Peter's words echo the philosophy of his father Henrique, who was equally famous in welcoming strangers to those shores. Their fame has travelled far and wide; the magazine *Newsweek* listed Café Sport among the world's best bars and the modest café has been featured in several television programmes. Besides the countless dedications, Peter and his father Henrique also had a book dedicated to them, 'No traveller ever found better friends' appearing on the flyleaf of Bernard Venable's 'Baleia', a book on Azorean whaling.

Straddling the transatlantic migration routes of whales as well as yachts, the Azores have a long tradition of whaling, which is reflected by Peter's other passion, a unique collection of scrimshaw. Hundreds of beautifully inscribed whale's teeth form the core of a personal collection which he now has turned into a museum. Café Sport's middle floor has been fitted with display cabinets to house Peter's scrimshaws, as well as his most cherished yachting mementos.

'Although I get a lot of satisfaction out of welcoming visitors to my café, I would like to leave behind something durable, both for myself and for this island.' Now in his mid-sixties, Peter has good reason to show concern for the future as a severe stroke a few years ago almost left him disabled. Now recovered, he is back in the café, but only for a few hours a day. However, there is no danger of the Azevedo welcome drying up as Peter's son José has stepped into his father's shoes to carry the family tradition into the fourth generation.

A Pacific priest

One man who epitomizes the true spirit of friendship towards the worldwide yachting community is Father George Kester, who has welcomed yachts to the Cook Islands for forty years, first on the island of Rarotonga and then in Aitutaki until his enforced retirement in 1987, when he returned to his native Holland for medical treatment.

The winding pass through the reef into Aitutaki lagoon is shallow and meandering, with a strong current always running out, not easy to negotiate at the best of times. Like many others before and after me, it was a great pleasure to see the tall angular figure of Father George on the wharf, ready to take my line and give me good advice on mooring. An invitation to visit him in his home was his spontaneous friendly greeting. Later on he bundled my family into his pick-up truck along with the half a dozen children that seemed to follow him everywhere like the Pied Piper, and he took us for a memorable tour of the island.

During the ten days we spent in Aitutaki, we visited Father George several times, his home a witness to his special friendships with yachtsmen, strewn with letters, magazines and books from all over the globe. Pride of place, however, was given to the seven large volumes of his guest book, which records the yachts visiting the Cook Islands for some thirty years. The books are not just a list of arrivals and departures, but full of poetry and drawings, photographs and stories, cartoons and route maps. They are nautical works of art, to which the less artistic like myself are diffident to add. But add I did, for like so many others I did not want to miss the chance to be recorded for posterity as a friend of Father George.

When in his late seventies, Father George retired as parish priest and returned to Holland for an operation, I took the opportunity to ask this exceptional man how he came to be involved with yachts and yachtsmen.

Growing up near Rotterdam and the Hook of Holland, as a young boy he was always fascinated by the sea. From the harbour he could watch ships coming and going across the North Sea to the rest of the world. Although wanting to become a cadet officer, his father insisted that he join the family business market gardening instead. Like many young men of his era, his life changed dramatically with the advent of the Second World War and he joined the army. Modest about what he did in the war, it takes some persistence to discover that during the German occupation he was a link in the lifeline helping those who wished to escape to gain the safety of the Allied lines.

It was during these wartime experiences that his desire to become a priest grew stronger and he was inspired by a quote from Msgr Kepler, that the greatest satisfaction in life is to make others happy. Wishing to share his faith with the world, he decided to become a missionary and with a love of the sea still running in his veins, he chose the Pacific. 'I had a look at the map of the Pacific and the Cook Islands were right in the middle of the "pond" ', is how Father George simplifies the story of how in 1947 as a newly ordained priest he made his way via New York, San Francisco, Honolulu, Canton Island, Fiji and New Zealand to the Cook Islands.

From the very beginning of his life on Rarotonga, he took a great interest in all the yachts that called. In those days there were not that many. As Father George says, 'In the beginning after the Second World War, yachting on the high seas was regarded as new and dangerous and it took many years before people found out that it was not, and that it was a great opportunity to see the world.'

In the early sixties, as the number of yachts calling at Rarotonga increased, Father George heard that a hotel on Bora Bora kept a visitors' book, which logged the names of all the yachts that called. This inspired him to start his own guest book. For Father George it was a perfect excuse to call on yachts and offer his hospitality. By the time he left Rarotonga in 1977, he had five volumes and records of some 800 yachts.

It was not just friendship that he offered, for over the years he has married couples, baptized children, mourned the dead and been the confidant of many a sailor who needed an ear into which to pour his troubles. Believer or unbeliever were welcomed in the same way, he accepted all yachtsmen as they were.

In 1977, he moved to the parish on the smaller island of Aitutaki, where fewer yachts called, until the 1980s when the rebuilding of the harbour on Rarotonga sent many more through

Aitutaki's winding pass in search of the man, who by then had quite a reputation on the yachting grapevine.

Over the years Father George has noticed many changes in the cruising scene. In the early days he observed that the yachts were larger, almost always over forty feet and usually had all male crews. He witnessed quite a lot of troubles with the men, especially when they hit the bars in town after a long slow passage or bad weather. In the sixties and seventies he remarked that smaller yachts appeared and many more sloops and cutters. 'People found that sailing on the high seas was not so dangerous and it did not make that much difference if one had a smaller yacht.'

Another change that was welcomed by Father George was the increased number of women sailing and with their presence, better behaviour from the men. In his opinion, 'The best team on a yacht is a man and a woman.'

In the 1970s the multihulls started arriving and this acute observer of the yachting scene says, 'They were often made in the backyard and anyone could become a shipbuilder. But they paid for that and several poorly built trimarans disappeared with all hands. It took a while before people found out they were dangerous on the high seas.' From the early 1980s until 1987 Father George did not see any catamarans or trimarans arrive in Aitutaki, then in 1987 three trimarans visited. 'Maybe they are safer now,' he added hopefully.

The loss of yachts and crew pains this deeply religious man. One of the most memorable yachts that called was the six foot long *Wind's Will*, skippered by Bill Dunlop. He left Aitutaki in June 1983 bound for Australia and was never seen again.

One of his amusing stories is of the friendship he struck up with the skipper of the British yacht *The Spurwing.* In his typical fashion, Father George had taken the yachtsman home on the back of his motorbike for a meal and evening of conversation, finishing with the two men washing and drying the dishes together. Only later did he discover that his guest was Sir Percy Wyn Harris, ex-governor of the Gambia and a famous mountaineer. 'Fancy an English Knight drying my dishes!' Even today he cannot quite believe it.

In 1984 it was his own turn, for Father George was invested with the Dutch order of Orangje-Nassau by the Netherland Embassy in New Zealand. 'It makes me a sort of knight,' he says in his modest way, adding, 'quite undeserved.' There are many yachtsmen from his worldwide parish who would disagree.

Chapter 2

THE OFFSHORE CRUISING YACHT

Almost everyone who has been cruising and even those who just dream about it, have in their mind a picture of the perfect offshore cruising yacht. That this picture is not the same for everyone is clear from the enormous variety of different yachts one sees plying the oceans of the world. While some people have very clear ideas about the essential features of a cruising boat and how it should be equipped, many others, particularly the less experienced, find the choice bewildering.

The basic parameters of size, construction material, displacement, rig and keel configuration all have to be decided before one comes to the even more complicated decisions over equipment. This is not helped by the fact that even designers are not always agreed on the optimum characteristics of an offshore cruising yacht. It was to try and find some consensus on this subject, or the reasons for a lack of consensus, that I first started questioning experienced cruising skippers in my surveys. While some of them had bought or built their boats specifically with an offshore cruise in mind, others had just set off in the boat they happened to own at the time, which may have been purchased originally for a different kind of sailing. To try to assess the essential features of a cruising boat qualitatively, in my earlier surveys the skippers were asked to give a rating to the various features of the boat they were sailing on, while in the ARC surveys they were questioned on what they would consider ideal, not on what they already had. In some cases these coincided, as the skippers were already sailing on what they considered to be their ideal boat.

The search for the ideal cruising boat can be a complex and difficult task, fraught with doubts, especially as the choice confronting the modern buyer is so enormous. In the early seventies when I was faced with this decision myself, searching for a boat to take me, my wife Gwenda and our two young children on a circumnavigation, the choice was much more limited. The fibreglass revolution had resulted in a wide range of boat designs being available, but the number of boats designed specifically for offshore cruising was very small. After scouring the market for a suitable boat, we finally chose a Trintella IIIA, also known as Victory 36, a 36 ft centre-cockpit ketch designed by E. G. van de Stadt. Our first *Aventura* incorporated what I considered to be the essential features of a sturdy and comfortable cruising boat. In view of my lack of offshore experience at the time, the mistakes in my choice were surprisingly few and she served us very well during six years of life afloat, during which time we covered some 60,000 miles.

Although I felt I had come close to that elusive 'ideal' cruising boat, I soon realized that my *Aventura* was not perfect and so I continued looking around at what my fellow cruisers were sailing. This gave me the idea of asking them if they were happy with their own decisions and so the first of a long series of cruising surveys was born. I started my work in the Fijian capital Suva, which is one of the major transit points for boats cruising the South Pacific. Later I joined the annual exodus to New Zealand, a favourite place to spend the cyclone season, where I continued talking to other sailors about what makes a good cruising boat.

New Zealand is a focal point for many of those sailing on a world cruise and so I had a chance to see some of the best production boats available at the time, as well as a large number of self-built boats. Among the latter there were two outstanding steel boats, both built in Australia, *Hägar the Horrible* from Sydney and *Tarrawarra* from Melbourne. Later I was to cruise thousands of miles in their company in the South Pacific and so came to appreciate their sailing qualities. Picking out the most highly rated aspects in the early surveys, I featured the Joe Adams designed 40 foot *Hägar* in my book *Ocean Cruising Survey* as being closest to the perceived 'ideal' cruising boat for the reef-strewn Pacific. *Hägar* was strongly built, but still fast, comfortable and spacious below, while with its centreboard it was able to reach places denied to other cruising boats.

Following my surveys in the Pacific, I turned my attention to the Atlantic, choosing as my starting point one of the major transit ports, Las Palmas de Gran Canaria. The Canary Islands have been a traditional staging post for Atlantic voyagers ever since Columbus started the trend almost five centuries ago. On his four transatlantic voyages Columbus set off from the Canaries like his present day followers, to take advantage of the northeast trade winds. In order to find out more about these modern voyagers and their boats, as well as their preparations for the crossing, I interviewed the skippers of fifty boats in the Canaries who were getting ready for their transatlantic passage. The sample included boats of all types and sizes as well as a great variety of people of different ages and nationalities. The Atlantic Survey was continued in the Caribbean among an additional fifty boats that had just completed their transatlantic voyage.

The findings of that survey were put to good use the following year in the preparations for the first ARC (Atlantic Rally for Cruisers). The success of that first transatlantic rally for cruising boats made the decision to turn it into an annual event almost inevitable. Hundreds of participants have taken part in successive ARCs, providing a constant source of data on various aspects of offshore cruising. From standard production boats to luxurious custom built yachts, from light displacement cruiser-racers to heavy classics of yesteryear, the variation in the ARC boats is only matched by that of the skippers, from those on a tight budget to millionaires, from those making their first ocean passage to veterans of many transatlantic voyages. Nevertheless, compared to the boats surveyed in other parts of the world, the majority of the yachts taking part in the ARC are production boats. Walking down the dock in Las Palmas one can see among them some of the latest offshore cruising yachts from the drawing boards of the best naval architects in the world today. There is no doubt that great strides have been made in offshore yacht design since my first survey and both designers and builders have learnt a lot from earlier failings.

The 400 yachts taking part in ARC 86 and ARC 87 provided such a perfect cross-section of ocean cruising yachts, that I could not resist the temptation to explore the latest state of the cruising scene by means of a survey. Participants in both events were asked to complete detailed questionnaires covering various aspects of offshore cruising. This was backed up by discussion and observation before and after the Atlantic crossings and I hope that the distillation of this mass of experience may answer some of the questions that preoccupy those who plan to sail offshore. The ARC surveys were particularly directed at areas where there have been major changes and development in recent years.

However, rather than restrict the object of the ARC surveys to existing boats and equipment, I also tried to find out what kind of boats, equipment and instruments the skippers would prefer if they had the choice. The object of the ARC Ideal Boat questionnaire was not to design an ideal boat as such, but to try and find some agreement on the most important parameters that ought to be incorporated into any long distance cruising boat. In order to force the skippers to keep their suggestions within the bounds of realism, each was allowed to spend on his or her ideal boat a maximum of £100,000 (US $150,000) or the equivalent in their own currency. The sum available was the only restriction imposed and all other facets of boat design were left entirely to each skipper.

The idea was highly appreciated by most participants and brought to light a wealth of interesting suggestions; 160 skippers rose to the challenge and handed in completed questionnaires at the end of ARC 86, many of them having obviously given a lot of thought to the points raised. The results of the Ideal Boat Survey, as well as the many valuable suggestions made by the skippers, will be examined below in parallel with the findings of the other ARC surveys. Whenever relevant, these findings will also be compared with those of earlier surveys, particularly when discussing the development of specific items over the last ten years.

SIZE

Undoubtedly the first decision to be made by anyone contemplating acquiring a boat is its size. The length itself depends on many factors, such as the number of crew, the length of time intended to spend afloat, the cruising area envisaged and, of course, the depth of one's wallet. For most people the latter reason is the determining factor and I know of many cases where a larger boat would have been acquired if the funds available had allowed it. Nevertheless, financial considerations must not be permitted to override all other criteria in the choice of boat for an extended cruise. As Ian Allmark, who had cruised for many years on his 35 ft *Telemark*, advised, 'Don't go for a bigger boat than you need and most certainly do not buy a large boat just because you can afford it.' These words of wisdom were echoed in a letter I received recently from another sailor, who has contributed to several of the surveys, Mike Bailes of *Jellicle*. His faithful Folkboat has been his home for quarter of a century and they passed the 100,000 mile mark a long time ago. As Mike remarked concerning the optimum size of a cruising boat, 'Too many of my friends follow the erroneous belief that a yacht should be as long in feet as the years of your age. Admittedly, neither I nor the cockroaches would like *Jellicle* any *smaller*, but nor do we want her any bigger!'

With all respect for Mike and his loyal cockroaches, 25 feet does not suit most people's requirements and even that useful yardstick, one's own age, may not necessarily coincide with what is best. As a more objective approach to this subject, the findings of my various surveys point to a remarkable consensus between what is regarded as the optimum and the actual size of cruising boats.

The optimum size of a cruising boat was investigated for the first time in Suva, when the most popular size in a sample of 62 long distance boats was the 35 to 40 ft group, which not only was the largest individual group but also attracted the highest rating. In the Suva Survey, the skippers were asked to rate the size of their boats by taking into account the number of permanent crew. Interestingly enough, the findings of that first survey were confirmed again and again over the next ten years and even the Ideal Boat Survey came up with virtually the same 'ideal' size.

In the Atlantic Survey, the average length of the boats also worked out at 38 feet, which surprisingly has been the average length in *all* of my four previous cruising surveys and shows a remarkable consensus for the length of an offshore cruising boat. Indeed, almost all the cruising boats in the Atlantic Survey fell between 30 and 45 ft (10 to 14 m), most larger boats being used for chartering, while smaller ones were often singlehanded.

Although the ARC is open to any cruising boat over a minimum of 24 ft, the majority are between 35 and 45 ft LOA and in every one of the first three ARCs over half the boats fell between these two lengths. Although there are still plenty of smaller boats cruising the oceans, in recent years I have detected a definite move towards larger boats and the ARC is a reflection of this. Whereas in the 1960s 30 to 35 ft was considered a good size for cruising, in recent years the bracket has moved upwards to 35 to 40 ft, the latter rapidly becoming the most popular size among offshore cruising yachts. This observation was borne out by the results of the Ideal Boat Survey, the first part of which dealt with the ideal overall length.

Although the specified sum of money allowed did preclude the upper end of the market, the skippers taking part in the Ideal Boat Survey still had a relatively unrestrained choice of size. The vast majority indicated the ideal length to be between 35 and 45 ft, with 40 ft LOA being the most popular choice. The extremes attracted only a minority, with only five skippers, or 3 per cent of the total, making their choice under 35 ft, while only a few more would have liked their boats to be 50 ft or longer. Although a few skippers were carried away by overspending the budget, some of those who specified larger boats pointed out that they would build the boats themselves so as to make the money go further. Nevertheless, the Ideal Boat Survey confirmed my feeling that financial considerations are often the determining factor in the choice of a particular size and only rarely is the final decision based on factors such as a 30-footer being easier to handle than her 40 ft sister.

The size of crew also has a certain bearing on the size of boat, but a change of attitude has occurred in this respect too and many people are now prepared to handle boats, which until not so long ago were considered to be fit only for a crew of Tarzans. This is particularly obvious in the ARC in which many boats over 40 ft LOA are sailed only by a couple, many of them not even that young. Comparative boat sizes are shown in Table 14 which includes data from all the surveys conducted during the last decade. The figures show the percentages of boats of a certain size in each particular survey. As can be seen, the sizes of some 400 cruising boats surveyed in the Pacific and Atlantic over a number of years as well as the 600 yachts which took part in the first three ARCs, are evenly spread between 30 and 45 feet.

Table 14. COMPARISON OF CRUISING BOAT SIZE

	Percentage of Total			
	Pacific Surveys	*Atlantic Survey*	*ARC 1986–88*	*Ideal Boat*
Under 30 ft	7	12	8	–
30–35 ft	20	21	20	3
35–40 ft	30	19	28	55
40–45 ft	21	28	24	24
45–50 ft	10	10	9	14
Over 50 ft	12	10	11	4

Most of the boats in the various surveys did suit their owners' requirements, whether large or small, yet in every survey there were some disgruntled crews. A few complained that their boats were too large to handle, but the vast majority of dissatisfied owners complained about their boat being too small. The feeling of being overcrowded or the lack of space can have a negative effect on morale and lead to friction among the members of the crew. Another cause of complaint was not having enough space to store all the gear necessary for a longer voyage. Often this meant that surplus gear was stowed on deck, which can lead to a potentially hazardous or unseaworthy situation. Having been on the dockside in Barbados watching boats coming stern to after their Atlantic crossing, I have been amazed at the clutter on the stern of some boats, as the person throwing the line ashore struggles to clear a forest of obstructions, from wind generator pole to danbuoy, self-steering gear, radar mast, fishing rods and reels, flagpole, spare anchor, satnav aerial, outboard engine or a barbecue. In an emergency, one might need to throw a line to a man overboard or launch the liferaft past all such obstructions. Undoubtedly there is a great safety factor in having clear uncluttered decks. However, it does not follow that larger boats necessarily have tidier decks, but that the amount of cruising gear to be carried and how it will be stowed should be given serious consideration when acquiring a boat for lengthier cruising.

Larger boats also mean more living space and many of the owners of smaller boats taking part in the Ideal Boat Survey stressed the importance of privacy, particularly on long passages. A separate cabin for each crew member would be the ideal solution, or at least a provision to shield a bunk from the rest of the boat. Having a separate cabin for the children was stressed as extremely important by several parents. Another interesting suggestion concerned those who may be planning to set off on a joint adventure with another couple, in which case the boat should be designed in such a way as to give privacy to either couple. An aft cabin with through access to the rest of the boat was mentioned as perhaps the best solution, although on most boats, the provision of an aft cabin of reasonable dimensions depends on the position of the cockpit.

In the Ideal Boat Survey the skippers were also asked to indicate their preferred position of the cockpit, but without going into detailed design considerations. Aft cockpits still had more adherents (84) compared to 70 centre cockpits, while six skippers were undecided. As some sort of cockpit protection is high on most cruisers'

Makiki III *amongst a mixed fleet of all types of cruising boats at the start of the Canary Islands Rally.*

list of priorities, the skippers were also asked to say if they would choose a canvas dodger or a more permanent arrangement. With the majority preferring an aft cockpit, permanent protection for the steering position is not so practical and 93 voted in favour of a canvas dodger, 12 skippers being undecided. However, 55 skippers specified a permanent structure providing shelter to a centrally placed cockpit. Going further in their quest for comfort, 29 skippers indicated that they would also like a secondary steering position. In some instances, it was suggested that a dual steering arrangement could incorporate a wheel inside and a tiller outside. Ideally, several skippers specified that the tiller should be linked directly to the rudder stock, so that it could also be used to activate the self-steering mechanism, if that gear was of the type which had lines going to the cockpit. Another suggestion concerning a secondary steering position inside a wheelhouse referred to the latter as being expendable in an extreme situation, all essential controls being duplicated elsewhere inside the boat.

KEEL SHAPE

The configuration of the keel was examined in a number of the surveys, usually in conjunction with draft. Over the years there has been a decrease in the number of boats with long keels, which used to be regarded as the best type of keel for a long distance cruising boat. Most modern production boats feature a medium length or fin keel, although a few designs continue to have a long or full keel. The predominance of the long keel was striking in the Suva Survey, in which out of a total of 62 boats, 39 had a full keel (63 per cent). The popularity of the full keel has been losing ground in the intervening years as can be seen from Table 15, which compares the different types of keel found on the boats taking part in various surveys.

Table 15. COMPARISON OF KEEL SHAPE

	Percentage of Total			
	Pacific Surveys	*Atlantic Survey*	*ARC 1986/87*	*Ideal Boat*
Long	34	27	30	27
Medium	37	36	31	38
Fin	19	31	19	11
Centreboard	9	4	5	15
Other	1	2	5	9

A major feature examined in the Ideal Boat Survey was the optimum keel shape. Skippers were asked to indicate both their preferred keel shape and the maximum draft they would consider acceptable. The most popular choice was a medium length keel with a skeg and rudder configuration, suggested by 38 per cent of the skippers. However, slightly over one quarter (27 per cent) still considered a long keel the optimum solution for cruising. For their ideal boat, eleven per cent of the skippers chose a fin keel. Probably being concerned by the vulnerability of a fin keel on a cruising boat, three of these skippers stressed that the fin keels should be matched with well supported rudders protected by strong skegs. Two of them went even further and also specified a watertight bulkhead forward of the rudder stock and skeg.

A drop keel or centreboard was the choice of 24 skippers, who were also among those who preferred the draft of their boats not to exceed 4 ft (1.2 m). In fact several skippers qualified both their choice of keel and maximum draft by pointing out that a final decision would depend on the particular cruising area the boat was being built for. Otherwise, for normal cruising, 110 skippers considered 6 ft (1.8 m) to be a reasonable maximum draft but 30 were not prepared to accept anything above 5 ft (1.5 m). The remaining 20 were all in favour of a centreboard or retractable keel.

The Ideal Boat Survey did not produce any surprises in the choice of keel with the exception of a concern for shallower draft, achieved either by designing a shallower keel, a centreboard or retractable keel, or by choosing a catamaran. One of the keels developed primarily to reduce draft is the Scheel keel, which interestingly was not chosen as the ideal keel by any skipper, not even those whose present boats featured this type of keel. This reluctance was explained by one owner of a brand new yacht who had agreed to fit a Scheel keel on the advice of the designer and builder. The keel performed satisfactorily when sailing off the wind, but on the wind he found that the amount of leeway was excessive and did not think that the modest reduction in draft achieved by the Scheel keel justified the sacrifice in the windward capabilities of the proven design of his boat. However, not all Scheel keel owners seem to share this view. During ARC 88 I had the opportunity to discuss the keel's advantages and disadvantages with two participants who had this type of keel on their yachts; each of them agreed that the Scheel keel had many advantages – indeed, the had only words of praise for it.

Two skippers stressed the advantage of being able to dry out upright and both were prepared to let the shape of the keel be dictated by this requirement. The boat should therefore have a fairly flat bottom and be provided with either a centreboard or swing keel. The rudder itself would have to be either retractable or one might choose a twin rudder configuration. The other alternative was to choose a catamaran.

Among those for whom a catamaran was the ideal cruising boat, low draft appeared to be one of the main attractions. Another attraction of catamarans outlined by their supporters was the possibility of providing them with sufficient positive buoyancy to render them unsinkable. Three of the existing catamaran owners would make sure that their ideal cats would incorporate extra buoyancy chambers, which could keep them afloat even if the boat was partially flooded.

It was interesting to note that among the 14 multihull owners, 11 chose a multihull again, but three specified a monohull as their ideal choice, whereas there was no switch in the other direction and none of the monohull owners made a multihull their ideal choice. It is interesting that in spite of the undeniable advantages of multihulls for cruising, particularly catamarans, their popularity is still limited. There are several reasons for this, mainly the reservations many people seem to have about the safety of multihulls in offshore cruising. The well publicised disasters involving racing multihulls have certainly not helped the cause of cruising multihulls, in spite of the fact that several outstanding voyages have been accomplished in cruising catamarans.

DISPLACEMENT

The variety in boat design that I came across in the first two surveys conducted in the Pacific prompted me to examine more systematically the factors which can influence the choice of a cruising boat. These aspects were investigated further in both the Pacific and Atlantic Surveys, which led to some interesting conclusions. One conclusion which I drew at the end of the Pacific Survey, and which was reinforced by its Atlantic counterpart, was that a large number of people do not consider displacement to be of sufficient importance to influence greatly the choice of their future boat. It seems that many people are quite happy to have this decision made by the designer, particularly such niceties as the displacement to ballast ratio. When asked if they were satisfied with their present ratio, a considerable number of skippers did not even know what their displacement to ballast ratio was, let alone comment on it.

The fact that displacement is something that many cruising skippers treat with indifference is reflected every year by the number of blank spaces or obviously incorrect figures given for displacement on the ARC entry forms. I can offer no explanation for this, although I am convinced that the performance of many cruising boats would be significantly better if their owners had given displacement the consideration it deserves when they were in the process of choosing a suitable boat for their cruising plans. Often it is only when they start cruising and meeting other boats that this aspect of design attracts their attention, often too late to do anything about it. This attitude was summed up by Erick Bouteleux of *Calao*, who never failed to show his disdain for his fellow Frenchmen, who had slavishly copied Moitessier's ultra-heavy *Joshua*. 'What fun can anyone get from sailing in a floating safe?'

Displacement was also examined in the Ideal Boat Survey and the majority of those questioned favoured a medium displacement boat, able to carry sufficient stores and provisions, but without being sluggish. The average displacement quoted as ideal for the entire sample came out at 10.6 tons. Although this figure has little meaning without reference to the construction material and other factors, but bearing in mind that the mean length of the sample was 41 ft, it points nevertheless to a demand for lighter displacement boats among long distance sailors, a move away from the heavier craft of the past.

One valuable suggestion concerning displacement underlined the importance of the designer taking into account the additional weight of water, fuel, stores and gear which are carried by every cruising boat, when calculating the displacement of the fully laden boat. This would then determine the amount of ballast to be added. Obviously with production or secondhand boats, the prospective owner can do little, but otherwise it is in the owner's interest to inform both designer and builder of his weight requirements and how it will be distributed, especially heavier items such as extra anchors or the amount of chain.

Construction material

Most people have a fairly precise idea about the kind of construction material they prefer long before they choose the actual design of their boat. As far as standard production boats are con-

Roter Baron *beats* Oyster Lady *by only two seconds in the first ARC to show that well designed steel boats can be fast.*

cerned, the choice boils down to any kind of material as long as it is fibreglass. A wider choice is available to those who can afford a one-off, who plan to build the boat themselves or who decide to circumvent all these problems and buy a used boat.

Although fibreglass continues to be the dominant construction material for the large scale production of offshore cruising boats, other materials still have an assured slice of the market. A tendency highlighted by the three surveys in the Pacific was the increased popularity of metal hulls, which rose as high as 30 per cent in the 1984 Pacific Survey. Many sailors who cruise among the reefs and coral atolls of the South Pacific feel safer in a metal boat and approximately one fifth of all the boats surveyed in the Pacific were made of metal. (See Table 16.)

The preference for strong hulls is not such a priority in the Atlantic, where the overall proportion of metal boats is lower. Yet, although the actual number of metal boats in the Atlantic and ARC surveys were lower than in the Pacific, the concern for strength was still manifested by 44 per cent of the skippers participating in the Ideal Boat Survey making a metal hull their ideal choice. Among these, there was a preference for steel rather than aluminium, the latter usually being the choice of skippers who wanted to combine strength with light displacement.

Table 16. COMPARISON OF CONSTRUCTION MATERIALS

	Percentage of Total			
	Pacific Surveys	*Atlantic Survey*	*ARC 1986/87*	*Ideal Boat*
GRP	47	69	77	52
Wood	27	11	7	3
Plywood	4	3	–	½
Steel	17	11	9	28
Aluminium	2	1	6	16
Ferro	3	–	1	½

As mentioned in the section on displacement, the Ideal Boat Survey revealed a shift towards lighter displacement boats. However, from talking to many of the skippers, it was clear that they were not prepared to sacrifice strength for the sake of speed, but rather it was the other way around, they expected designers to produce cruising boats that were fast as well as strong.

Fibreglass or foam sandwich continued to be the favourite construction material, being chosen by 82 skippers, while 5 preferred wood, one plywood and one ferrocement. Of the 71 skippers choosing a metal hull, 45 preferred steel and 26 aluminium. Although the majority still consider a GRP hull to be the ideal construction material, a rising proportion of metal boats, particularly steel, have become apparent among those undertaking world voyages. In the ARC fleet, the proportion of metal hulls is not very different to other surveys, which makes it even more significant that such a large number of skippers indicated a metal hull as their ideal choice. The fact that more metal hulls were specified as the ideal material than were found in reality, is probably because for most buyers a production boat is the only feasible option and metal hulls are not so easy or economic to produce on a mass scale as is a moulded hull, although some French boatyards have made strides in this direction by producing competitively priced aluminium boats.

The main reason for the current concern with the strength of the hull among world voyagers is the fear of collision with an unidentified object, of which there seem to be rather too many lurking on or just under the surface of the ocean. Several skippers reported such collisions, either before or during the ARC, and one yacht on her way to the start suffered severe damage to keel and rudder after hitting a submerged object in the Irish Sea, forcing her to withdraw from the ARC. Four ARC yachts collided with whales during the Atlantic crossing, fortunately with little damage to themselves. These examples show that such fears are not exaggerated. Not surprisingly, every one of the skippers who had experienced such a collision, indicated either steel or aluminium as the preferred construction material of his ideal boat.

Rig

Another tendency which has manifested itself in recent years among cruising boats has been the switch to a one-masted configuration on even the largest yachts. The reasons are many, although the single most important contributing factor has been the improvement in furling gear, both for headsails and mainsails. The rig of the boats taking part in the various ARCs confirmed the findings of previous surveys with over two thirds of the boats under 40 feet having single masts and only a handful being ketches. Even above this length, more than half the ARC boats were either sloops or cutters. This also confirms the trend towards single masts on all but the largest cruising boats and spells the end to the old theory that a two-mast configuration is to be preferred because smaller sails make handling easier. Smaller sails are indeed easier to handle, particularly in strong winds, but jib furling gears, which are now used on many cruising boats, have taken care of that aspect. For long distance cruising it is just as important to have a rig that is efficient to windward and this is where a sloop or cutter wins hands down.

The Ideal Boat Survey confirmed this tendency towards single-masted boats as three quarters of the skippers gave a single mast as their ideal choice (43 sloops, 77 cutters) while the remaining quarter preferred two masts (32 ketches, 2 yawls, 2 schooners, one luna and 3 cat rigs). An interesting phenomenon was the large number of skippers who gave a cutter as their preferred rig. The increasing popularity of cutters was not restricted to single masted yachts as 15 of the 'ideal' ketches would also carry a staysail. The increasing preference for single masts is apparent from Table 17, which compares the findings of previous surveys and ARC participants with the ideal rig.

Table 17. COMPARISON OF RIG

	Percentage of Total			
	Pacific Surveys	*Atlantic Survey*	*ARC 1986/87*	*Ideal Boat*
Sloop	33	50	53	26
Cutter	23	21	17	48
Ketch	38	25	26	21
Yawl	3	2	1	1
Schooner	3	2	2	1
Other	–	–	1	3

Several skippers pointed out that whichever rig was chosen, it should be of ample proportions, as there is nothing more frustrating than an undercanvassed boat. Their views were defined by Peter Ibsen, an experienced Danish sailor whose Sigma 41 *Baldur* took part in the first Canary Islands Rally, ARC 87 and TRANSARC 88, during which I had the opportunity to discuss with Peter various aspects of cruising boat design. Having led the fleet on many occasions, both in strong and light winds, he stressed the advantages of a generous sail plan. 'In light airs one can set a good spread of sail, while in a blow one can always reef down to manageable proportions.'

This ability to perform satisfactorily in light winds is obviously not a matter that many people consider seriously when choosing the rig of their boat. Usually heavy weather preoccupies them more and in fact many skippers admitted that initially they had thought a ketch rig would make life easier in heavy weather, only to find later that they did not meet much heavy weather along the trade wind route and that their boats were slow and undercanvassed most of the time. Having made exactly this mistake myself when fitting out our first *Aventura*, I have a particular interest in this subject. It pains me to see well designed cruising boats that simply cannot move at any

The cutter has been a popular rig for a long time, particularly in the USA, and received highest marks in the Ideal Boat Survey.

speed once the wind drops below 10 knots. This was quite apparent during the second Canary Islands Rally in October 1988, which attracted a score of very different boats. In strong winds their performances were fairly evenly matched, but when the wind was light, which it was most of the time, many of the cruising boats were left wallowing far behind the cruiser-racers, who continued sailing at a fair pace. Gauging the right amount of sail area for a particular boat is something that some designers are obviously far better at than others. Philip Owen, skipper of the Evasion 37 *Cormorant* vented his frustration when he said, 'For comfortable cruising there is little to fault our boat, but why hasn't the designer added another five feet to the mast to make her into a perfect all-rounder?' It was a question that probably went through the minds of several others taking part in the rally as they watched some participants don their spinnakers and show a clean pair of heels.

Not just the rig, but light weather sails were also deemed important by many skippers. Another aspect of the rig preferred by some with long distance cruising in mind was the provision of twin forestays and possibly twin backstays as well. Whereas the latter is primarily a safety feature, the former can be very useful when running before the wind with twin jibs or genoas, although it was pointed out that the added safety factor should not be neglected either.

Interior

Many suggestions concerned the galley, such as the provision of more gimballed facilities apart from the cooker. A good suggestion was a gimballed shelf for serving and stowing prepared food in plates, cups or mugs. The table itself might also be gimballed and possibly one of the berths. The importance of good comfortable sea berths at any angle of heel was stressed by many and it was also suggested by one skipper that if the saloon bunks were not used for sitting at sea, they should be easily convertible to coffin shaped berths on passage. The attraction of a double berth in port was also underlined by many and rather graphically by one singlehander!

Good ventilation was considered essential throughout the boat, which should have several opening portholes and reversible hatches. Some skippers went as far as providing their ideal boat with air conditioning, whereas others praised the advantages of good hull insulation, which many boats lack, and which can make life on board more comfortable both in hot and particularly in cold climates. Adequate sound insulation for the engine room was also recommended, as was the provision of good ventilation for the engine itself. On the subject of ventilation, it was also suggested that the stowage area should be adequately ventilated as fresh stores kept much better if air circulation was not restricted. Particularly in the galley area it might be better to fit wire baskets instead of shelves.

The heads attracted a whole range of comments, from some who would be prepared to pay anything for a good quality toilet, which did not break down at the most inconvenient moment, to others who swore by the bucket-and-chuck-it principle. Next to reliable heads, a shower was also deemed by many as a desirable feature. One interesting suggestion was to provide the shower tray with a high sill so that it could be used as a tub for bathing children or even for soaking laundry. One of the conclusions I drew early on in the Ideal Boat Survey was that many boat owners appear to be obsessed with everything on board having a double function. For instance, among some rather unusual comforts listed was a sauna, which could double up for stowage when not in use.

The need for ample stowage space was often repeated as was the suggestion to use the forecabin for stowage, but to provide it with collapsible berths which could be used for extra crew if necessary. The foc's'le was also suggested as a possible workshop, several skippers stressing the importance of having a work bench on a cruising boat. Other desirable features mentioned for a well thought out cruising boat were a cockpit table and, if space allowed, full size chart table or at least a table which could take a chart folded only once. Concerning the navigation table it was also stressed that ideally the navigator should always face forward and have a properly shaped seat which provides firm support even when the boat is heeled.

Safety

An overall concern for safety was apparent from the large number of suggestions made by the skippers on this subject. The provision of collision bulkheads and watertight compartments was a common suggestion as it was felt that more should be done to reduce the risk of losing the boat as a result of collision. Also with this consideration in mind, it was suggested that water or fuel tanks should be built into the sides of the hull to reach above water level so as to act as a second skin in case of collision. Another improvement in safety was the suggestion that ideally there should be only one sea water intake through the hull and that generally, the number of through hull openings should be kept to an absolute minimum. Criticism was levelled at boat designs with a bottom so flat that there is no bilge, although even on flat bottomed boats a provision should be made for a well. The ideal boat should therefore have a bilge and be provided with good bilge pumps, one of which should be engine driven. That the engine should be easily accessible in an emergency was a requirement mentioned by many skippers. Another interesting suggestion was to make the engine compartment watertight so that the engine could continue to operate even if the rest of the boat was partly flooded. An engine driven large capacity bilge pump could possibly save the boat in such an eventuality.

Many interesting features were suggested, some adding to safety while others making life more comfortable for the crew. Nonslip floors, especially in the galley area, were recommended as contributing to safety as was the absence of sharp edges anywhere below decks. Several skippers pointed to the convenience as well as safety of having all furling lines brought back to the cockpit. Permanent boarding steps on the transom were suggested by many as a safety feature, as was the provision of a transom platform. This latter feature also serves as a bathing platform and could also be designed in such a way as to protect the selfsteering gear.

After having processed all data and worked my way through the results I had no doubt that if most suggestions were put into practice, the consensus of the Ideal Boat Survey would be a very attractive cruising boat. The first to benefit from this survey was myself, as my new *Aventura*, designed in close consultation with Bill Dixon incorporates many of the interesting suggestions made by the ARC skippers. My own 'ideal' cruising boat, and the way many of these valuable suggestions became part of her, will be described later in the book.

A CRUISING IDEALIST

After having reached a consensus on the most important features of the ideal cruising boat, perhaps it would have been logical to continue with the story of an ideal boat. Yet that perfect blend of so many requirements remains elusive, for so much depends on personal factors. So instead of an ideal boat, I decided to introduce a man who has found an ideal to pursue, not in the shape of a cruising boat, but by using his boat to achieve something more valuable than just a cruise.

The first time I met Pierre Ribes, a 55 year old French singlehander, was in Las Palmas. His battered 26 ft *Sphinx* with a large yellow dinghy upturned on deck stood out among the scores of smarter yachts getting ready to sail across the Atlantic to the Caribbean. Slipping her lines one sunny morning, *Sphinx* set off for a very different destination. As Pierre had explained to me the night before, the one month long voyage would take him to an unusual rendezvous off the coast of West Africa. A mini-armada of five yachts from ports on both the Atlantic and Mediterranean coasts of

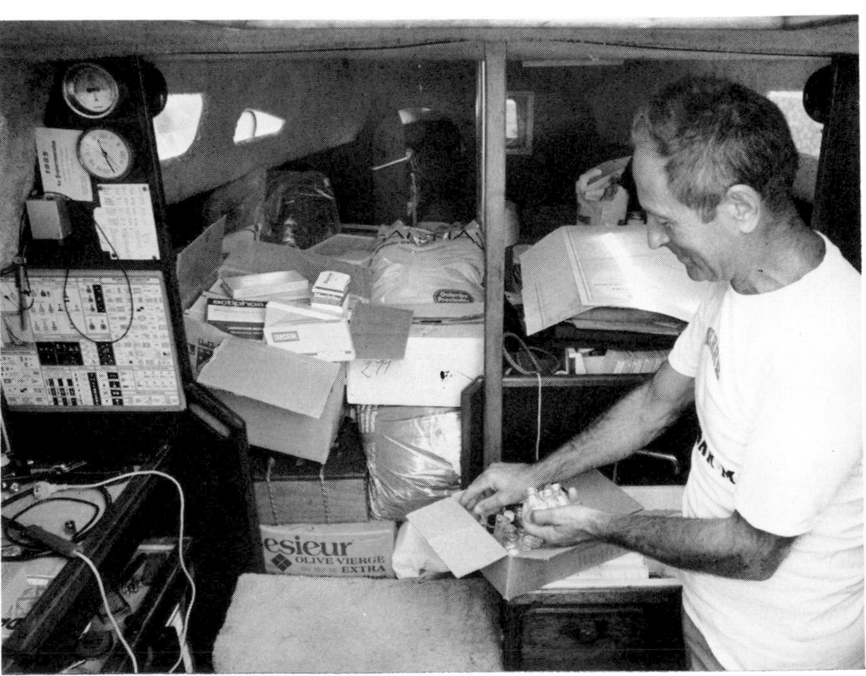

Pierre Ribes' floating dispensary.

France had agreed to meet there and deliver six tonnes of medical aid to Senegal.

Pierre Ribes, the soul of the operation, had sailed the round trip from France to Senegal every year for the previous five years, logging over 35,000 miles. In 1984 his efforts were instrumental in the birth of a voluntary group, La Fédération Humanitaire des Associations Maritimes. The purpose of FHAM was to encourage long distance sailors to carry small loads on behalf of development agencies in Europe to Third World destinations. As many cruising boats sail to places and islands that are rarely visited by regular supply ships, the idea was welcomed by those who, in the past, had seen many valuable projects collapse because of lack of transport. Another aim of the Association was to forge links between those who give and those who receive.

Pierre Ribes's personal story is quite remarkable. A serious work accident, which broke his spine, left him paraplegic in 1958. With iron determination, he slowly taught himself to walk again, although he still only walks with some difficulty. Unable to continue his work as a market gardener, he looked around for some activity which he could pursue which did not require too much walking, and sailing appeared to be the ideal solution. He bought the bilge-keeled *Sphinx* as a bare hull and fitted her out himself in a simple, functional manner. The boat is powered by an outboard engine and a bank of solar panels supply his modest electricity needs, mostly consumed by the amateur radio, for Pierre has no electronic instruments and navigates by traditional methods.

The first offshore voyage took place in 1981 when *Sphinx* sailed via Portugal and the Canaries to Senegal, where Pierre had offered his services as a voluntary advisor on vegetable farming to the government, a subject that had been his speciality. While working in the marshy region of Casamance, in the southern part of Senegal, he was shocked by the lack of even the most basic medicines and medical equipment. He remembered that huge amounts of medicines were destroyed every year in France because their date of expiry has passed, yet he knew that in many instances, certain drugs could still be used safely after the expiry date, although the dosage might have to be increased. The waste in Europe compared to the needs in Africa appalled him.

When Pierre sailed back to France, he contacted the French Red Cross, as well as hospitals and pharmacies in his native region near Bordeaux. After a winter of incessant effort, *Sphinx* left France loaded with over one tonne of medicines. All drugs had been checked, repacked and relabelled by a voluntary team of pharmacists. As space was at a great premium on *Sphinx*, the bulk of the supplies had been reduced considerably by repacking the drugs in a more efficient way.

A brief stop in the Canaries, before carrying on past the Cape Verde Islands without stopping, brought *Sphinx* once again to Senegal. Fearing that the drugs might be resold and not reach where most needed if he simply handed them over to the Ministry of Health, when he arrived in Senegal, Pierre got on a bicycle and started visiting rural dispensaries to assess their needs. Then he would return to the boat, load the required drugs on his bicycle and deliver them to the village. By the end of the dry season, the tonne of drugs had been distributed in an efficient manner to where they were most needed.

Encouraged by his success, Pierre sailed back to France via the Azores and started collecting again. As well as drugs, he also began looking for other useful items, such as discarded spectacles which he obtained from old people's homes and clubs in French villages. The lenses were often perfect as the glasses had been discarded for other reasons, a faulty frame or a changed prescription. Thinking that the glasses would be welcomed by many an elderly African villager, Pierre persuaded an optician friend to check all glasses and label the lenses with the correct dioptries.

Although his initial efforts had fallen on stony ears, most well known aid and development agencies not even bothering to reply to his letters, gradually his activities caught the imagination of various organisations, such as Rotary Clubs in both France and Senegal, and help started pouring in. A victim of his own success, Pierre found the mountain of medicine growing and also expanding by donations of all kinds of medical equipment, electric scalpels, a dental chair, laboratory equipment, even an anaesthetist's table. It was too much for poor *Sphinx* to carry, so an appeal was launched and FHAM was born. In the summer of 1985 *Sphinx* was joined by four larger boats for the voyage to Senegal. As Pierre had imagined, there were plenty of people willing to help those in need, provided someone showed the way. Pierre also knew that many sailors enjoyed putting some purpose into a voyage, setting off on what he called 'a useful adventure'.

It has not been always plain sailing, however, and during one return trip home, *Sphinx* was dismasted on the passage to the Azores. Pierre had only three weeks' rations on board, the length of time it normally took him from Dakar. He managed a rig a jury mast but the rest of the voyage took him a long 67 days. Now he buys more stores, although space is still at a premium, particularly on his outward trips. This is the main reason why he always sails on his own, not because he particularly likes solitude, but because a crew would take the space of valuable medicines. Brimming over with boxes of drugs, disposable syringes, blood pressure gauges and countless spectacles, when I first visited Pierre's floating pharmacy, only the quarter berth had been left uncluttered with just enough space for him to squeeze in.

A keen radio amateur, Pierre keeps in constant touch both with supporters back home and his many friends in Senegal. With only his disability pension to finance him, he leads an extremely simple life, but one he enjoys to the full. 'Because of my disability, the sea is a perfect environment,' he says. '*Sphinx* has become my home and I have a very special relationship with my boat. The fact that I can come to the aid of people who are less fortunate than me has made my own life so much more meaningful.'

As an inspiration to us all, Pierre Ribes is obviously a very special man. He represents the best qualities of a cruising sailor, modest and generous, unbiased and with a great sense of humour. He is also an excellent navigator and has given me many useful tips on the routes and weather systems between Europe and West Africa. The fact that he is also French will hopefully prove to some people that in spite of the bad reputation French cruising sailors have acquired in some places, there are many exceptions. Pierre Ribes is undoubtedly one of them.

Chapter 3

GEARING UP FOR OFFSHORE CRUISING

In the relatively short span of fifteen years since I fitted out my first boat for an ocean voyage, there has been an incredible explosion in the amount of boating equipment available, which would have been impossible to imagine then. Now there seems to be a special piece of equipment for every conceivable job, from telling how much water is left in the tanks to how far the boat is heeling over. The choice and variety is truly bewildering, making it almost impossible to decide which pieces of equipment are really *necessary* on a cruising boat. Finding a way through this maze is not easy and although a few general guidelines can be prescribed, it is finally up to each person to decide what is needed for his or her boat.

People go cruising for a variety of reasons, although I suspect that for many it is a search for peacefulness and a yearning for the unspoilt face of nature. Even those who at the outset of a voyage are convinced that they could not possibly live without the modern conveniences of contemporary society, gradually come around to a different point of view, in which values are reassessed and the quality of life itself is found to be measured by different standards. It is perhaps a question of mind versus matter and, in spite of the aggressive intrusion of material values into our lives, I find that particularly among cruising sailors, it is mind that eventually wins. This is the reason why in this chapter, and in the book generally, I have tried to concentrate more on the essential items, that are common to every boat, such as sails and rig, a reliable auxiliary engine, an efficient reefing system, adequate ground tackle, and less on things which are not so vital but more a matter of personal choice. However, I have tried not to go to the other extreme and I most certainly would not advise anyone to return to the lead and line when an electronic depth sounder does the job so much better. With the equipment explosion a lot of useful gadgets have been developed as well as unnecessary ones, but I shall deal first with the items that every boat must have.

SAILS

Tremendous strides have been made in recent years in the design and making of sails, an area where the cruising market has benefited enormously from the advances made in racing. Although some of the newest materials may not be found on cruising boats, nevertheless designing sails by computer is now commonplace. All the developments have resulted in much better quality sails, particularly in the case of furling sails, both headsails and mainsails. Light weather sails are also much better designed and cut, while the provision of socks or dousers on spinnakers have made these exciting sails manageable even by short-handed crews.

In spite of the general improvement in the quality of sails, both in design and manufacture, I still find that many cruising skippers do not pay this subject the attention it deserves. This is particularly obvious on the starting line of the ARC, where I have a grandstand view of some two hundred boats. The contrast is enormous and while some sails seem to have been cut and put together by a trainee tent-maker, others are perfect examples of the present state of the art.

Standard sails were examined in several surveys and it was interesting to compare the sail wardrobe of various boats. Thus, in the Pacific Survey, many boats carried a complete second suit of sails, almost half the boats in the sample having a spare mainsail on board. Among the 50 boats surveyed, exactly half also had a trisail to be used in strong winds. Some of these were kept bagged at the foot of the mast ready to be hoisted on a separate track if necessary. An even larger number of boats (43) also carried a storm jib. Without counting the storm jibs, the total number of foresails worked out at an average of almost four foresails per boat. This is a fairly high number for cruising boats, although it must be pointed out that jib furling gears were not common in those days, whereas now many cruising boats sail with a one and only roller furling genoa.

In the Atlantic Survey standard sails were not examined, but being aware of most cruising sailors' dislike of going to windward, I tried to find out what kind of preparation skippers had made for downwind sailing. Several people told me that they had made special provision for extended downwind runs, nine having twin jibs or genoas to be set on poles of equal length. On three of these boats the twin jibs were of the furling type and were used with existing furling gear.

Over half the boats had spinnakers on board, many of them

fitted with a sock or douser, as were some of the eight cruising chutes. Not all the owners of the chutes were totally satisfied with their performance, some stressing that these sails were not as good as expected when the wind is forward of the beam and that it was a mistake to regard them as an all-round light weather sail. Another criticism levelled at the chutes was that often these were advertised as a hybrid spinnaker, but with the great advantage of being set without a pole. However, several skippers mentioned that if there was any swell combined with a light wind, the sail tended to collapse and the only way to overcome this was to pole it out, in which case one might as well have a proper spinnaker.

Downwind sailing techniques were investigated more closely in the second part of the survey after the boats had completed the Atlantic crossing. The sails used, their setting arrangements and the effect on automatic pilots or selfsteering gears were discussed in detail with the skippers. Although just over half the boats (26) had spinnakers, these had been used very little during the transatlantic crossing. On 14 boats their spinnakers were not used at all, while on the remaining 12 boats their use amounted to an average of only 14 per cent of the time. Cruising chutes were set just as infrequently on the 8 boats that had them, three not being used at all and the other five about 13 per cent of the time. The main reason given for the limited use of spinnakers and cruising chutes was the need to steer by hand, or at least keep a watchful eye on self-steering gears when these sails were in use in boisterous trade wind conditions. The fact that most boats had small crews was another reason why spinnakers were used so little. One short-handed skipper who tried to fly his spinnaker only managed to get it wrapped around his jib furling gear. He was forced to climb the mast to get it untangled and protected himself from the constant banging against the mast by wearing a life jacket.

On most boats the preferred running technique was to use the mainsail, often reefed, in conjunction with a poled out foresail. This arrangement worked reasonably well on 24 boats, although in some instances the mainsail had to be well reefed to balance the jib or to minimize weather helm. On some cutters the staysail was also set, but sheeted hard in so as to stop some of the rolling. The constant rolling was in fact the main criticism levelled at the recommended trade wind technique of running with twin jibs poled out. Nineteen boats had provision for setting twin jibs or genoas, either on separate stays or by alternate hanks on the same stay. One boat had an excellent system of twin furling genoas set in separate grooves in the same extrusion and poled out on booms of equal length so that they could be reefed simultaneously with the help of the roller furling gear. In most cases, the twin jibs had to be dropped when the wind exceeded 20 knots and a smaller jib set, either with or without a reefed mainsail.

Another running technique used on four boats was to match a furling jib with another foresail of roughly the same size set either flying or on a jackstay. On two cutters a poled-out jib was used in conjunction with a staysail sheeted to the end of the main boom, but without the mainsail being set. On *Svanhild*, the largest boat in the sample, two squaresails were used for running, which had been specially cut in the Canaries for the crossing.

Although standard sails were not examined in detail in the Ideal Boat Survey either, skippers were asked to rate the importance and usefulness of cruising chutes and spinnakers, particularly as the latter are not so popular among cruising folk. However, in the ARC even some hardened cruising sailors underwent a sudden metamorphosis into a racing mentality and tried to gain that elusive extra half knot by flying a spinnaker, even at night if necessary. In the survey itself, only 21 skippers considered spinnakers to be very important, almost half (77). as not important and 32 rated spinnakers as outright useless. Cruising chutes were slightly more popular than spinnakers, although not as popular as twin jibs which were considered very important by 59 skippers.

Any questionnaire, however wide ranging, has its limitations and many skippers wished to make points not included in the questions. These were often added on the back of the forms and some of the most valuable suggestions were made in this way. For instance, the importance of carrying storm sails, which could actually drive the boat to windward in a blow was mentioned by several skippers. A feature one skipper would like was some provision to make it possible to hank boltrope sails on an ordinary forestay in case of trouble. Undoubtedly the most desirable feature to be appreciated by most cruising sailors was that suggested by Werner Eichholz of *Dresden*, who hoped that someone would invent an anti-beating device.

Skippers were also asked to comment on the effect their particular downwind sailing arrangement had on the behaviour of self-steering gears or automatic pilots. Windvanes appeared to function best in conjunction with twin jibs, even if the rhythmic rolling induced by this particular set of sails was not appreciated by some crews. Mostly because of the rolling, but also due to stronger than expected winds, even on boats fitted with twin jibs, a reefed mainsail and poled-out jib were often substituted for running. Self-steering gears generally coped better than automatic pilots with extended downwind runs and usually when they were thrown off balance it was not because of the wind and sails, but the swell. On some boats which were less well balanced, the danger of gybing the mainsail while running on self-steering meant that the watchkeeper had to be close on hand all the time.

The wear and tear of cruising sails was examined in the Circumnavigators Survey, in which the average mileage per sail worked out at almost 30,000 miles, although this does not mean that every single sail was actually used for all those miles. Some of the circumnavigators taking part in that survey completed their voyage on one suit of sails, which reflects the kind of care they gave to their sails.

The longevity of sails depends on two main factors, both of them equally important; firstly, the quality of the material and workmanship and secondly, the care taken in looking after those sails. Continuous exposure to the sun, particularly in the tropics, exerts a heavy toll on any sail, although some brands of materials appear to be more resistant to ultraviolet rays than others. Usually it is the stitching that disintegrates long before the material itself and one way to overcome this is to have cruising sails provided with triple stitching, ideally by using one of the ultraviolet resistant threads.

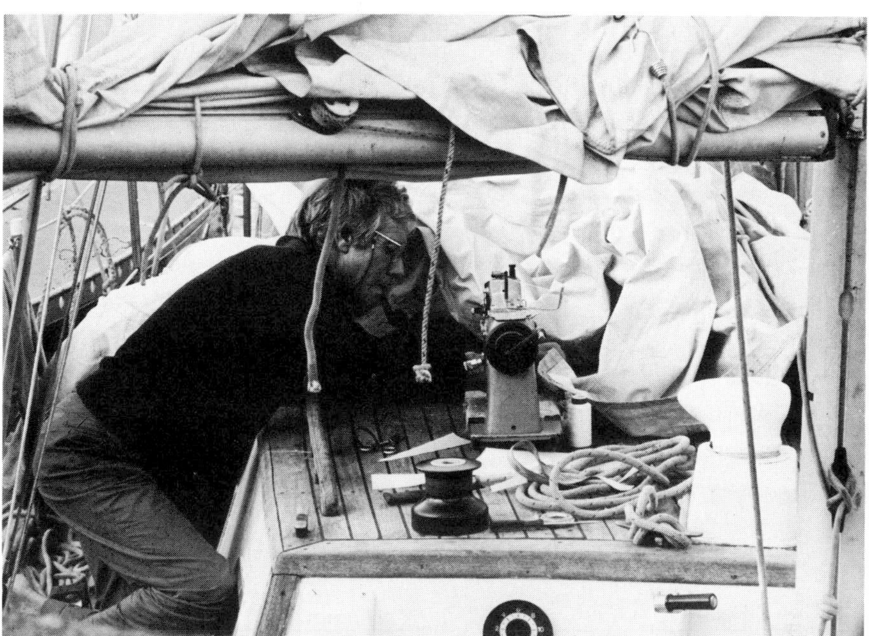

Prompt sail repair can avoid serious damage later on.

Taking good care of sails can undoubtedly prolong their life considerably, but still one sees boats left in marinas for long periods of time with their mainsails left unprotected without a sail cover. It is an operation that rarely takes more than a few minutes, but one which pays dividends in the long run. The most meticulous people I came across in this respect were Herbert and Illa Gieseking of *Lou IV*, who always put on the sail covers immediately after dropping anchor, folding away carefully the sails which had been used and giving all sails a rinse ashore with fresh water when this was possible. After four and half years they completed their circumnavigation of 46,000 miles with all their original sails intact.

Furling gear

The preference for single masts discussed earlier has undoubtedly been helped by the proliferation of jib furling gears. Over a quarter of the boats in the Atlantic Survey had such gear, two among them also having furling gear for their mainsails and mizzens. The more advanced among the latter was the French-built Amel Mango *Avanti* on which all reefing and furling was done from the cockpit by the push of a button, as all gears were electrically operated. On *Deles*, a Hallberg Rassy 49, all furling gear was hydraulically operated also by remote control. The proportion of furling gear was even higher in the ARC, which is a clear sign of the speed with which these developments are spreading through the cruising market. In ARC 87, 42 per cent of the boats were equipped with jib furling gear, although only 8 per cent also had furling mainsails. Pride of the fleet was the magnificent 128 ft schooner *Gloria* on which all sails were handled by remote control making the crew almost redundant.

In the Ideal Boat Survey comfort and ease of handling were high priority items for most skippers and many of the features specified by them as essential indicate that they would like sailing to be a pleasure, not a chore. The presence of women on most of the ARC boats probably has an influence on this, as well as the fact that the majority of boats had small crews, whether family or not. In order to find out how much importance skippers attached to various types of equipment, they were asked to rate the importance of the equipment with 3 if they considered it very important to have on their ideal boat, 2 important, 1 not very important and 0 useless.

Jib furling was rated as very important by 89 skippers, important by 43, not very important by 23 and useless by 5. However, although over three quarters of those questioned would like their ideal boat to be equipped with jib furling, only a handful would also choose mainsail furling gear, which was regarded by many with a certain reservation, only 13 considering it very important, 37 important, 82 not very important and 28 as useless. A possible explanation for this reluctance was the fact that the survey was conducted at a time when there had been various press reports extolling the virtues of fully battened mainsails, lazy jacks and other rapid systems of mainsail reefing and stowing, which were being promoted as a better answer to mainsail reefing than the various systems of mainsail furling. My personal feeling is that in spite of such misgivings, furling mainsails will come into their own and soon become a regular feature on long distance cruising boats, just as jib furling has done.

There is no doubt that the main attraction of furling gear, both on headsails and mainsails, is the ability to reduce sail area quickly and with the minimum of effort, a particularly attractive feature for shorthanded or less muscular crews. Several skippers who had used this equipment extensively pointed out that they sailed their boats much more efficiently, because they always carried the right amount of sail for the situation. Although the shape of some specially cut sails or the absence of battens and roach on furling mainsails were the main criticisms levelled by their detractors, owners of such furling gears argued that those disadvantages were more than compensated for by the ease of handling even the largest sails

Routine inspection can detect potential trouble before it occurs. The skipper of Tenga *making adjustments to his furling gear at the end of the Atlantic crossing.*

by a small crew. A skipper who fully supported this point of view was Manfred Kerstan who sailed his Swan 61 *Albatros* across the Atlantic in 14½ days with only Vera Schmidt as crew, their task made significantly easier by the furling gear fitted to both mainsail and headsails. Another ARC skipper who admitted having been opposed to mainsail furling in the past was Tim Aitken who nevertheless agreed to have the gear installed on his new Swan 53 *Airwave*. After completing the second ARC and cruising in the Caribbean for two months with a short-handed crew he told me that he had changed his mind completely and that he never had any problems in handling the boat with just one other person. He also stressed a point made by several other owners of mainsail furling gear of the type made by Hood that because of the ease of adjusting sail area from the comfort of the cockpit, the boat was sailed at maximum efficiency under any conditions. In this context it is therefore interesting to note that nine out of the first ten arrivals in the first ARC had jib furling gear.

Windvanes and Autopilots

There used to be a time, not so long ago, when long distance cruising boats could be instantly identified compared to their coastal cruising cousins by the windvane selfsteering gear mounted on their sterns. Yet among the yachts taking part in the Equipment Survey, conducted among ARC 87 participants, only 43 per cent were equipped with these gears. This fact confirmed my conclusion from earlier surveys that the proportion of windvanes on cruising boats had been declining. There are several explanations why so many offshore sailors choose autopilots instead of wind operated selfsteering devices, perhaps the most important reason being the fact that autopilots are more user-friendly. Indeed it is much easier to set a compass course on the autopilot, which on the more advanced systems is by the push of a button, than adjust the selfsteering gear to the required course. In spite of this however, once the windvane has been set, it does look after the boat without a continuous drain on the batteries. This was the observation made by many people during their first ocean passage and by the time they had reached Las Palmas for the start of the ARC, many of those without self-steering wished they had made different arrangements before leaving home.

The debate about the use of electronic autopilots as opposed to wind operated gears in offshore cruising is of such importance that it was examined in particular detail in the ARC 87 survey. Skippers were asked not only to rate their equipment for performance and usefulness but also to indicate how much it had been used on the Atlantic crossing. They were also asked to estimate the daily electricity consumption of the autopilot and how this affected their energy requirements generally.

Two thirds of the boats (67 per cent) had autopilots, which were rated an average 7.5 for their performance. A similar rating was given to their usefulness and it was not surprising to note that the longer the pilot was in use, the higher the rating given for its usefulness. The average time the autopilots were in use during the Atlantic crossing was 75 per cent. Individual figures were greatly influenced by the size of crew, the availability of an alternative self-steering device and also by how seriously that particular skipper took the ARC to be a race or just a friendly rally. For the competitively minded, steering by hand was the rule rather than the exception and on some of these boats the autopilot was hardly used at all. At the other extreme, on 20 per cent of the boats, maybe those in the fun rally mode, the pilot was in use over 90 per cent of the time.

The number of hours the pilot was in use obviously affected the amount of electricity consumed, which came to an average of 34 Amps per boat. This daily average was reached by presuming that the autopilot was in constant use and the resulting hourly consumption of nearly 1.5 Amps was very close to the estimated consumption given by most manufacturers. In most cases, the existing battery capacity was able to cope with this demand, but 15 per cent of the boats were obliged to generate electricity for their autopilot alone. Some of the boats had to run their engines once or twice a day to top up the batteries.

The commonest make of automatic pilot was Autohelm, 45 per cent of the boats surveyed having one of the various models on board. Rated for their performance, the 49 Autohelms under scrutiny averaged 7.4. Neco fared better, being rated on average 8.9 for performance, although there were only seven in the sample. Other makes attracting high ratings were Robertson and Alpha Marine.

Wind operated self-steering devices were also examined in ARC 87 and the 47 different units were rated an average 7 for their performance, although some makes were rated much higher than others. Almost half the gears (22) were Aries which were rated an average 7.6. Among the other 13 makes, higher ratings were awarded only to the three Windpilot (8) and the two Monitor (8.5) gears. Overall, the windvane gears were used 59 per cent of the time, although in the case of the Aries, these were used an average 76 per cent. Aries owners seem to put their units to good use as on ten boats they were in use over 90 per cent of the time. On the whole, the worse the performance rating of a particular gear, the less it was used. On nine boats, the gear was used less than 10 per cent of the time. In almost all instances, these were lesser known or home-built gears, which indicates that it pays to invest in a proven model. However, it must also be pointed out that most of those who used their windvanes very little also had autopilots, which they used considerably more than those skippers who were equipped with an efficient and reliable windvane gear. Even so, the majority of owners agreed on the usefulness of wind-driven self-steering gears, an aspect which was rated an average 9, as compared to the 7.5 rating given for the usefulness of autopilots.

The increasing preference for autopilots as opposed to wind operated self-steering gears can be seen by looking at the findings of the various cruising surveys undertaken during the last ten years. In the first survey of this kind carried out in the South Pacific in 1978, 68 per cent of the boats in the sample had some kind of self-steering gear and only 44 per cent had autopilots. In a follow-up survey undertaken later in the same area, 72 per cent had self-steering gears and 36 per cent autopilots. This tendency was later reversed, mainly as a result of the development of reliable low cost autopilots for yachts. The preponderance of autopilots became apparent in the Atlantic Survey in which 76 per cent of the boats were equipped with autopilots and only 32 per cent had self-steering gears, with a few boats having both. In the ARC 87 fleet, the proportion of autopilots was even higher (82 per cent) while windvanes were found on 44 per cent of the boats. Table 18 shows the distribution of autopilots and windvane self-steering among the various sizes of boat in ARC 87.

Boat length (ft)	*50–80*	*45–50*	*40–45*	*35–40*	*30–35*	*24–30*	*multi hulls 25–50*	**Total**
Self-steering	1	–	4	5	9	4	1	**24**
Autopilots	17	10	24	18	14	3	10	**96**
Both	4	6	9	18	17	6	–	**60**
Neither	3	2	3	–	2	–	–	**10**
Total	**25**	**18**	**40**	**41**	**42**	**13**	**11**	**190**

Table 18. DISTRIBUTION OF AUTOPILOTS AND WINDVANE SELF-STEERING IN ARC 87

Almost one third of the boats (32 per cent) were owned by believers in the 'belt and braces' philosophy and were equipped with both an automatic pilot and a wind operated gear. Some boats even carried a second smaller autopilot as a standby in case the main unit failed. On the other hand, the few boats that had neither pilot nor windvane were usually skippered by keen racing enthusiasts who were prepared to steer by hand. In most cases they could also rely on larger crews.

The subject was also examined in the Ideal Boat Survey when the skippers were asked to rate the importance of having vane self-steering and/or automatic pilot. Although 112 skippers considered vane self-steering to be very important on a cruising boat, and implicitly more important than an autopilot, there were some who held the opposite view and would rather have their boats steered by electronic means. On a point for point basis, autopilots scored higher than wind-operated devices, which is a reflection of the current attitude among many sailors who seem to have more faith in an electricity hungry pilot than an energy saving vane gear.

Diesel engines

No modern boat is complete without its 'iron staysail' and so diesel engines were examined in various surveys, when both the performance of individual makes and the availability of parts were discussed. Whereas in every survey undertaken in the Pacific there was at least one boat without an engine, engineless boats are much more a rarity in the Atlantic. Indeed, the number of people prepared to set off on a cruise in a boat not equipped with an adequate engine is extremely small. Personally I consider those who do to be a danger both to themselves and to other sailors. Whatever arguments these purists use to justify their decision, the fact is that most modern ports and marinas cannot be entered safely under sail and an engine is essential to be able to manoeuvre in confined spaces. What usually happens is that the engineless boat asks to be towed in or out by another yacht, which lays bare the whole pretence of not 'believing' in engines. There is undoubtedly great satisfaction to be gained from being able to manoeuvre a boat under sail alone, but there is no reason why this cannot be done with the engine switched off.

The attitude of contemporary sailors to engines was reflected in the findings of two surveys undertaken among ARC participants. In the Equipment Survey conducted at the end of 1987, all skippers agreed that a diesel engine was essential on a cruising boat. Although no one expressed doubts about having an engine, several skippers pointed out that they were perfectly able to handle the boat without resorting to the engine under most conditions. That they were indeed able to sail without an engine was shown by those who willy-nilly had to fall back on sail power because of a broken engine or, more commonly, flat batteries. Perhaps the best example is that of *Sea Spell*, a Nicholson 32, who sailed in ARC 86 and returned from the Caribbean to Europe with the TRANSARC in the summer of 1988. When the engine, which had broken down during the leg from Bermuda to the Azores, could not be repaired in Horta in time for the start of the last leg to Falmouth, the MacAllister brothers decided to leave with the rest of the fleet, undaunted by the prospect of neither engine nor electric power on the 1200 mile passage to Falmouth which they reached successfully at last, after three weeks bedevilled by head winds.

Optimum power

Most skippers taking part in the earlier surveys agreed that a sufficiently powerful engine was essential on a cruising boat. This is particularly true in the Pacific where passes into lagoons are often subject to strong outflowing currents and, as most of the passes are quite narrow, tacking in is often almost impossible.

The question of optimum engine size was examined for the first time in detail in the Pacific Survey. Every skipper was asked if he considered his engine to be powerful enough both for his boat and the particular requirements of the cruise he was undertaking. Although the majority considered the power of their engines to be sufficient, or even in excess of their requirements, one quarter of those interviewed stressed that the engines were not powerful enough. For the entire sample, the power rating per boat came to an average of 40 HP. As the average length of the boats taking part in that particular survey was 38 ft, the power ratio seemed reasonable. However, a more meaningful conclusion could be drawn by looking at the boats whose engines were considered underpowered by their owners. Although the average length of these boats was 37 ft, which came very close to the overall average, their average engine power was only 24 HP, which their owners did not regard to be sufficient for the kind of cruising they were doing at the time.

The subject of optimum power was also put to the skippers taking part in the Ideal Boat Survey. Three quarters indicated an engine power of between 35 and 80 HP to be their ideal choice, with the remainder equally split between some who would go higher and others who would settle for less. Looking at the figures closer it became obvious that many skippers would like their boats to be equipped with more powerful engines than the accepted standard and in fact almost half of the ideal boats would be fitted with engines rated at between 50 and 80 HP. The average engine power for the entire sample came out at 52HP. If this figure is applied to the average length of 41 ft and even to the average displacement of 10.6 tons, it does show that most people regard a powerful diesel engine to be a desirable feature of a cruising boat. Although these are hypothetical figures, they confirm the findings of earlier surveys which indicated a trend towards more powerful engines. The figures also agree with the rule of thumb which says to allow at least 1 HP per foot length of boat.

Probably the main reason why most people would like to have a more powerful engine is not only to get them out of difficulty or potentially dangerous situations, but also to use the engine in calms or light wind conditions. Yet in spite of this willingness to turn on the engine rather than wait for the wind, in both the Atlantic and Equipment Surveys, less fuel was used for propulsion than for electricity generating purposes. The figures show that as much as 76 per cent of the fuel was consumed by the main engine while charging the batteries and only 24 per cent while actually driving the boat. There is little doubt that using the main engine to charge the batteries is a costly exercise, nor is it very efficient, particularly as most boats were equipped with powerful diesel engines.

Various interesting suggestions concerning engines, apart from adequate power, were made in the Ideal Boat Survey, unfortunately not all of them practical. Thus, several skippers would like to have a hand starting facility for their engine, although as some of these had also expressed the wish to equip their boats with powerful units, starting them by hand would be out of the question. Other suggestions concerned the type of propellers, many skippers choosing the folding type in order to reduce drag. On the other hand, rather than eliminate propeller drag some skippers would prefer to put it to good use by driving a shaft generator. The ideal solution suggested by one skipper was to fit a variable pitch propeller, which would ensure maximum efficiency either when used to propel the boat or when turning the generator attached to its shaft. Yet another alternative was to fit a separate shaft with its own propeller, which would drive a generator independently of the engine propeller.

In parallel with auxiliary engines, fuel capacity and range under power were also examined in various surveys. The boats taking part in the Pacific Survey had an average fuel capacity of 90 gallons, although in some instances additional fuel was taken in jerrycans for longer passages or when cruising in areas where diesel fuel was difficult to obtain. The average range under power, if motoring in calm conditions, was 750 miles per boat. In the Ideal Boat Survey most skippers indicated a requirement for adequate fuel capacity, which ranged from 60 to 120 gallons. The optimum fuel carrying capacity quoted was on average 110 gallons.

Reliability

The reliability of diesel engines was examined for the first time in the Suva Survey when an overall satisfaction was shown by the average rating of 8.8 given to the engines. Nevertheless, some makes were rated consistently higher than others, which did not always reflect the better quality of the engine in question, but often the availability of spare parts or the quality of service. Among the most common makes, the highest average rating (9.5) was awarded to Perkins, followed by Ford (8.9) and Volvo (7). The higher marks attracted by Perkins was due both to the reliability of this make and also the worldwide availability of spare parts, as in many cases the same parts are used in heavy plant or truck engines as in marine engines. The same is generally true in the case of Ford, whereas many owners of Volvo engines complained about the difficulty of finding parts for their engines outside the main centres.

The findings of earlier surveys were confirmed in the Equipment Survey when the performance of the most common makes of diesel engines was again examined. The make which was consistently rated best was Perkins, both for performance and the availability of parts worldwide. Ford was also rated high on both aspects, whereas Yanmar, although rated well for performance, attracted less points for parts, as in some areas of the world spares for Yanmar engines are difficult to obtain. This was again the main criticism levelled at Volvo and Bukh engines, whereas for less common makes parts were almost impossible to find. Because of this, it was suggested that a selection of common spares should be acquired before a longer cruise, which should include at least one complete injector, a head gasket and other essential seals and gaskets, a belt for the alternator and impellers for all pumps. Just as important is to carry a set of tools for the engine, a workshop manual, a diagram showing all part numbers and a list of agents worldwide for the particular make. Another useful suggestion, which had in fact been put into practice by several skippers, was to attend an induction course covering the basic principles of maintenance and servicing of one's engine. The makers of some diesel engines run such courses for new owners and from the comments made by skippers who had attended them they appear to be extremely valuable, particularly when one bears in mind that during a longer cruise the engine might break down hundreds of miles from the nearest repair facility.

Although diesel engines are considered to be one of the most reliable machines invented by man, their rate of failure on sailing boats is surprisingly high compared to diesel engines operating on land. Having owned a car with a diesel engine for several years I can vouch for their reliability and I am puzzled why their performance is so much less reliable on boats. There are various reasons for this, not least the fact that marine diesel engines operate in a corrosive environment, which takes its toll even on units that have been properly marinized, which is something that cannot be said for all engines installed in yachts. Another reason for the frequent breakages is the fact that on most yachts the engines are used irregularly and for short periods. Often when they are used, they are not put under sufficient load, particularly when the main engine is used to charge the batteries.

I had a long discussion on this subject with the skipper of *Honeymead*, Chester Lemon, an excellent diesel mechanic, who had left his farm in Queensland to travel the world by sea. Chester had complete faith in diesel engines and as his livelihood as a farmer had depended on such engines, he knew both how to run them and how to put them right. The valuable point which he made, and which I have followed religiously ever since, both in cars and boats, is that diesel engines *must* be run under load. Running a powerful diesel engine just to turn a small alternator is simply not enough and so, when underway, the propeller should always be engaged to put some load on the engine. Running the main engine just to charge the batteries is unfortunately not recommended and a lot of problems have their origin in this widespread practice. Just as bad is the practice of turning on the diesel engine to leave a dock or anchorage, but using the engine for only a few minutes and turning it off before it has had time to reach the recommended working temperature. Repeatedly submitting the engine to this kind of treatment will eventually take its toll on even the most reliable of engines.

Engine breakages

Looking at the engine breakages that I have come across over the years, particularly those in the ARC, of which there are at least half a dozen each year, in most instances it is not the main engine which is faulty, but auxiliary equipment, such as water pumps, starter motors and alternators.

A source of serious difficulty is often the inadequate provision made for the exhaust. For instance, on *Aeolus* which took part in ARC 87, water found its way through the exhaust into the manifold causing the engine to seize up. Skipper Michael Parkin managed to free the pistons by pouring a mixture of paraffin and oil into the cylinders and leaving it for three days. He then tapped the top of the pistons until they started moving, cleaned everything thoroughly and the engine started first time. He advised other skippers to make sure that a one way valve was fitted to the exhaust or some kind of trap, which does not allow water to siphon into the engine when sailing before large following seas. His point is extremely valid as in several previous instances that have come to my attention, the cause of engine failure was narrowed down to sea water ingression via a faulty exhaust system.

Another source of engine seizure also caused by sea water finding its way into the engine sometimes occurs on units having a direct cooling system. On such units, raw cooling water circulates around the engine block and any broken seal or gasket allows the water to find its way into the engine itself. Yet another cause of serious engine problems is dirty fuel, which can contain either impurities or water. Both of these should be separated out if the engine has been provided with an adequate filtering system, which many production boats do not possess. Some boats are not even provided with a separate water trap, while on others the filter element provided as standard can only cope with a small amount of dirt in the fuel. The best way to avoid these problems is to install a large filter and water trap in addition to the fuel filter provided by the manufacturers. The water trap should be in an easily accessible place where it can be inspected regularly. The fuel intake from the tanks should always be set sufficiently high above the level of any water and sludge accumulated in the bottom of the tank, which should be drained off regularly through a tap set in the lowest part of the tank. Most of the water that is found in fuel tanks has not got there with the fuel, but by condensation. On most boats, an overflow pipe from the engine returns excess fuel into the tank. Particularly on fibreglass boats, the warm returning fuel causes a certain amount of condensation, the resulting water gathering in the bottom of the tank, from where it must be drained before it finds its way into the fuel system.

A little known culprit which can seriously damage injection pumps is a fungus which grows inside diesel tanks. A few drops of a special antifungal solution added occasionally to the tanks will keep the fungus under control, but not many people seem to be aware of this problem. One of the boats taking part in ARC 87 had to have its injection pump rebuilt at great cost after it had been seriously damaged by this fungus which had clogged up the entire fuel system.

Outboard engines

Another noticeable change that has occurred during the last decade is the increased proportion of tenders equipped with an outboard engine. Compared to earlier surveys, more boats now have an outboard engine and those who row their dinghies are very much in the minority. The main reason for this change is the proliferation of inflatable dinghies, most of which are difficult to row. An outboard engine is almost essential for an inflatable dinghy, especially if used over longer distances.

In the Pacific Survey, 80 per cent of the boats had an outboard engine for their tenders. Among the eight different makes, the highest average ratings were given to Yamaha (9.1) and Suzuki (8.9). The other ratings were: Mariner 8.2, Johnson 8, Evinrude 7.6, Seagull 7.3, Volvo 7 and Mercury 7. When asked if they considered an outboard engine to be an essential piece of equipment on a cruising boat, almost half the skippers (42 per cent) replied in the negative. Among those who took the opposite view, several skippers stressed the usefulness of an outboard engine when anchoring far from the shore, or when wishing to explore reefs or rivers.

Although in the ARC 87 fleet, the percentage of outboard engines was slightly higher (82 per cent), a smaller proportion of skippers went as far as describing them as essential. The probable explanation for this is the fact that in most of the ports en route to the Canaries boats come alongside and there is little need to use the dinghy, let alone an outboard engine. On the other hand, cruising boats in the Pacific spend more time at anchor and commuting to the shore can sometimes be an expedition in itself. A reliable outboard engine is then indeed useful if not essential.

TENDERS

In earlier surveys I was hoping to find out whether a hard or a soft dinghy would make the ideal tender. Mostly because of the lack of space to stow a hard dinghy, the majority of skippers are now opting for an inflatable tender, which does not mean that they regard inflatables as necessarily the best.

In the first survey conducted in the Pacific, preferences were evenly divided between rigid and soft dinghies. The skippers were asked to rate their dinghies from the point of view of an overall yacht tender. Among the 83 tenders that made up the sample, the 43 rigid dinghies received an average rating of 8.6 compared to the 40 inflatables which were given an average 7.8. The rigid tenders included all types of material, wood, plywood, fibreglass or aluminium.

The subject was re-examined in the later Pacific Survey, in which the 39 inflatables received an average rating of 7 compared to 8.7 for the 31 rigid tenders. Several skippers explained the higher rating given to the hard dinghies by pointing out that they were easier to row and stood up better to rough treatment such as landing on coral or rocky beaches. Hard dinghies also hold an outboard engine better, although it was mentioned that, precisely because they are easier to row, it is possible to dispense with an outboard engine altogether. On the other hand, the disadvantages of hard dinghies were also pointed out, such as the fact that they take up too much space, also that they can be a hazard in heavy weather, are not much use for diving and have the annoying tendency to bang against the boat or self-steering gear when at anchor. Several of the tenders, particularly among yachts surveyed in the Pacific, were equipped with mast and sails. A few skippers explained that they planned to use them as lifeboats in an emergency.

In the ARC fleet, the proportion of inflatable dinghies had risen to 88 per cent as more and more people decide to acquire a one-and-only inflatable. Although dinghies as such were not the object of the Ideal Boat Survey, a few skippers did not miss the opportunity to describe their 'ideal' dinghy. In most instances these proved to be made of rigid materials and, being aware of the inherent stowage problems, their prospective owners specified that they would make sure that the yacht was designed in such a way as to allow the stowage of a dinghy on deck. This was one of the reasons why a flush deck was advocated by some, while others looked for the solution in the dinghy itself, possibly by making it in two parts. The other solution suggested was to use davits, although this idea does not seem practicable except on much larger yachts than those which were chosen by the majority as being of an ideal size, i.e. around 40 ft LOA. Wherever stowed, some ideal dinghies would also be provided with a transparent bottom panel. Another desirable feature of a hard dinghy was the facility to convert it for sailing by providing it with a mast, centreboard and rudder. This option was mentioned not only by those who enjoyed the idea of having a sailing dinghy, but also by some who regarded the use of the dinghy as a lifeboat as a safety feature in case the yacht had to be abandoned. The suggestion of adapting the mast and sail of a windsurfer for dual use on a dinghy made a lot of sense.

Ground tackle

As docking facilities in most ports outside Europe and North America are rather limited, cruising boats spend more time at anchor than alongside a dock or pontoon. The ground tackle on long distance cruising boats was examined in great detail in two surveys undertaken in the Pacific. In the Cruising Survey, the majority of boats (85 per cent) used only chain with their main anchor. To qualify as 'only chain', the boat in question had to have at least 100 feet of chain for its main anchor alone, although I found that in most cases boats carried twice that amount and even more.

The proportion of boats anchoring with only chain was even higher in the Pacific Survey (92 per cent) and practically all of them were provided with more than 100 feet of chain. The average amount of chain carried by those boats was 240 ft, several skippers pointing out that they carried additional lengths of chain for use with their second and even third anchors. The insistance on more than adequate ground tackle shows the importance that long distance voyagers attach to being securely anchored under all conditions.

The skippers taking part in the Pacific Survey were asked to assess the performance of their main anchors and, as in the Cruising Survey, by far the most common type in use was the plough. In the majority of cases, the anchors were genuine CQR, although a few skippers warned of poor imitations of this type. The average weight of the plough anchors on the boats over 40 ft LOA was 52 lbs, while on the boats under 40 ft, the average was 45 lbs. Most boats were equipped with anchors whose weight was in excess of what is considered to be adequate for a particular length. This was equally true for the other types of anchors, as the average weight of Danforth anchors on boats over 40 ft was 65 lbs and 53 lbs for boats under 40 ft. The weight of Bruce anchors on boats under 40 ft averaged 37 lbs. Several boats carried additional anchors of heavier weights (average 75 lbs) to be used only in case of severe storms or hurricanes. The majority of boats carried on average three anchors of different types and weights and these did not include light folding anchors.

To cope with the heavy ground tackle most boats surveyed in the Pacific were equipped with windlasses, either manual (56 per cent) or electric (30 per cent). Several owners of manual windlasses complained that they were not powerful enough and were of little use in deep anchorages. Electric windlasses performed better overall and were recommended as being very useful by several skippers. One common complaint which concerned both types of windlass was that non-calibrated chain tended to slip on the chain gipsy.

One of the main reasons for this is that American chain, such as BBB, Proof Coil or High Test, is made from so-called 'trade size'. This means that American chain is 1/32″ larger than the nominal size, whereas British chain is manufactured from material of the nominal size. In Table 19 the nominal size of British and American chain is reduced to metric values. The last column shows the percentage increase in weight.

Table 19. COMPARISON OF BRITISH AND AMERICAN ANCHOR CHAIN

Nominal size (inch)	*Equivalent metric size*		*Increase in weight (per cent)*
	British	*American*	
5/16	7.93	8.73	21.0
3/8	9.73	10.32	17.4
7/16	11.11	11.91	14.8
1/2	12.70	13.49	12.9
9/16	14.29	15.08	11.4
5/8	15.88	16.67	10.3

An International Standard (ISO 4565) for yacht anchor chain aims to standardize sizes to 6, 8, 10 and 12 mm. The purpose of the standard is to achieve dimensional interchangeability of chain on windlass gipsies to ensure a proper fit. Although the manufacturers in Europe and the UK will most probably adopt the new standard, American manufacturers may continue with trade size and Imperial dimensions, which means that there may never be interchangeability of chains made on the two sides of the Atlantic. Unless this standard is accepted by everyone, the compatability of chain and windlass gipsy should be checked if they are bought separately and especially if they have been bought in different countries.

Although anchoring techniques as such were not investigated in any of the surveys, various comments and valuable suggestions were made when discussing ground tackle generally. Tony van der Velde of *Athabasca II* mentioned that many people with little cruising experience seem to be unaware of the well proven method of checking and setting the anchor by putting the engine into astern. After the anchor has been dropped and the required scope paid out, the engine is put into astern until it is felt that the anchor has bitten and is holding. This method is particularly valuable in exposed anchorages or where strong gusts of wind can be expected, such as those experienced in the lee of high hills. It is also a good idea to go through this procedure if the boat is going to be left unattended for any length of time.

Other anchoring methods were also recommended for specific circumstances. Among these was the Bahamian moor, which is very useful when anchoring in tidal estuaries, rivers or where there is a strong current that changes its direction. Two anchors are used, both set from the bow, and the principle is to set one anchor forward and the other astern, so that the boat pivots in a relatively small arc to be held by either one or the other of the anchors, depending on the set of the current. Probably the easiest way to set this type of mooring without having to resort to the dinghy is to drop the secondary anchor first, then pay out sufficient scope so that one can go far enough forward to drop the main anchor in the desired place, the excess scope on the secondary anchor being taken in until the boat rests between the two anchors. As the tide changes, the boat will gradually swing into the opposite direction when the secondary anchor will become the primary one and vice versa.

The usefulness of a stern anchor came up as a topic of conversation on many occasions, some people swearing by them, while others considered them a waste of time. Several skippers who were advocates of stern anchors suggested that permanent anchor stowage should be provided at the stern. If mounted on the guard rail, a Danforth type anchor is preferable as it stows flat. For a plough anchor, a special fitting with a roller is more convenient and in fact some production boats feature this arrangement as standard. Usually the stern anchor has only a short length of chain attached to it and the rest of the scope is made up of line, which ideally should be kept on a reel. On some boats the reel is mounted on the rail, while on others the reel is removable and stowed elsewhere on the boat. Stowing the spare anchor warp is not always easy and a solution to this problem is to use one of various makes of flat polyester braid on their own reel which take up less space and are easier to handle.

Boarding platform and a neat stern anchor stowage on this self-built steel boat.

As well as anchoring techniques, the art of coming stern to the dock was another topic which attracted comments from some skippers. Those who had spent any length of time in the Mediterranean had learned to live with this style of mooring, which usually requires a bow anchor to be dropped some distance from the dock and then the boat to be manoeuvred astern, usually into a tight space between two other boats. It is not always an easy operation, particularly in strong winds. Because of the reverse flow of water from the propeller, the rudder itself is of little use in steering the boat astern, which calls for a different technique. The skill lies in getting the boat lined up in the desired direction by going forward and then taking her slowly astern. Several quick forward manoeuvres may be necessary to straighten the boat up, all the while getting closer to the dock, paying out enough chain to allow the boat to move astern unhindered. It is also a good idea to have coiled mooring lines prepared on both quarters to be thrown ashore as soon as the dock is within heaving distance. Having helped to dock countless boats in the various events I am involved with, I have witnessed many disastrous docking manoeuvres, usually caused by haste as much as lack of experience. The most important thing is to have everything prepared before starting the manoeuvre, with fenders and lines all in place and every crew member assigned to a precise function. Just as important is to keep calm, ignoring the superior smiles of the 'experts' ashore and if the manoeuvre does not proceed the way it should, the wise thing to do is to abort and start all over again.

ANCILLARY EQUIPMENT

Various suggestions concerning ancillary equipment were made by the skippers taking part in the Ideal Boat Survey. A permanent provision for a stern anchor was one suggestion made by several skippers. It was also suggested that bow anchor stowage and handling could be improved by the addition of a short bowsprit. Several skippers stressed that ground tackle should be of ample size, but also easily handled. An electric windlass was deemed important or very important by more than half the skippers designing their ideal boat. Selftailing winches were also considered worth having if the budget allowed it. Another feature often recommended was a Bimini top or some other type of sun awning, ideally incorporating a rain catching facility. A good supply of drinking water was a priority for many skippers and several listed a watermaker among the items they would install on their ideal boat. One important item, which is absent from most boats, is a gauge showing the amount of water left in the tanks. Gauges for both water and fuel were specified as essential on several ideal cruising boats.

Various safety items were mentioned as desirable on an ideal boat, such as a provision for night lighting, not just at the chart table but also in the saloon, toilet and galley. During a night watch, the watch keeper might wish to prepare a cup of coffee or use the heads, and even a brief exposure to white light could spoil his night vision.

An essential piece of equipment on any boat is a radar reflector. As a result of suggestions made by several ARC skippers, radar reflectors have now become compulsory on all ARC boats. The decision was also influenced by my own observations made in the past. During ARC 87, as the smaller boats started from Las Palmas three days before the rest of the fleet, many of the larger yachts were overtaking smaller yachts all the way to Barbados. The skipper of one large yacht equipped with a powerful radar was surprised to find that several small yachts he passed in visual range did not show up on his radar. Calling up the skippers on VHF he was surprised when some admitted to having dismantled their radar reflector, as they considered it unnecessary during the Atlantic crossing, while others did not have a reflector at all. There is indeed an impression shared by many sailors that an aluminium mast gives such a good signal on a radar screen that it is unnecessary to also mount a proper reflector. It is unfortunately a fallacy, which has led to a false sense of security. During the first Canary Islands Rally, which was held among the seven islands of the archipelago prior to the start of ARC 87, I had the opportunity to follow the entire rally from the bridge of various Naval ships kindly provided as escort by the Spanish Navy. Having to deal with only a small number of yachts, I thought that it would be a rather simple matter to keep track of them, either visually or by radar. It did not take me long to realize that even on an advanced naval radar, a small yacht gave an insignificant signal when a few miles off, which was easily lost in the sea clutter, particularly when the sea was rough. On the other hand, the yachts that were equipped with properly installed radar reflectors gave a good signal even from several miles away.

Many skippers used the opportunity offered by the Ideal Boat Survey not only to design their ideal cruising yacht but also to provide it with features, some seemingly minor, but which would make life on a longer cruise more comfortable and also much more enjoyable. On the entertainment side, a stereo installation with a compact cassette player was mentioned by some skippers as being the kind of equipment which should be installed at the fitting out stage as the wiring for the speakers, for instance, could be routed out of sight. Also in the audio field, a good quality radio receiver in the short wave bands makes it possible to tune in to the long distance sailors' favourite, the BBC World Service, and also listen to weather forecasts, such as those broadcast by France International or to the storm and hurricane warnings issued by WWV and WWVH. Television sets are also becoming more popular on sailing boats and if tempted, one should make sure to buy a set which can receive in the various systems, PAL in the UK, most of Western Europe and Australia, SECAM in France and its dependencies in the Caribbean, NTSC in the USA, Canada and the English speaking Caribbean islands. Even a video tape recorder is no longer regarded as unusual on a boat and there are even some available which can run off 12 volts.

Another pastime which combines safety with pleasure is diving and in two earlier surveys I found that most boats had snorkelling equipment on board and about 10 per cent also had diving tanks as well as a diving compressor. There is no doubt that the ability to dive is a major safety feature as I can vouch myself. On several occasions I had to don a mask and snorkel to untangle a line from the propeller, to escape the clutches of a lobster pot, to free a fouled anchor, to check if the anchor had set properly or even to set the anchor by hand if it did not look as if it was going to hold. Retrieving objects that had been lost overboard was another use to which the diving tanks were put, as was the ability to give the hull a scrub before a long passage, not to speak about the more pleasurable side of diving, shell collecting, spear fishing, or just being part of the aquatic environment by enjoying the beauty of the underwater scenery.

Another wet pleasure mentioned by skippers in regard to the ideal boat, was the importance of having proper bottle stowage. This reminded me of the results of my first survey in which two skippers described their bottle openers as the most important instruments on board their boats. Like in every other respect, it is a matter of priorities, and an ideal boat should also reflect the owner's whims. It would be boring if all boats were the same. One skipper, obviously fond of his glass of wine, suggested installing a stainless steel tank which would make it possible to buy the wine in countries where it was cheap and easily available, such as in France or Spain, and have an assured supply in places where wine was expensive or difficult to find, such as some of the islands in the Caribbean or South Pacific. Another skipper was even more precise in his requirements, expecting his ideal boat to serve British Tetley bitter on draught!

A BOAT FOR ALL SEASONS

After a six year circumnavigation and hundreds of interviews with long distance sailors on every aspect of cruising under sail, I was faced with an almost impossible task when it came to designing my own new boat. I felt that I knew almost too much about the things that had to be avoided and there was a real danger of ending up with a boat incorporating a lot of useful features but not sufficient original thought. In order to avoid such an outcome, I drew up a list of priorities and tried to push the less important features out of my mind. The list of priorities was finally honed down to three aspects: speed, seaworthiness and comfort.

A fast, strong and comfortable passage maker is most people's idea of a long distance cruising boat, yet it is surprising how many boats do not meet all these basic requirements. There is a whole range of fast cruisers on the market, but their degree of comfort on a long ocean passage is debatable as is their intrinsic strength. Conversely, many strongly built comfortable cruisers can be infuriatingly slow and add many days to a long passage. A totally different approach was therefore needed and in close cooperation with Bill Dixon, one of Britain's leading naval architects, we have succeeded in designing the Aventura 40 to satisfy those three basic requirements. The prototype of this design is my new boat *La Aventura.*

Beside speed and strength, there were other features which I considered important enough to be added to the list of priorities. The first was shallow draft. Having been denied access to many anchorages in my previous boat because of its draft, I was very attracted to a centreboard configuration. However, following on from the developments in 12-metre boat design and the advantages of a winged keel, I decided to fit *La Aventura* with a winged daggerboard. The wing section is attached to the daggerboard by bolts so that it can be removed for repair. This allows the board to be retracted upwards through a slot in the deck normally covered by a waterproof plate. The lifting board ensures draft of only one metre (3′ 3″) with the board up, while about 1000 lbs (450 kg) of lead ballast in the wings, contributes considerably to the stability of the boat as the weight is concentrated as low as possible. It also means that with the board down the boat is very comfortable in a rolly anchorage as the wings dampen both pitching and rolling. With the board up, the boat can dry out resting on the wings and twin skegs. The twin rudder configuration was chosen not only because of the shallow draft, but also because of the better steering and tracking capability of a hull fitted with two rudders.

Speed

In the past there seems to have been a contradiction between a steel boat and speed. Yet there is no real reason why steel boats should not be fast, except the tendency to build steel boats much heavier than necessary. Both Bill Dixon and Brian I'Anson, the builder of Aventura 40, took it as a challenge to build a light steel boat and the construction methods employed ensure that the hull is as strong yet as light as possible. This, combined with the underwater profile of the hull, has made *La Aventura* a fast boat for her size and displacement.

The sail plan has also ensured that *La Aventura* has a good turn of speed under most conditions. A tall rig was essential to keep her sailing well in light winds, while the cutter rig offers maximum flexibility under any conditions. Because of our original cruising plans as well as the fact that the crew would usually consist of only Gwenda and myself, Hood roller furling gear was fitted on both mainsail and headsail. These features, combined with self-tailing winches and the fct that all lines lead back to the cockpit, means that the boat can be handled by one person alone.

Seaworthiness

Seaworthiness goes hand in hand with strength and one of my main priorities was a strong hull. The fact that many of the boats lost on the high seas recently have gone down after hitting some unidentified object, made the choice of a metal hull the logical solution. Nor had I forgotten the impact of hitting a large tree trunk at night when crossing the Indian Ocean in the previous *Aventura*. Although running before the monsoon at about six knots under twin jibs at the time, the impact was enough to stop the boat in its tracks and take a large chunk out of the keel. For this and other similar considerations, the choice of a metal hull became inevitable. Although attracted for a long time to an alloy hull, I finally chose steel, both for its higher strength and lower cost.

Other features contributing to the overall seaworthiness of *La Aventura* which have been included in the design are a watertight collision bulkhead between the forward cabin and the rest of the boat, an uncluttered deck layout, protected steering position, no opening portholes in the sides of the hull as well as a minimum number of through hull openings. Also the stern has been designed with a platform which makes boarding from the water easier and serves as stowage for the liferaft. It also protects the self-steering gear and acts as a crumple area in case of collision from astern.

Comfort

La Aventura's interior is designed for maximum comfort for a crew which will rarely exceed four people, but will usually consist of only two. The daggerboard casing has dictated the layout of the interior, with the saloon and galley being located in the aft section of the boat. The living area is an open plan arrangement which adds to the feeling of spaciousness. Forward of the companionway are two separate cabins with a watertight bulkhead dividing them from the forward cabin. As storage is a major problem on any cruising boat, the forward cabin is used for storing the inflatable dinghy, outboard engine, spare sails, diving gear, tools, portable generator, fenders, ropes, etc. Because of the anticipated weight forward, the ballast aft has been adjusted accordingly.

One of the features inherited by *La Aventura* from her older sister is the fixed wheelhouse. During six years of living aboard, we had learned to appreciate the protection given by the wheelhouse from rain, spray and sun. The shelter it provided also meant that the watchkeeper was always in a dry and comfortable position regardless of the conditions outside. This protection contributed greatly to the overall safety, as even in the worst gale we were able to stay in the cockpit either to steer or just to keep an eye on things.

One of the more unorthodox features of our new boat is the positioning of the steering wheel under the shelter of the wheelhouse. This is another outcome of our long life at sea. An efficient self-steering device meant that we hardly ever steered by hand and on the rare occasions when we did, it was during rough conditions when the sheltered steering position allowed us to take over from our self-steering gear. As *La Aventura* is fitted with both self-steering gear and a powerful Brookes & Gatehouse automatic pilot, there seemed to be no reason to have a secondary steering position outside the wheelhouse, so we finally chose to have only one.

Another innovation concerning the self-steering gear was to incorporate it in the overall design of the boat rather than add it on as an afterthought. The rudder shaft of the Hydrovane self-steering gear passes through a hole in the floor of the transom platform, which not only protects the gear, but also allows for it to be mounted more efficiently; it operates independently of the main steering system by using its own auxiliary rudder, which can also act as an emergency rudder. As the Hydrovane is fitted with a short tiller arm, this could also be used in conjunction with a small autopilot.

As one of the main disadvantages of a twin rudder configuration is the difficulty of steering at low speeds in confined spaces, we decided to equip *La Aventura* with twin engines fitted with Teignbridge folding propellers. Having two small diesel engines rather than a single large unit has many more advantages than just improved manoeuvrability. The safety of having a second propulsion and charging unit is paramount when one considers the number of yachts that get into trouble either because their engine has broken down or it cannot be started as the batteries had been discharged. With a twin engine installation one can be used as a workhorse by having it drive a large alternator or freezer compressor. One major advantage of this arrangement is that one only needs to run a smaller unit for charging the batteries and doing all the work, but when more power is necessary, the two engines can be run in parallel. Most of the time it is more efficient to run only one engine and when motorsailing to windward, for instance, only the lee engine is nor-

The aft cabin on La Aventura *is spacious and light.*

mally used. *La Aventura* is fitted with two identical Perkins Perama 29 HP diesel engines, one of which had its standard alternator replaced with a 90 Amp alternator. The charging system operates via a TWC regulator which ensures maximum output from the alternators.

La Aventura incorporates many other rather unusual features, some inspired by suggestions culled from the various surveys that I have conducted over the years, others being the result of my own cruising experience or inherited from *La Aventura*'s predecessor. Our new boat was designed very much to suit our own cruising plans and so some of her features may well not agree with other people's requirements. Many skippers taking part in the Ideal Boat Survey specified that the design of their boat would very much depend on their cruising plans and the area they were planning to sail in. In our own case, our plans included a voyage to the South Atlantic and then into the Pacific by way of the Straits of Magellan. We then planned to sail via Tahiti and Hawaii to Alaska and down the coast of British Columbia to California. The islands of Micronesia were to be our next destination, possibly followed by a foray to Japan. A year's delay in the building and fitting out of *La Aventura* followed by several new commitments resulted in a drastic change of plan and our ambitious cruising plans had to be shelved. The only compensation was that we did end up with a very able and attractive cruising boat, even if she has been confined to the Atlantic Ocean for the time being.

Chapter 4

ELECTRONICS SURVEY

Cruising boats used to lag far behind racing yachts in the range of instruments and equipment carried, but this is no longer the case and some of the most sophisticated gear can be seen on boats equipped for offshore cruising. Many of the ARC boats are equipped with the latest navigation devices and their range of instruments would put many a racer to shame.

Yachting electronics were examined in several of my earlier surveys as well as among the ARC fleet, but before going into the findings of these surveys, it may be useful to have a brief look at the present state of marine electronics. The range of instruments and devices is now so wide and changing so rapidly that many people find it difficult to keep up with the latest additions to a never-ending list of new equipment.

SATELLITE NAVIGATION

There is little doubt that the most important addition in the field of navigation has been the satnav. The Transit Navigation Satellite System came into general use in 1968, but another fifteen years went by before units were developed that were both compact and cheap enough to be installed on a cruising boat. In the last few years, satnav has become the most reliable navigation system mariners have ever known and there are almost 100,000 marine users in the world today, the majority being yacht owners.

The Transit system, launched and operated by the US Navy, relies on several satellites in polar orbit 550 miles above the earth, of which six are normally in use. Every two minutes each satellite broadcasts data, which gives its exact position, this then being used by the receiver on board a vessel to calculate its own position. The relatively low orbits of the satellites mean that each one is in view of the receiver for only about 15 minutes and the average wait for a satellite pass in mid-latitudes is 107 minutes. In high latitudes the frequency of passes is more frequent, whereas near the equator the passes are much more rare and a satnav may not be able to give an updated fix for several hours. Apart from working out an accurate fix, satnavs also include a dead reckoning computer to keep track of the vessel's progress between satellite passes. Most satnavs can also be interfaced with other instruments, such as an automatic pilot, so as to make the navigator's role almost obsolete.

Whereas most people would agree that for an ordinary yacht on an ocean passage the present Transit system is perfectly adequate, for military purposes its accuracy is not deemed to be satisfactory and therefore the US Navy is in the process of replacing it with a much more accurate system, the Global Positioning System (GPS). The potential accuracy of the new system is incredible, but its use will be restricted almost exclusively to the military. Nevertheless, a slightly less precise version is available to civilian users, including pleasure craft.

Initially GPS was expected to become operational in the late 1980s, but problems encountered with the shuttle programme caused some delays and the present Transit system has been given a new lease of life. In the meantime, some of the more advanced satnavs can operate in both systems, but as their cost is still prohibitively high, most cruising skippers will probably make do with the present Transit system, which will survive at least until the mid-1990s.

Kjell Heiberg of Makiki III *at his well equipped navigation station.*

Hyperbolic systems

The global satellite navigation system was preceded by several years by two regional radionavigation systems, which after many years of being used almost exclusively by military and commercial vessels, are becoming increasingly popular with yachts too. The older of the two is Decca, which has been in commercial use since the end of the Second World War and covers the Atlantic coast of Europe as well as parts of the Mediterranean. Its North American equivalent is Loran (Long Range Navigation), which was introduced in the 1970s and is used mostly for coastal navigation as its accuracy decreases rapidly over 100 miles offshore. Both systems use a network of regional groups or chains and their accuracy depends on how good the system's coverage is of a certain area. Recent improvements both in receiver design and the transmitters themselves have greatly enhanced the accuracy of both systems. This is one of the reasons why Decca and Loran units are becoming more popular among yachtsmen, the other reason being that the units suitable for yachts have been miniaturized and now include many features common in satnavs. Their reasonable price is yet another attraction appreciated by cruising sailors. It is estimated that by the end of the 1980s, Decca will have some 100,000 users, well over half of which are European yachtsmen. Loran is used by a much larger number of sailors, particularly in the USA, and the total number of users is estimated to reach half a million in 1990. There has been talk about the Loran system being extended to encompass the entire North Atlantic and give the same coverage to Western Europe as it does to the other side of the Atlantic. If such a decision is taken, it may mean the end of Decca, although it is very unlikely that this would become a reality before the end of the century.

One long range system, which has not caught on among yachts, is Omega, which provides worldwide position fixing with an accuracy of two to four miles. Omega is used almost exclusively by aviators and the high cost of the receivers has kept the number of yachts equipped with this system to a minimum.

Radar

Yet another navigation device developed originally for military use, which is proving increasingly popular with yachtsmen is radar (Radio Detection and Rangefinding). Radars used to be seen only on the largest yachts and it took many years before the bulky scanner and the equally large set were brought down to a size that could be fitted on the average cruising boat. However, the development which really introduced radars to the cruising scene was the change from a phosphorous to a raster scan display. The latter shows a positive non-fading picture of everything that surrounds the vessel and produces a high definition colour picture. The latest radar models can receive integrated information from Loran, satnav, depth-sounder as well as other equipment, all the pertinent data being displayed on the screen. It is also possible to receive automatic alerts if a target enters a predetermined distance and bearing, which is an extremely useful function for collision avoidance.

The only serious drawback is that in spite of all the improvements to the receiver and display unit, the antenna itself must remain between two and three feet long to obtain a good definition of the target and therefore on smaller yachts the siting of the scanner is a major problem. This may not have been such a problem when many cruising boats were two-masted and the mizzen could be put to good use, but the present trend towards one-masted yachts complicates matters for those who wish to fit a radar. Siting the scanner in front of the lower spreaders is one solution, the other alternative is to fit an 8-foot pole at the stern which, on some yachts, also doubles up as a support for a wind generator. Neither solution is ideal and

On some sloops the radar is mounted on its own pole at the stern. On Second Wind *this also serves as a mount for the wind generator.*

this is probably the explanation why in spite of its undoubted attractions many cruising boats are not equipped with radar.

ELECTRONIC CHARTS AND PLOTTERS

One of the greatest innovations in recent years has been the development of electronic charts. For the time being, however, they provide only a limited amount of information and cannot be used for accurate coastal navigation. The main drawback is that the immense amount of information included on a conventional chart needs a computer with a huge memory to present it graphically on a screen. Although in its present form the system can be useful for route planning purposes and greatly simplifies the task of the navigator on offshore passages, its usefulness for detailed navigation is doubtful. For the foreseeable future the use of electronic charts for cruising will therefore be limited.

Particularly in coastal navigation, the old-fashioned paper chart is still hard to beat. Personally, I consider the main disadvantage of the electronic chart to be not its lack of detail (a drawback which most probably is going to be overcome soon) but the need to peer into a screen whenever one has to refer to a chart. This can be irritating and also potentially dangerous, particularly at night when one's night vision would be greatly affected by the need to use a screen rather than consult a chart lit by a red light. However, the perfect answer to these doubts seems to be the electronic plotter as it combines all the advantages of the latest microprocessor-based position fixing systems with the accuracy of a conventional paper chart. An electronic plotter, such as Navstar's Yeoman, is capable of working out its own latitude and longitude on a regular chart and can also plot ranges and bearings to and from any point on the chart in use. It also shows instantly the present position of the vessel if interfaced with a compatible position fixing receiver such as Loran, Decca or satnav. In offshore navigation it can be used to work out great circle routes and will even provide the necessary information for an autopilot. In coastal navigation its greatest advantage is that it makes dead reckoning extremely simple and also as accurate as possible.

INSTRUMENTATION

Whereas some of the latest navigation systems mentioned above may be regarded as optional, few people like to sail offshore without some basic instruments on board. This area has also witnessed tremendous advances over the last decade and today's instruments, unlike those of only a few years ago, can be used either individually or as part of a fully integrated system. The amount of computed data being generated by wind, water and navigation instruments is put to more and more use and virtually any information can now be obtained at the push of a button.

Depthsounders

Depth or echo sounders are probably one of the most useful instruments on a cruising boat. The basic sounder is a simple sonar device using ultrasonic waves emitted by a transducer mounted in the hull. The signal is reflected like an echo, which is picked up by the transducer and converted into an electrical impulse. This is then translated into the depth of water on a liquid-crystal (LCD) or light-emitting-diode (LED) display. There are various types of depthsounders available and those using an LCD display are considered not only easier to read but also preferable, as they use less electricity. When choosing a depthsounder, perhaps the most important question for the offshore navigator is to decide how deep the sounder should be able to read and also how many ancillary features are needed. The design of the hull will dictate the choice of one or two transducers. A digital sounder is probably a better choice for a cruising boat as it has several useful features, such as the ability to choose feet, fathoms or meters as well as an alarm for high or low water depths.

Speedometers

Just as the lead and line have been overtaken by the electronic sounder, so the days of the trailing log are numbered. The majority of cruising boats use electronic speedometers or knotmeters, most of which are fairly simple devices. A paddlewheel mounted through the hull has a number of magnets embedded in its paddles. As they spin past a sensor, they create electric pulses, which are translated into nautical miles per hour to show either speed or the distance covered since the log was last checked.

Although the majority of speedometers use paddlewheel transducers, there are several other types available, all of which have both advantages and disadvantages compared to the former. One type which is fairly common has a propeller type spinner on a small skeg, while some of the latest speedometers use solid state transducers which have no moving parts and can use either electromagnetic or sonic impulses.

Wind indicators

Most wind speed indicators work on the same principle as the basic speedometers in that the wind is measured at the top of the mast by a spinner, which sends an electric impulse to a counter at deck level. Most masthead units have a three cup anemometer, on top of which sits a slender indicator or fly. Electro-mechanical windspeed indicators share some of the same problems as speedometers and they also suffer because of the fragility of the sensitive moving parts. Therefore it will not be long before they are replaced by solid state masthead units, some of which are already available.

Integrated systems

In a world of microchips and data processing, cruising yachts could not remain unaffected for long and soon boats not equipped with their own computer will be the exception rather than the rule. The first area to be computerized has been data collection by various instruments. The interested navigator now has access to a whole range of information provided by separate processing units to which all individual instruments are connected. The basic computed functions are true wind direction, true wind speed and velocity made good (VMG). The latter is not only useful when racing around the marks but also, for instance, when sailing downwind, as it shows instantly at what angle of wind the boat is making best speed. Much more complex data can be computed with the aid of inputs from other sources, such as an electronic compass, automatic pilot, satnav, Decca or Loran as the integrated systems are being continually expanded and refined.

Satellite navigation in practice

Atlantic Survey

The successful completion of an Atlantic crossing, or for that matter the crossing of any ocean, depends on many factors, accurate navigation being foremost among them. Navigators' skills in astronavigation used to be put fully to the test during an Atlantic crossing, but with the widespread use of satellite navigation, the daily navigation routine on cruising boats is very different to what it used to be in the past. An increasing number of people with little experience are setting off on ocean passages feeling that their worries over navigation have been taken care of by the satnav on board. In the Atlantic Survey over half the boats (52) among the 100 boats surveyed on both sides of the Atlantic were equipped with satellite navigation and 33 skippers described satnav as their principal means of navigation, the other skippers using satellite navigation in conjunction with their sextants. All 100 boats had a sextant on board and these were used to a greater or lesser extent, usually depending on the presence of satnav.

Satellite navigation was investigated in more depth in the second part of the Atlantic Survey when 50 skippers who had just completed their transatlantic passages were interviewed in the Caribbean. Six of them admitted that they had not touched their sextants once during the crossing, four of them being experienced navigators, who assured me that they could have easily reverted to the old ways had their satnavs failed. On the other hand, several skippers, both experienced and not, used their satnavs not just for position fixing, but also to improve the accuracy of their celestial navigation, 15 of the satnav owners regularly comparing their own results with the position given by the satnav. All of them praised this practice, as it often showed them how poor their accuracy had been before. One skipper, who in the past had always believed his margin of error was only one or two miles, found that he was usually five to six miles out. He attributed this to the big swell, which made it difficult both to keep the sextant steady and sight the true horizon. Another skipper went even further and checked both his own navigation and the accuracy of his satnav, by obtaining position updates over the VHF from passing ships.

On the 44 boats on which the sextant was used at least occasionally, the average number of sights was two per day. In most cases these included a noon sight, which on 18 boats was taken daily.

On another 11 boats noon sights were taken less frequently, while on 15 boats they were never taken at all, either because they were considered inaccurate or difficult to take on a constantly rolling boat. Sunsights were used almost exclusively for the calculations and on only 13 boats were star sights taken from time to time, but rarely more than once during the entire passage. The other celestial bodies proved even less popular, planets being used by only two navigators and the moon by an additional three, usually when a moon sight could be crossed with the sun.

Among the satnav owners, only a few kept the units on all the time, the majority using them intermittently to save electricity. Usually the satnavs were switched on once a day for an average of four hours, but this time was increased with the approach of landfall. The most widely used function was that of waypoints, other satnav functions being used much less. Several skippers pointed out that they would have used more of the functions if their satnavs had been interfaced with some of their instruments or automatic pilots.

Although a large proportion of skippers relied on the satnav alone to fix their position, sextants were still carried on board and every single boat taking part in the Atlantic Survey had at least one sextant available, accompanied by the relevant reduction tables. The nautical almanac is slowly being replaced by navigational computers, which store the data contained in the almanac for many years. Fifteen boats carried one of these computers. Several navigators used computers for their calculations, some of whom had written their own programs to work out the sights. However, 44 skippers still carried an almanac for the current year and 23 also had the almanac for the following year. Several of those who had not had the foresight to obtain next year's almanac in good time realized too late that these were not easily available either in the Canaries or Caribbean and were hoping to make do with the old almanac to which a correction can be applied.

Every single satnav owner stated that the availability of these instruments had not influenced their decision to take up ocean cruising. As one skipper put it, 'Satnav or not, I would have gone cruising in any case, but I am happier because I have it. Anyway, one can hardly miss America, Columbus didn't and he didn't have satnav.' Another skipper, who did not know any astronavigation at all, was planning to learn it during the crossing by using his satnav as a useful check. In fact one skipper had bought a satnav specifically to help him improve his astronavigation results. He ended up using the sextant more than he used to and considered satnav to be less useful on a cruising boat than radar.

The majority, among both satnav owners and those who did not possess one, had learnt their astronavigation from books. Some had picked it up from others, usually during previous offshore passages on other boats, while one third of all skippers had done a special course on astronavigation and these included three qualified navigators, two of whom had served in the merchant navy and one in the airforce. Often those who had taken a course were skippers who had planned their voyage for many years.

Satellite vs astronavigation in the ARC

In both ARC surveys particular attention was paid to satellite navigation, which in a relatively short time has become the most important means of navigation in offshore sailing. Whereas in the Atlantic Survey, satnavs were found on 52 per cent of the boats, in the first ARC, which took place one year later, the proportion had already increased to 68 per cent. By the second ARC, 85 per cent of the boats had satnav on board and the time cannot be far off when virtually every offshore cruising boat will rely on satellite navigation as the main source of position fixing.

Undoubtedly one reason for satnav's increased popularity is the low cost of some models. Fortunately the considerable reduction in price that has occurred in recent years has not been achieved at the expense of quality. In fact the reliability of most makes has actually improved and there were only a few reports of malfunctioning satnavs among the ARC yachts. Even when there was a problem, the manufacturers or their local agents managed to put it right speedily.

This relatively happy state of affairs is reflected in the high performance ratings awarded to the various satnavs. In order to compare the performance of various makes, the 110 skippers taking part in the ARC 87 Equipment Survey were asked to give ratings from 1 to 10. Similarly they were asked to rate the usefulness of a particular device on the same scale.

Nine different makes of satnav were used in the ARC fleet, their owners giving them an average 9.1 for performance. The most popular make (40 per cent) was Navstar, whose various models scored an average rating of 9.3. The second most popular make was Walker (12 per cent) with a rating of 9, while Magnavox and Shipmate, although proportionally fewer, scored a maximum 10. It was interesting to note that whereas in the first ARC the most common make was Walker (42 per cent) followed by Navstar (25 per cent), the position was reversed in the second ARC, probably due to the success of the low price models introduced by the makers of the Navstar range.

The proliferation of satellite navigation among offshore sailors does not seem to have resulted yet in the demise of astronavigation, as every ARC yacht still had a sextant on board and, with a few exceptions, the necessary sight reduction tables and current almanac as well. According to the skippers, there was at least one person on each boat who could work out an accurate position using the sextant. In fact, on almost half the boats, the skipper was not the only person who had mastered the art of shooting heavenly bodies. However, this does not mean that their skills were put to the test, as position fixing on the transatlantic passage was left entirely to the satnav on 40 per cent of the boats. The sextant was used on a regular basis on less than half the boats (45 per cent), and only rarely on the remaining 15 per cent.

The importance attached to satellite navigation was also shown by the fact that in this survey satnav was the only piece of equipment whose usefulness was consistently rated higher than its performance. On a scale of 1 to 10, the usefulness of satellite navigation was rated an average 9.5. The fact that 75 per cent rated the usefulness of satellite navigation a maximum 10 speaks for itself and presumably means that the majority of offshore skippers now regard satnav as indispensable.

Another significant factor is that on the majority of boats (63 per cent) the satnav was left on all the time. Some boats had a battery dedicated to the satnav alone, which was kept separate from the other batteries. On one of them, the wind generator was hooked up directly to this battery, which ensured that the satnav had a constant source of electricity unaffected by general consumption.

RADIONAVIGATION

Radar is also proliferating on small boats, although not at the same rate as satnav. One quarter of the boats in the Equipment Survey had radar, the most common make being Furuno, the performance of the 13 Furuno radars being rated an average 7.8 by their owners. The only higher rated makes were Decca and Raytheon, of which there were five altogether in the sample. The usefulness of radar on a small boat was rated an average of only 5.3, which reflects the doubts some users have about the actual need for radar on an offshore sailing yacht, the main drawbacks being the relatively high consumption of electricity and the difficulty of siting the scanner.

The consensus was even more striking when the relative merits of RDF were assessed by the ARC skippers, the verdict for its usefulness being an average 4.9. This low figure was borne out by the fact that less than half (46 per cent) of the boats were equipped with RDF. The most common make was Lokata, the 18 instruments being rated an average 7.4 for performance. The 12 Seafarer RDFs were rated 7.7, a higher average rating of 8.8 being awarded to Sailor, of which there were seven in the sample.

The low rating for usefulness was influenced by the fact that there is little call for RDF in the middle of the ocean, where most of the time one is out of range of radio beacons. Similar low ratings for usefulness were given to the Decca navigators, mainly because the area between the Canaries and Barbados is outside the range of Decca. Although Decca attracted a mere 4.9 for usefulness, the 10 Decca units were rated 7.7 for their performance.

Weather facsimile

Weatherfax did not fare any better in the Equipment Survey, the 12 units being rated an average 5.7 for performance and even less (4.6) for their usefulness. Several owners complained that the transcripts were often unintelligible, making it impossible to draw up a weather prognosis. The poor quality of the printout was usually caused by the state of propagation at that given time, although the quality of some printers did not help matters either.

In the earlier surveys, only a few boats were equipped with weather facsimile, but most owners had rated weatherfax highly, an attitude which contrasts with the findings of the Equipment Survey and for which there is no obvious explanation. Several skippers who did not have weatherfax in the earlier surveys pointed out that they used their amateur radios to contact other boats that had weather facsimile on board to obtain the necessary information, while some people had made their own weatherfax by using decoding machines. Morse decoders were also used by other sailors to decode the more comprehensive weather information transmitted in morse on the marine bands. Many of the owners of yachts equipped with amateur radio equipment pointed out that one of the main uses of their equipment was to obtain weather information, and this particularly applied to those who did not possess a license to transmit.

Instruments

The standard instruments of wind speed, wind direction, speedometer and log fared better, both in respect of performance and perceived usefulness. Table 20 shows the average rating awarded to the most common makes in the ARC Survey. By far the most common make was Brookes & Gatehouse (69 per cent), which was rated consistently higher than the other makes with the exception of Datamarine equipment, which was found only on a handful of American boats.

Table 20. QUALITATIVE ASSESSMENT OF INSTRUMENTS IN THE EQUIPMENT SURVEY

	Wind speed	*Wind direction*	*Speedometer*	*Log*
Brookes & Gatehouse	8.8	9.1	9.2	8.8
Stowe	5.2	8.3	7.3	7.7
VDO	9.0	7.8	7.8	8.2
Walker	8.7	8.5	8.7	9.3
Datamarine	10.0	10.0	10.0	10.0
Sumlog			7.3	7.6
Performance (overall)	8.0	8.7	8.4	8.7
Usefulness (overall)	7.4	8.5	7.4	8.2

Radio equipment

Until not so long ago, long range radio transceivers on cruising boats were quite rare, mainly because of their high cost. The situation was changed by the proliferation of amateur sets, which are often very reasonably priced. For short range communication, most boats are now equipped with VHF radio and the point has been reached where a cruising boat *without* some sort of radio equipment is unusual. Figures speak for themselves and the data gathered in various surveys shows a steady increase in the number of boats equipped with radio transceivers, from VHF to long range SSB and amateur radio.

VHF radio

Very High Frequency (VHF) marine radio has been the standard means of coastal and ship to ship communication for the last two decades. Since the demise of the 6 and 12 channel radios, manufacturers have competed to offer more and more channels. Only a single crystal is needed in present sets, as the inbuilt microprocessor can synthesize any number of frequencies from it. In order to be able to use all available channels, manufacturers have added scanning circuits and memory chips. Most models have a dual watch function, which allows the set to simultaneously scan channel 16 and one other channel chosen by the operator. Some more sophisticated sets are able to scan the entire frequency band or just a group of channels, while a memory bank allows the operator to store certain frequencies, usually private, for instant recall. Another interesting development in recent years has been the miniaturization of the transceivers, some hand held models being incredibly compact.

The proliferation of VHF radio has been indeed remarkable and the stage has almost been reached where every single cruising boat has a VHF transceiver on board. The increased usage of this means of communication is most noticeable if a comparison is made between the results of various surveys. Among the earlier surveys, the usage of radio equipment was considered in particular detail in the Pacific Survey. Among the smallest boats, only one in four had a VHF radio and rarely used it. Among boats over 30 ft, three in four had VHF (76 per cent), but more than half their owners specified that they did not use this equipment very often, mostly when coming into port or to talk to friends on other yachts. In fact, when the skippers were asked to rate the usefulness of various pieces of equipment, several thought that their VHF radios were the most useless piece of equipment on their boat. Approximately one third used their VHF more frequently, including one skipper who kept it on 24 hours a day and another who organized a VHF net in New Zealand waters. Some people mentioned that they used their VHF for calling up ships in mid-ocean, either for a position update or to avoid a collision course. Three skippers mentioned that their usage depended on which area they were cruising in, pointing out that they used their VHF radios very little in the Pacific, but all the time when in US waters or the Caribbean. This regional difference probably explains why the ratings awarded to VHF were much lower among yachts sailing in the Pacific than in the Atlantic and Equipment Surveys.

The opportunity to use VHF among the smaller islands in the Pacific region is indeed very limited.

The higher proportion of VHF possession among participants in ARC 86 (93 per cent) was due to the fact that VHF facilities are more developed in Europe, North America and the Caribbean and also to the increased availability, selection and relative low price of this equipment. The ARC sample was the only one in which the range of frequencies or available channels was examined. Apart from a few boats, which had only a limited number of channels available, usually older models, most of the equipment had the full range of international, USA and other marine channels. In ARC 87, the number of boats equipped with VHF radio had increased to 95 per cent.

The proliferation of VHF radio among cruising boats is explained by the fact that in many parts of the world, especially in North America and Western Europe, VHF has become an essential piece of equipment as more and more port authorities, customs, marinas and yacht clubs expect to be contacted by arriving yachts on VHF. Safety considerations are another reason for the purchase of a VHF radio and an increasing number of yachts are equipped with a portable VHF radio which can be taken by the crew into the liferaft in case the yacht has to be abandoned. In some recent cases the rescue of shipwrecked crews was effected more rapidly when a portable VHF radio was used than by resorting to flares.

Citizens Band (CB) radios have not made significant inroads into the cruising market, although there were a number of boats equipped with CB radio in all surveys. In virtually all cases, these had been used in the past while engaged in coastal cruising but were of limited use in offshore sailing. In all later surveys the number of yachts with CB radios was small, with only one in the Pacific Survey and seven in the first ARC.

SSB marine radio

The greatest disadvantage of VHF radio is that it can only be relied on for communications over distances of not more than 20 to 25 miles, although shore based stations equipped with powerful directional antennae can reach further than that. Therefore the alternative for offshore sailing is single side band radio (SSB) which, in theory at least, has a worldwide range. Under certain conditions the 2 to 23 Mhz bands, which have been allocated for marine use, comprise frequencies which can reach any point in the world.

Depending on the frequency used, the groundwaves bend over the horizon for up to 150 miles, while the skywaves are reflected off the ionosphere and bounce back to earth thousands of miles from their source. The knack of long range communications is to know exactly which frequencies to use at certain times of day or night and under which conditions to ensure optimum propagation. The operator's task has been made much easier by advances in radio design and on most sets the frequencies are now selected digitally rather than by twisting a dial. Just as on VHF radio, frequencies are synthesized, which gives a wide choice of channels. To make the operator's life easier, most manufacturers programme the frequencies most likely to be used, the choice depending on the area to be sailed as well as the destination of the calls. Some of the set frequencies are the International Telephone Union channels, which are used for making calls through the international telephone system. Another development which contributes to better propagation are automatic antenna tuners which ensure the most efficient transmission. The antenna no longer needs to be tuned manually to the frequency used as an automatic tuner or coupler does all this at a press of a button.

In spite of these developments, the number of SSB marine radio users on cruising boats is still small. There is little doubt that the main contributing factor to the relatively low number of boats equipped with SSB transceivers has been the higher cost of this equipment compared to the price of both VHF and amateur sets. In the Suva Survey, 20 per cent of the boats possessed marine transceivers, most of which were not rated very highly by their users. The relatively high percentage recorded in that survey was due to the large number of yachts from the Antipodes possessing double side band radios, which have now been phased out, but used to be compulsory for Australian boats sailing offshore.

In the Pacific Survey, the number of SSB operators had dropped to less than 10 per cent and only one of those yachts used the radio extensively, almost every day. Two other owners hardly used their radios at all saying that they had installed them mainly for emergency use and had no need to use them regularly. In the first ARC, the number of SSB radio was slightly higher (13 per cent), a percentage which is close to the average number of ocean going yachts equipped with marine radio. As might be expected, the number of yachts equipped with this type of radio was higher among larger boats and in the ARC two thirds of the yachts over 50 ft had SSB equipment.

Amateur radio

An alternative preferred by many cruising sailors for long range communication is amateur radio, which is a global communications system with a clearly defined purpose. The frequency bands allocated to amateur operators are interspersed with those used by the SSB marine radio system, as both of them use the same type of transmission and even the sets are very similar. The major difference is in the price, an amateur set costing half or even less of its marine equivalent. This cost factor and the feeling that in an emergency an amateur will always be able to raise another amateur somewhere in the world has persuaded many sailors to equip their boats with an amateur set. One serious impediment, however, is the requirement to have a full licence in order to operate an amateur set legally. The practical examination, which requires proficiency in morse code as well as technical knowhow, is quite stringent and as a result many owners of amateur sets do not possess a licence. As most of them had acquired the sets only for safety reasons, they often listen but do not transmit, and those who try to do so without being licensed are quickly detected by other operators who usually tell them to get off the air. However, I have not heard of any case of a real emergency where the amateur fraternity refused to help a sailor in distress just because he did not have a valid call sign and the necessary piece of paper to go with it.

The proportion of yachts equipped with amateur radio in the earlier surveys conducted in the Pacific was relatively high, reflecting the view among many yachtsmen that in remoter areas of the globe, amateur radio is the most efficient and reasonable way to keep in contact with the rest of the world. More than anything else, the popularity of amateur radio among cruising sailors is due to the presence of well organized maritime mobile networks, operated by shore based enthusiasts. These nets are geared to vessels at sea and as well as logging the position of yachts checking in on the net, they also relay weather reports and general information. Receiving accurate information on weather, especially long range prognoses, is of special interest to anyone undertaking a long ocean passage and many cruising yachts have been equipped with amateur radio because of this service provided by the nets.

An interesting development in the latest models of all band amateur radios is that they are also equipped with marine frequencies and therefore can receive SSB weather information. At the present time it is illegal for an amateur operator to use these sets to transmit on the marine radio frequencies, although some amateur sets have been modified to transmit in those frequencies as well.

In the earlier surveys, which were conducted among boats that were away from home for long periods of time, amateur radios were to be found on approximately one third of the boats. Asked to rate the reliability and usefulness of their equipment, almost all operators rated amateur radio with the maximum 10 points. When asked about the amount of time the equipment was used, over half the operators stated that they used their amateur radio extensively, often every day and even twice daily. Even those who used it less rated it as extremely useful to have on board in case of any emergency.

In ARC 86 the proportion of yachts equipped with amateur radio was slightly lower at 25 per cent, probably because many of the yachts were not planning to leave the North Atlantic for a world cruise on which an amateur set would have been more useful. One striking feature of the distribution of amateur radio is the high possession of it by those flying the American flag. This became apparent first in the Suva Survey, which included a higher proportion of American boats than the other surveys and where 16 out of the 30 American boats carried amateur radio. All three Canadian boats in the same survey also had amateur radio. This trend was also apparent in the Pacific Survey, where 9 out of the 14 American boats were equipped with amateur radio. Among the remaining nationalities

For Giancarlo Damigella of Coconasse, *a senior instructor with the Italian Offshore Club, amateur radio allows him to keep in touch with his wife Rosy during his long absences from home.*

the proportion of radio amateurs was much lower. In the Atlantic Survey, although Americans were not the most numerous nation, they still possessed the highest number of amateur sets, whereas in the first ARC, exactly half of the American and Canadian boats (24 out of 48) were equipped with amateur radios.

The large proportion of amateur radios on American cruising boats is probably explained by the fact that it is somewhat easier to obtain an amateur licence in the USA than in some European countries. Regulations concerning the use of amateur radio in many countries, particularly in Europe, are more stringent. Another significant difference is that in the USA, it is possible to patch into the telephone system via an amateur radio contact. Usually the marine operator chooses a contact near to the person that he wishes to call. The land based radio amateur is then asked to patch the caller from the yacht into the telephone system, which means that often a call can be made home from the middle of the ocean for little more than the price of a local telephone call. Many of the American yachts use this facility to talk regularly with their family and friends back home while cruising anywhere in the world. This facility to use the amateur radio as a telephone is illegal in most other countries, but if it were allowed, there is no doubt that many more non-American yachts would carry this equipment.

Ideal Boat Survey

Applied to the field of electronics, the ideal boat exercise showed beyond doubt that what is essential for some is dispensable to others. The ARC fleet itself was a true reflection of the present state of yachting electronics, with some yachts bristling with the latest equipment and others relying on basic instruments. The skippers were asked to rate the importance of various items of electronic equipment for their ideal boat and in this way it was possible to draw up a list of priorities. Top of this list came VHF radio, considered by the majority as a very important piece of equipment. This is not so surprising as a VHF communications and emergency net operated very successfully within the ARC fleet during the crossing of the Atlantic. However, it was interesting to note this change of attitude towards VHF radio, which only one decade earlier had been described by many skippers taking part in a survey in the Pacific as a useless piece of equipment on a cruising boat.

Almost as highly rated as a VHF radio on an ideal cruising boat was satellite navigation, considered by almost two thirds of the skippers (102) to be very important. The ratings given to other equipment in descending order of importance were electronic speedometers, wind speed indicators, amateur radio, radar, SSB marine radio, weather facsimile and Decca navigation. Although the latter scored least points because of its regional limitations, some skippers gave Decca a higher rating for specific areas, which was also the case with Loran.

Electricity Consumption and Generation

One of the main conclusions of the Atlantic Survey was that the consumption of electricity was causing many skippers serious concern and often the only solution they could think of was to turn off the power hungry gadget. Automatic pilots are one of the pieces of equipment which are used increasingly on cruising boats and put up the consumption of electricity dramatically. Although satnavs use comparatively less energy, several skippers told me that they had their units on permanently when they left the Canaries, but decided to switch them off once they noticed how much drain was put on the batteries. Considerably less skippers went as far as switching off the autopilot as well, which shows that in choosing between an accurate position and a stint at the wheel, most people would opt for their comfort.

Among the subjects investigated on both sides of the Atlantic were battery capacity and charging methods and some interesting results came to light. Most boats carried either two or three batteries and usually they were sufficiently large to cope with a normal load. The average battery capacity per boat worked out at 336 Ah, although it must be pointed out that this high average included eight boats with an excess of 500 Ah, which is rather unusual for ordinary cruising boats. Without these high powered consumers, the average dropped to 260 Ah per boat. The average capacity per battery was 105 Ah, due to many skippers replacing their standard models with heavy duty batteries, usually because the boatbuilders had equipped their boats with standard automobile batteries. Rated at only 50 or 60 Ah, they may be sufficient for weekend sailing requirements, but were inadequate for an extended offshore cruise where electricity consumption was much higher.

The boats which had two batteries on board, usually split them between general use and engine starting, while the boats with higher electricity consumption had at least three batteries, two for general consumption and the third for engine starting. The majority of the boats in the Atlantic Survey normally used their main engines for battery charging; four large consumers had fixed diesel generators and one boat with modest requirements relied on solar panels.

As electricity consumption is a cause for much concern for those planning an ocean voyage, I asked each skipper for suggestions based on his personal experience. One traditionally minded sailor insisted on a return to paraffin lamps, although he was very much in the minority. Less reliance on electricity was also advocated by James Starling of *Windshift* who considered it a mistake to rely solely on an automatic pilot and stressed the advantage of a wind operated self-steering gear on long passages. He also thought that an alternative means of generating electricity should be a priority. His views were reflected by almost a quarter of the skippers, who agreed on the advantages of wind and water generators, or solar panels if deck space was available. Keith Hill had been using solar panels for five years on his *Currikee* and they provided sufficient electricity to run his satnav two or three times a day. Sven Holmberg of *Annatria*, an electronics engineer by profession, recommended installing a dedicated battery for the satnav alone, which would be charged when the unit was not working and would supply stable current when needed. Wind generators were also praised, especially if the unit could be adapted to operate in conjunction with a water generator. Robert Bittner of *Lorebella* had used his towing generator extensively until its propeller was bitten off by a hungry fish, always a hazard for towed objects such as trailing logs or generators.

Electricity consumption was also examined in more detail in the Atlantic Survey than in earlier surveys. Apart from navigation lights, the main consumers of electricity were autopilots, satnavs and freezers, in that order. Equipment that was switched on only as needed, such as amateur radio, rarely came in for criticism as a big consumer. Many skippers were annoyed that their autopilots consumed more than they had been led to believe. This may be explained by the fact that the pilots had to work much harder to keep a yacht on course in the vigorous downwind sailing of an ocean passage, when compared to the smaller swell met with during most coastal cruising. Several people mentioned that they would increase their power capacity before another voyage and also provide an alternative means of generating electricity so as not to be dependent on a single source.

Electricity in the ARC

As energy demands are on a constant increase on cruising boats, electricity consumption and generation were examined closely in the Equipment Survey conducted during the second ARC. The skippers were asked to comment on electricity consumption, different means of generation and methods of charging. They were also asked to make suggestions and many valuable tips came to light in this way. Several skippers stressed that they knew much more about this subject by the time they reached Barbados than when they had left home and with hindsight would have made very different arrangements for their voyage. However, compared to the findings of previous surveys, offshore sailors seem to be learning the right lessons and most ARC boats were better equipped to deal with the heavy demands made on their batteries. However this was not always the case as some skippers found to their cost.

The ARC yachts carried on average three batteries with a capacity of 90 Ah per battery. The total battery capacity worked out at 290 Ah per yacht. As the majority of skippers (82 per cent) found their energy provisions satisfactory, it may be a useful yardstick when assessing one's own requirements.

Although some production boats continue to be equipped with ordinary automotive batteries, on most boats these had been replaced with heavy duty models. Unfortunately even batteries that had been sold as heavy duty were sometimes substandard, as their owners discovered after a season of hard use. Several skippers pointed out that the battery level should be checked more frequently in hot climates, especially as on most boats the batteries are kept in warm confined spaces. Even the so-called maintenance free batteries proved disappointing as on inspection some were found to have dried up.

However, the quality of the batteries is not always to blame, as the demands put on them on cruising boats often exceed the norms for which the batteries had been designed. In many instances charging was carried out erratically, allowing batteries to run dangerously low. Both in the ARC and the TRANSARC several boats were unable to start their engines after having crossed the finishing line, due to flat batteries. In most cases the demand on the batteries had been heavier than usual during the last day or two before landfall and when the time came to start the engine, the batteries were too weak to turn it over. As the majority of boats charge their batteries from the main engine this usually meant a tow into harbour.

In the Equipment Survey, 93 per cent of the boats charged their batteries with the help of the main engine, which was run on average 1 hour 45 minutes per day. Although several yachts ran their engines for considerably more hours each day, over half the yachts in the survey ran their main engine for less than two hours each day for charging purposes.

In spite of an increased consumption of electricity compared to earlier surveys, only 24 per cent of the yachts had auxiliary generators, either diesel or petrol driven. In all cases the latter were portable and were used mainly as a standby. The fixed type diesel generators on some large yachts were used both for charging batteries and running various appliances, such as 110 V or 240 V cookers, microwave ovens, television sets and even video games.

An increasing number of cruising yachts are being equipped with alternative means of generating electricity, the most popular being wind generators. Twenty-eight yachts in the Equipment Survey had wind generators, the majority being mounted permanently. As most of these boats were single-masted, the generator was usually fitted on its own pole mounted at the stern. In some instances the same pole was also used as a mount for the radar scanner. Several wind generators were acquired shortly before the start as skippers had realized on their way to Las Palmas that their existing arrangements could not cope with a higher demand for electricity than anticipated.

Most skippers were satisfied with the performance of their wind generators in keeping the batteries topped up both in port and at sea, although it was pointed out that when running downwind the apparent wind was often too light to produce a reasonable charge. On the other hand, in very strong winds, especially at anchor, some generators had to be disengaged either because they tended to burn out the diodes or more often because of the irritating vibration transmitted to the entire boat.

Water generators were used on seven boats and althugh they performed well in producing a good charge, some owners had reservations, mainly because of the drag which they estimated reduced their speed by between half and one knot depending on the size of boat. It was also pointed out that at higher speeds it was very difficult to haul in the generator. Another disadvantage of towing a generator is that one cannot tow a fishing line at the same time. This can be a serious consideration as fresh fish makes a welcome addition to the menu on a long passage, as many ARC participants found during their transatlantic voyage.

Another type of generator deriving its energy from the flow of water are special generators which are fitted directly to the main engine shaft. They appear to be most efficient and the few ARC skippers who used them spoke highly of them. However, they also induce a certain amount of drag.

Although solar panels seem to provide the solution to some of these problems, only 12 per cent in the Equipment Survey used them. Their limited popularity is due to the need to find sufficient space on deck and for this reason some panels were not mounted permanently and were only used in port.

CONCLUSIONS

This chapter dealt with what I regard as giving the greatest amount of aggravation on board cruising boats, namely electronic equipment and the electricity it consumes. A logical first step for anyone equipping a boat for offshore cruising is to draw up a realistic list of priorities before actually buying anything. It is also essential that instruments and equipment requirements are matched to the area where one intends to cruise. This is also where the old adage, 'Only rich people can afford to buy cheap things' has an undoubted validity, as in the long run it will probably pay to choose instruments made by reputable firms, some of whom give a worldwide guarantee valid for several years.

The impression that I have gained from being in close contact with hundreds of offshore sailors every year is that an increasing number expect their equipment to do everything for them. This results in some people becoming virtual slaves of their hardware, which can take a lot of the pleasure out of cruising. A certain push-button mentality is also becoming prevalent among today's seafarers as shown by the increasing number of cruising boats using autopilots in preference to wind operated self-steering gears. The main drawback to this is the constant need to generate electricity to keep the autopilot going.

It was interesting to note in the Ideal Boat Survey, that although the skippers had been given virtually a free hand to design and equip their ideal boats, several experienced skippers stressed the need of keeping things as simple as possible, or praised 'simplicity at all cost'. Maurice Pilkington of *Maid of Moraira* reflected the views of these skippers when he said 'The more electronics one has, the more problems, and if something goes wrong at sea with this type of equipment, there is little one can do about it. Cruising boats should be self-sufficient in every respect and what cannot be put right with your own means must not be regarded as an essential piece of equipment.' He then gave the example of a skipper whose satnav had broken down in mid-ocean and who could only guess his position to within 60 miles. It is cases such as this which show the value of suggestions made by many skippers that no matter how much equipment one piles on a boat, it is the skill of the crew that is ultimately the guarantee of a safe voyage.

Concerning radio equipment, a VHF transceiver has become almost standard on a cruising boat and bearing in mind their comparatively low cost, there is no reason why everyone should not have a set. The only dilemma is whether to get a portable or permanently mounted unit. The simplest answer, if one can afford it, is to get both. Hand held sets can be extremely helpful when cruising as they allow you to communicate with the yacht either from the dinghy or ashore. In the extreme, hand held VHF radios can also be taken into the liferaft and many people equip their panic bag with one. A decent waterproof bag should be acquired for a portable set as those advertised as splash-proof do not like sea water. Finally, the fixed set should have a permanently mounted antenna at the masthead which gives a noticeable boost to its range.

As far as long range communications are concerned, the ultimate choice of a marine SSB or an amateur set will depend on each user's individual priorities. SSB radio has two clear advantages over amateur radio. Firstly, it can be operated legally with little more trouble than is involved in obtaining a VHF operator's licence. Secondly, although the amateur fraternity operates a huge number of nets run by shore based enthusiasts, a proper 24 hour safety net is only operated on certain marine frequencies. Apart from that, to communicate with shore based parties who are not amateurs themselves can only be done via SSB radio, with the exception of the USA and Canada where so-called patching is allowed. Also marine SSB radio does allow the use of the radio for business calls, which are not permitted on amateur radio. Another advantage of SSB radio is the ability of most sets to receive weather information, which can be printed out on a weather facsimile printer. Finally, most SSB sets can also be used to listen in on the amateur frequencies.

Therefore, acquiring an SSB set depends on several factors, primarily the need to be in constant touch with land, which for many cruising people is not a vital priority. The cost itself is no longer so prohibitive as over the last few years the price of SSB transceivers has dropped to a very reasonable level. If the decision is taken to acquire such a set, it should be matched with an automatic antenna tuner. However, one important aspect that must be considered very carefully is the high energy output required by most SSB radios. This applies equally to amateur sets, which are an alternate solution that suit many sailors' requirements for long range communications.

If after having taken all these matters into consideration amateur radio continues to be more attractive, then the only solution is to acquire one, but also the proper licence to go with it. What is certainly wrong is to regard amateur radio as the poor man's SSB, which it is not. The concept of amateur radio is fundamentally different and some marine users of amateur radio, often the loudest exponents of its virtues, seem unaware of the basic tenets which motivated the early afficionados and led to the creation of this truly international association. Founded at the dawn of radio communications, its basic function was and still is to enable amateur enthusiasts to communicate with each other over the airwaves. Keeping it as an exclusive club by forcing those who wish to join it to go through the rigmarole of an examination in morse code, which is then never used again, seems out of place nowadays in the era of voice communications. On the other hand, I consider it equally wrong to use the set only as a means to make cheap phone calls home, which is not the purpose of amateur radio.

For the offshore sailor, the main attraction of amateur radio is its safety aspect. The amateur radio maritime nets that have grown up all over the world play a vital role in enhancing the safety of those who sail offshore and I believe that the easing of the licensing laws would bring about an increase in the number of yachts carrying this type of radio legally. Many boats have been equipped with amateur radio primarily for safety reasons, but their owners are forced to operate illegally. This happens especially in the remoter areas of the world, where there is little control, although the attitude of net controllers has hardened considerably in recent years and illegal operators are bluntly told to get off the air. Should there be a serious emergency involving a yacht with an unlicensed set on board, there is no doubt that other amateurs would do their best to help, but for the time being it would be safer not to leave home without a licence or, alternatively, to acquire an SSB set.

After more than a decade of investigating various aspects of offshore cruising, I consider the problems associated with electricity consumption to be among the most serious faced by long distance sailors. This observation is borne out by the fact that electricity generation and the problems associated with it was the most common cause of complaint among participants in the first two ARCs.

Although it would be rather difficult to draw one overall conclusion from all suggestions and observations made by the hundreds of skippers who contributed to the various surveys, there appears to be a consensus regarding electricity consumption, namely that it is a problem that must be tackled long before leaving on a voyage. The first requirement is to make a realistic assessment of one's projected daily needs and then double that figure for good measure. The battery capacity should be at least twice that amount, with the engine starting battery preferably kept separate. Consumption and battery capacity should dictate the size of the alternator, as often the standard alternator provided with the engine is not powerful enough.

Some sort of an auxiliary battery charger is almost indispensable on boats with heavy demands. The most efficient solution on yachts equipped with a freezer is to have an engine driven compressor so that the batteries are charged while running the engine for the freezer. Otherwise, on boats with a reasonable consumption, water generators appear to provide the better solution on passage and wind generators in port. Provided one has sufficient deck space, solar panels might be the answer, although the demands on boats that have room to accommodate them usually surpass the modest output of the panels.

THE TRANSATLANTIC NET

The popularity of amateur radio among long distance voyagers is partly due to the efficiency of the various maritime networks run and controlled by land based amateurs. Beyond being efficient, the net controllers and their associates more often than not come to be regarded as friends, their voices comforting many a lonely sailor worried about some problem on a long passage. My first contact with the camaraderie of the airwaves was in the South Pacific, where Colin Bush's voice sounding a welcome to New Zealand was a factor in persuading quite a few undecided sailors to take the route to the Bay of Islands. Not long afterwards in Vanuatu, I met the local net controller, busy dashing from work to get the day's weather forecast from the local French radio station to translate and broadcast to his waiting flock of maritime mobiles. The flavour of the numerous radio maritime nets that have blossomed round the world is best portrayed by one of the most important, the Transatlantic Maritime Mobile Net.

The nerve centre of the Transatlantic Net is on Grand Turk, a small island between Puerto Rico and the Bahamas. The main settlement on this little known and even less frequented island is Coburn Town, which has a population of four thousand souls and is also the capital of Turks and Caicos, one of the few remaining British colonies. It is a sleepy place where nothing ever seems to happen, except the occasional visit of yachts on passage to or from the neighbouring Bahamas. Grand Turk briefly hit the international news on two occasions in its history, once in the 1960s when the first American to be launched into space was brought ashore on Grand Turk after his historic flight from Cape Canaveral and some twenty years later when the Chief Minister was arrested and imprisoned in Florida on charges related to drug smuggling.

For Sheila Laing, VP5SL, the net controller, the chance to talk to sailors as they make their way across the Atlantic is a pleasant way to enliven daily life on a small tropical island since her retirement from an active business life. During five years as an ethereal agony aunt she has had to cope with almost every conceivable situation and request, from giving advice on medical matters, both to humans and their pets, to finding recipes when all bananas started ripening at once and even on how to avoid being hit by flying fish when taking a watch at night in the cockpit. Whenever she does not know the answer, such as when one skipper of a yacht in mid-Atlantic asked for the mathematical formula needed to calculate the volume of a cylindrical tank so as to be able to work out how much drinking water he had left, Sheila appeals to her other half, Robin VP5GT, also a keen amateur operator. This was one of the rare occasions when Sheila had to resort to outside help, although she has prepared for more difficult medical matters by persuading one of the doctors at the local hospital to give a consultation over the airwaves to a sick yachtsman if necessary.

After running a general import business in the islands for several years, on retirement Robin and Sheila have continued to reside on Grand Turk where they spend the best part of the year. The only time they try to be away is the summer, when the weather is at its most sultry and the North Atlantic is quiet, both on the airwaves and on the water. A 40 ft yacht based in Chesapeake Bay is their summer retreat, which they sail up and down the East Coast.

The net was started in the 1970s by Bill Trayfors, a US diplomat based in Morocco, who handed it over to Mel Cole, a Boston based enthusiast. Looking for a relay station to help out when propagation was poor, Mel discovered the Laings' hideaway and persuaded Sheila to help out with the net, which she ended up taking over completely in 1984. It operates daily from October to May between 1300 and 1400 GMT on 21400 Mhz.

The main function of the net is to keep track of the yachts making an Atlantic passage, as well as relaying to them all relevant weather information. The latest prognosis is obtained regularly from the US Coast Guard weather station in Portsmouth, Virginia; this is supplemented by data arriving on Sheila's own weatherfax direct from the US Navy headquarters in Norfolk, Virginia. Weather information covering the area south of 32°N and west of 35°W is relayed on the net every day at 1330 GMT.

The busiest time for the net is November and December, not only because this is the time when most yachts cross the Atlantic to the Caribbean, but also because the net has adopted the ARC, which brings into the net many new voices, some of whom remain with the net until the end of their voyage. From January onwards, the net starts picking up voices from the South Atlantic as European boats make their way to Brazil, an increasingly popular transatlantic destination, while others head northwards along the traditional route from the Cape of Good Hope. Traffic starts slowing down by the end of March and virtually ceases during summer as there are few cruising boats crossing the Atlantic during the hurricane season.

Sheila's 600 watt station is located in an optimum position on the very top of Grand Turk, which has a maximum altitude of some 75 feet. It is an ideal take-off point for radio waves and propagation is usually excellent as there is nothing between the small island and Africa. In case of difficulties in propagation or other problems, Sheila can call on the expertise of the assistant net controllers strategically located around the North Atlantic. To provide the best coverage possible, Laurie Mayhead in Southampton, Robin Page-Blair in Florida and Trudi Smyth in Barbados are occasionally helped from Nova Scotia by Douglas Conrad. Laurie Mayhead, G3AQC, is the veteran amongst them having been involved with amateur radio for over half a century. A keen sailor himself, keeping his 43 foot yacht in the Mediterranean at Dubrovnik, he plans to join one of the future ARC's now that he is retired.

The net's involvement with the first ARC was particularly significant for Trudi Smyth, as her son Martin was taking part in the rally as crew on board *Peter Rabbit.* Trying to keep a 'sched' with her own son was much more moving than talking to the usual disembodied voices to which the net controllers only rarely have the chance to put a face. Although most friendships made over the airwaves cease with a successful landfall, the net has a few regulars, such as Bob Salmon, a delivery skipper and several times participant in the Whitbread Round the World Race. Most other regulars are only known by their call signs, such as Peter G3FWB (Front Wheel Brakes). Veteran of two ARCs and two return Atlantic crossings is Ernst Torp, another regular on the Transatlantic Net.

The Transatlantic Net maintains a close contact with the UK Maritime Net operating on 14303 Mhz, whose controller Bill Hall, G4FRN, is based in Cobham, Surrey. During ARC 87 Bill became directly involved as a documentary of the event was being made by TVS from Southampton. Three ARC yachts had been selected by the film makers to record the Atlantic crossing, the British *Admiral's Lady*, the Australian *Drina* and the American *Bucephalus.* When the latter reported a malfunctioning of the video equipment, TVS director Bob Franklin dashed to Cobham to try and sort out the problem over the air. Bill's expertise in electronic matters came in handy and the problem was finally narrowed down to a battery charging fault. It was the kind of emergency preferred by Bill, who in the past had been involved in several life and death situations. One of the most dramatic rescue operations he had been involved with was when a catamaran began breaking up in heavy weather in the Bay of Biscay, while returning from the Azores to England. A Mayday call on 14303 Mhz was picked up by an amateur on a boat in the Solent, who alerted the Coastguards on VHF. A Nimrod aircraft was scrambled from Kinloss and flew over Biscay to locate the distressed yacht. A permanent contact was maintained between the Nimrod and the UK net on the amateur frequencies and eventually the catamaran was found 200 miles off Ushant. A Sea King helicopter from Culdrose in Cornwall tried to reach them, but as it was just out of range, a French helicopter from Brest also assisted and eventually took off the crew.

It is emergencies such as this, which highlight the advantages of amateur radio. Both Sheila and Robin Laing are convinced that the facility to always be able to raise someone on the air is what has persuaded many sailors to choose amateur radio. Although feeling quite strongly about illegal operators, who are not tolerated on the net, Sheila would not hesitate to assist anyone in a genuine emergency, whether licensed or not. Robin is in total agreement with the need for amateurs to make the effort to become properly licensed and quoted the perfect example in support of his belief in the importance of amateur radio.

A serious emergency occurred on board the 80 ft motor yacht *Honeybee III* when the captain died while on passage from the Virgin Islands to Florida. No member of the crew was able to navigate nor was anyone licensed to operate the radio, but the skipper's brother managed to put out a call on the amateur radio, which fortunately had been left tuned to the frequency of the US Intercontinental Net. The call was picked up by a Canadian amateur, who contacted Robin as the nearest station to the stricken vessel. Robin spent the entire night poring over a chart spread out on his floor and talking the boat through the reef strewn area. By morning the boat was safely at anchor off Grand Turk and Robin has no doubt that without the amateur radio, *Honeybee III* might have ended up on a reef.

Chapter 5

OFFSHORE ROUTINES

I have often been taken aback by the naïvety of questions asked by some coastal sailors, who seem to have great difficulty in imagining life on board during a long offshore passage. Often they seem surprised when I try to explain that most voyagers lead a normal life, with regular meals and the occasional sundowner, even if the nights are interrupted by the unavoidable watches. Although routine might sound the wrong term to describe life at sea, on any well run ship the daily activities of necessity have an element of routine about them.

WATCHKEEPING

Offshore routines were investigated in a number of surveys and every aspect that makes up a day on the high seas was discussed with the skippers and crews. Keeping watches is undoubtedly a demanding chore and the fellow who once asked me if we went to sleep every night was not entirely misguided, as a few people do indeed turn in for the night and leave their boat to be looked after by its self-steering and God above. However, these are the minority and on most boats somebody is usually awake to keep an eye on things.

Watchkeeping varies enormously from boat to boat, from a few who do not keep regular watches at all to those who run their yachts along Navy lines. Two of the factors which influence watchkeeping is the availability of an automatic pilot or windvane and the size of the crew. In the surveys carried out in the Pacific among 100 long distance cruising boats, I found that on most boats where watches were kept as a matter of routine, a fixed system of watches only operated at night. On boats with a crew of two, the night was usually split into four three-hour periods, with two watch and two rest periods. A similar arrangement operated on boats with a crew of three, so that on any given night only one crew member had to take two watches. Boats with larger crews generally kept two hour watches, especially those steered by hand. In most instances older children also took watches, although they were usually spared night watches.

Watchkeeping was also investigated in the Atlantic Survey. Trying to put their vigilance to the test, I asked every skipper how many ships he and his crew had seen during the passage, once they were well clear of the Canary Islands. The average number of sightings was almost four per boat, but looking at the answers more closely, it was perhaps not surprising that there were many more sightings on boats where watches were kept, than on those where the crew only kept the occasional lookout. Three of the singlehanders did not see any ships at all, whereas in contrast, on a boat that was handsteered all the way, there were 14 sightings. These sightings included about an equal proportion of large ships and yachts. As scores of yachts cross the Atlantic at about the same time, such encounters in mid-ocean tend to become the norm rather than the exception, even if this pleasure is sometimes one-sided. Both the skippers of *Nabulus* and *Freelife* had close encounters at night with yachts that were showing no lights and no sign of life. In both cases the yachts ghosted by about 100 feet away, kept on course by their self-steering gears.

Encounters with larger ships were usually limited to the airwaves, some skippers trying to contact passing ships on VHF. Such calls were not always returned and Cornelius Roon of *Springer* had to take avoiding action twice as the ship he was trying to contact bore down on him with no one on the bridge and apparently no radio watch being kept either. The old assumption among yacht skippers that the keeping of watches or the showing of lights is less crucial when one is out of the shipping lanes must be re-examined, especially as the current practice of weather routeing can take ships all over the oceans away from traditional shipping lanes.

On all boats, discipline became stricter on nearing land or when sailing close to known shipping lanes. At such times watches were usually kept even on boats which did not take watchkeeping too seriously in mid-ocean. This was certainly a wise precaution as my investigation into the loss of fifty cruising boats in various parts of the world in my previous book *Ocean Cruising Survey* showed that the single most common cause for the losses had been poor watchkeeping. Over half the disasters probably could have been avoided if somebody had been on watch.

Keeping a good lookout at all times can undoubtedly play a major part in reducing the risks and even if a navigational mistake has been made, a good pair of eyes can still avoid disaster. The fact that modern ships equipped with the latest instruments are still wrecked shows that even the most sophisticated gadgetry does not make a good lookout obsolete. One quarter of the boats whose loss was investigated in *Ocean Cruising Survey* were lost on reefs and at least half of them could have been saved if avoiding action had been taken in time. The New Zealand yacht *Maamari* was sailing at night along the coast of Papua New Guinea, relying on seeing a light before altering course. Unbeknown to the navigator the light was out of action and their course closed with a reef. The person on watch, however, saw and heard the reef and the boat had time to go about and avoid disaster. Although reefs do not show up well on radar screens, those on the windward side of islands always break, except in the calmest of weather, and are thus visible and audible even on the darkest night. Even on the lee side of an island, reefs are often visible, especially if there is some swell.

Another cause of small boats being lost at sea is collision with ships. The days are gone when power gave way to sail as a matter of course. Not only are a large number of ships reluctant to alter course, but larger vessels are unable to do so quickly even if they wanted to. Therefore it is safer to assume that any ship on a converging course is not going to give way and to take whatever avoiding action is necessary in good time.

Watchkeeping should not be neglected even when off known shipping lanes, as the most deserted areas of the ocean can be crossed by fishing boats, naval ships, research vessels, submarines and, of course, other yachts. In one particular incident, two cruising yachts did collide at night off Tonga, fortunately at low speed and without causing serious damage to each other. Both skippers were convinced that the area was so deserted that it was not necessary to keep someone on watch, nor was either of them showing any lights. When the skippers had got over the shock of the mild collision, they had the pleasant surprise of realizing that they knew each other and had not met since leaving California.

The tendency not to keep watches during an offshore passage is not necessarily a sign of lack of experience, as there are plenty of experienced skippers who admit to going to sleep at night, some of them following the practice since earlier days when yachts or ships outside of the shipping lanes were a rarity. Nor is the wrecking of boats the prerequisite of inexperienced sailors as the skippers of well over half the boats whose loss I investigated in *Ocean Cruising Survey* had sailed many thousands of miles before disaster struck.

A criticism that has been levelled at the ARC is that it attracts inexperienced sailors, for the safety in numbers it provides, who otherwise would not contemplate an Atlantic crossing. Although there may be some truth in this supposition, the actual situation in the first two ARCs was rather different. Over one third (39 per cent) of the skippers taking part in ARC 86 had actually crossed the Atlantic before, some of them more than once. Even among the 61 per cent who did not have a transatlantic passage to their credit, the majority stated that they would have crossed the Atlantic regardless of the ARC. Altogether 18 per cent of the skippers agreed that the ARC had stimulated them to cross the Atlantic, most of these being interested in the competition it provided. The situation was similar in ARC 87, which attracted a slightly higher proportion of skippers with offshore experience.

Among the various safety measures introduced by the ARC, probably the most appreciated were the daily VHF and SSB listening nets for emergencies. Those who joined the ARC for company also used the radio to keep in touch with other participants throughout the crossing and this worked well using VHF, SSB and amateur radio apparatus. Contact was maintained not only over the radio waves but also visually as almost all participants saw other yachts during the crossing, only three not seeing any at all. On average 10 yachts were seen during the crossing with a maximum of 53 sightings recorded by one fastidious skipper.

Again it was not surprising that many of the people who saw fewer yachts also took a more lackadaisical approach to watch-keeping. It underlined the truth of a statement made by a skipper interviewed in a previous survey who stated, 'It is only people who don't keep watches who never see ships at sea; we seem to meet them all the time.' A telling comment from Mike Morrish, who decided to sail his *Fortuna* around the world without self-steering gear for the precise reason of ensuring someone would be in the cockpit all the time.

Lights at Night

The showing of lights at night is another subject of varying opinion and practice. Half of the skippers in the Pacific Survey stated that when on passage and well offshore their boats showed no lights at all, mainly in order to save electricity. A number of skippers specified that they kept their navigation lights on when sailing in known shipping lanes. Over one third of the boats showed some kind of light from the masthead at all times, either an all-round white, the regulation tricolour navigation light or, in a few cases, a white strobe. On the remaining boats a storm lantern was hung in the rigging at night, although one skipper noticed that this light disturbed his night vision so he reverted to showing a masthead light.

The showing of lights is related both to watchkeeping practice and electricity consumption, so in the Atlantic Survey these aspects were examined in relation to each other. The main reason people fail to show lights at night is not that they do not wish to be seen, but the desire to conserve electricity. This concern is not limited to those boats equipped with a full range of electronic instruments. Seventeen of the skippers interviewed said that they rarely showed lights offshore, while an additional nine skippers specified that they only switched on their lights if they saw another vessel. However, in order to see another vessel, someone has to be on watch and, while on most of these 26 boats watches were kept at night, the skippers of an additional five boats admitted that they neither showed lights nor kept a regular system of watches. Although faced with the special watchkeeping difficulties of singlehanding, three of the seven singlehanders did not show lights either. The other four admitted that they often slept through the night, but tried to wake up every few hours to check if everything was all right. In fact proper night watches were kept on only two thirds of the boats.

Although lights were not shown in order to save electricity, some skippers solved this problem either by using paraffin lamps or by showing a masthead light with a less powerful bulb, often a strobe, and only switching on the regulation lights when necessary. Several people complained about the powerful bulbs in some tricolour masthead lights, which can flatten an average battery in two or three nights. This was one of the main reasons why many skippers eventually decided to switch off their lights altogether. For those worried at the consumption of electricity, Austin Whitten who took part in ARC 87 in *Discovery II* suggests replacing the standard bulb of the masthead light with a low wattage bulb prior to a long offshore passage.

The Atlantic in November and December has been compared to a busy four lane highway as many other yachts also cross at the same time as the ARC fleet. This profusion is appreciated by those who draw comfort from seeing other yachts en route, but is causing concern to some skippers who are not convinced of the safety in numbers argument, especially if some yachts do not keep proper watches. From the information provided by the ARC skippers, it would appear that almost all of them did keep watches, although they were more lax when it came to showing lights at night or displaying radar reflectors. Several skippers who showed lights commented on the practice of switching on lights only when another vessel was visible and described the surprise their watchkeepers had felt when suddenly a yacht was lit up close at hand on what had previously looked like an empty ocean. If two yachts are following this same practice on a dark night with a big sea, they could get dangerously close before they saw each other. All these factors have led to changes in the ARC rules, which now make both the showing of lights at night and the displaying of a radar reflector compulsory.

COLLISIONS

The single most common cause of yachts being lost offshore is collision, whether with ships, whales, containers, tree trunks and a whole range of unidentified debris, of which there seems to be plenty floating in the world's oceans. There are some boats which have disappeared without trace while on passage and the reasons for their disappearance will never be known. Some collisions can be avoided and the prudent skipper who insists on a proper lookout being kept at all times can narrow down the risk to a minimum. In spite of the undeniable dangers posed to yachts by all manner of unidentified objects, the main hazard continues to be the possibility of colliding, or more likely, of being run down by a ship. No one will ever know how many small boats have been sunk by large ships and this may be the most plausible explanation for many a mysterious disappearance over the years. In a few cases, the shipwrecked crew were rescued by the very ship that caused the sinking, but in most instances the unfortunate yacht disappeared without a trace. Usually the crew of the large ship are not even aware that they have struck something as witnessed by the story of the tanker which arrived in New York with the remains of a fibreglass yacht wrapped around its bulb. The only way to avoid this danger is to keep a permanent watch and to treat ships with the respect they deserve. Unfortunately even the greatest vigilance cannot avoid every type of collision, especially at night, and this is where a strong hull comes into its own. However, even the strongest hull may not be able to withstand the violent impact of certain collisions and the obvious example that comes to mind is the possibility of being struck by a submarine surfacing or cruising at periscope depth.

Several collisions with unidentified objects seem to point to this possibility, such as the loss of the 30 ft yacht *Nanesse*, which sank after colliding with something while on passage from the Caribbean to Bermuda. The skipper François Erpicum heard a strange ringing sound from outside the boat. As he went on deck to investigate, the boat struck something hard and started filling with water. He barely had time to launch the liferaft before the boat sank. Another mysterious collision which could be attributed to a submarine caused the sinking of the sloop *Napoleon Solo* on a transatlantic passage from the Canaries to the United States. Also lost in similar circumstances was the yacht *Misty Blue*, on passage from the Canaries to the Caribbean. Both boats struck underwater obstructions in mid-Atlantic and in both cases the damage was so grave that the yachts sank almost immediately.

A similar unexplained collision happened to the yacht *Traigh*, a UFO 31, on its way to join the ARC in the Canary Islands. In broad daylight with crew on deck, a large bang was the first indication that an unidentified underwater object had been hit. The impact was severe enough to sheer the rudder and seriously damage the keel, causing the boat to have to be towed into port by a local lifeboat. This happened in the Irish Sea, where there have been several documented incidents involving fishing boats and submarines. Submarines detect the presence of surface vessels by noise, so it may be advisable to motorsail when passing through an area known to be used by submarines or if ringing sounds are heard in the water immediately switch on the engine to announce one's presence.

Similar sinkings after a collision with an unidentified object occurred to two New Zealand boats in the South Pacific, *Southern Kiwi* and *Pono*. In all of the instances of sinkings quoted above, the crew managed to take to the liferaft, from which they were rescued and could tell the tale of their disasters. However, there are several cases of yachts that have disappeared without trace while on passage, such as *Ponsonby Express* lost between Fiji and New Zealand or *Valhalla* between Samoa and Tonga, and the cause of such sinkings will always remain a matter of speculation. From Joshua Slocum to Alain Colas, sailors and their boats have vanished at sea without explanation. Although structural defects or gas explosions cannot be entirely ruled out in some cases, collision remains the prime suspect. Even when the crew have been rescued, as in the cases mentioned previously, the real cause is rarely known, as strangely the majority of these unexplained collisions happened at night.

Many more examples of collisions have come to my knowledge, fortunately not all with disastrous consequences. In the first two ARC's there were several close encounters with other yachts, but no actual collisions. During ARC 87 there were two collisions with unidentified objects, both at night, one of which caused serious damage to the rudder of the yacht involved. A more dramatic incident involved the German yacht *Joy* which was caught up in and brought to a complete standstill by a huge fishing net drifting in mid-Atlantic, which was kept afloat by several plastic floats. The yacht became so enmeshed that the Kellner family were unable to free the yacht themselves. Their calls for help on the VHF radio were finally answered by a large motor yacht on its way to the Caribbean who came to their assistance. It took the combined efforts of two divers to cut the yacht free and *Joy* carried on to Barbados where it had to be hauled out and the rudder repaired.

There were several collisions with whales both in ARC 86 and in ARC 87, none with serious consequences for the yachts concerned, although in 1987 the Danish yacht *Electra* reported a collision which knocked some of the woodwork loose on the side of the impact. There was a lot of blood in the water and the whale appeared to be more hurt than the boat. Ironically, the design of *Electra* was a Spaekhugger, which means killer whale in Danish. Similarly *Northern Quest* reported more damage to the whale than to their boat after their collision. Both *Molla III* and *Summer Wind* who reported collisions in ARC 86 were concerned by the injured whales remaining around the boat. Both crews managed to disperse the whales by starting their engines. Sightings of whales have increased dramatically over the last few years due to the international moratorium on the hunting of whales. While some may enjoy seeing these creatures in the middle of the ocean, most skippers share the view that yachts and whales do not mix and prefer to keep their distance from the leviathans. Although whales did show an interest in some yachts, there was no report of actual aggressiveness, only a certain curiosity, which nevertheless can be rather unnerving when the beast is twice the size of the yacht.

In the past, mysterious collisions have often been blamed on whales, due mainly to their habit of sleeping on the surface, oblivious to everything around them, especially a sailing boat moving through the water with little noise. Although accidental collisions with whales account for some of the reported sinkings of yachts, the number of deliberate unprovoked attacks by whales is very small. One such case involved the New Zealand yacht *Dauntless* on passage home from New Caledonia. While motoring along in calm weather, three sperm whales were sighted at some distance. The smallest of them, a young calf, swam towards the boat. Perhaps sensing danger, the mother rammed the boat amidships, breaking through the hull. With blood spouting from the injured whale, the bull joined in the attack, lifting the boat right out of the water. Sinking rapidly, the damaged yacht was abandoned by the crew in two liferafts, from which they were picked up within 24 hours, having taken their amateur radio with them, for which they had had the foresight to prepare a portable aerial and battery in their panic bag.

Deliberate or accidental, the possibility of a collision with a whale causes considerable concern to many sailors, most of whom are of the opinion that whales are best avoided. Those who have had close encounters with whales advise that it is never too early to take avoiding action, such as altering course away from them as soon as they are sighted. If a whale does approach a vessel and certainly if it shows any interest in the yacht, everything possible should be done to discourage it, such as running the engine or pouring oil, diesel or paraffin in the water around the vessel. It has also been suggested that certain light colours of antifouling, such as white should not be used as this may make the boat resemble the underbelly of a large whale, which could lead to an attack by killer whales.

BREAKAGES

The various surveys dealing with equipment have brought to light a wide variety of gear failure. In the majority of cases the con-

Sad end to a transatlantic passage as the Italian yacht Elisa *arrives in St Vincent with a broken mast.*

sequences were not serious and the crew managed to effect temporary repairs on the spot. Fortunately only a small number of skippers suffered the loss of their mast, which is one of the most traumatic experiences for any sailor. In all of these cases, which occurred in the early surveys, the mast was lost because of rigging failure. It is comforting to know that the number of offshore cruising boats that lose their masts is extremely small and I suspect proportionately less than it used to be, given the increase in the number of yachts. From the wide range of breakages that have been reported in the surveys, I have selected only those which have some relevance to other yachtsmen.

The passage to the Canaries, whether from the Mediterranean via Gibraltar or direct from the English Channel across the Bay of Biscay, appeared to have been a good shakedown cruise for all untested boats and crews. In this way, many skippers were able to assess the seaworthiness of their craft during an offshore passage before setting off across the Atlantic and the results were not always satisfactory. A disturbingly high incidence of broken equipment or poor quality work was reported to me, often on some of the more expensive boats. Unfortunately there are a number of boatbuilders putting boats on the market, which are not capable of standing up to the rigours of an ocean passage, although sold as offshore cruisers. One such example was mentioned by the skipper of one of the boats surveyed, which was knocked down by a large wave while approaching Gran Canaria. The helmsman, who was wearing a harness at the time, fell against the lifelines and one of the stanchions was ripped out of the deck together with a piece of fibreglass. It was an unpleasant way for the skipper to discover that his stanchions had not been properly bolted on and that there was no backing pad or any strengthening under the bolts. Even more serious was the gross incompetence of a well known builder, who supplied a new boat with the backstays bolted through the aft deck, but not led to proper chainplates. While beating to windward, the entire aft deck lifted up and the mast was nearly lost. The builders tried to brush away their responsibility by claiming that the deck might have been weakened by the strong Mediterranean sun!

Yet another example of substandard work came to my attention during the 1988 Canary Islands Rally. The owner of a new production boat joined the rally in Arrecife at the end of a maiden voyage from the Mediterranean. Until it reached the island of Gomera, the boat had never been at anchor as all the ports visited en route had docking facilities. Shortly after dropping anchor in San Sebastian harbour, a strong gust of wind whistled through the anchorage and the skipper of the boat happened to be still on the foredeck. To his amazement he watched the anchor chain stretch, to be followed by the windlass lifting up, wrenched off the deck. On inspection, it was discovered that the windlass pad, a rectangular piece of marine ply, had been glassed to the deck and the windlass fixed to it by means of two 1 ¼″ wood screws.

This incident, fortunately with no serious consequence, reminded me of a report prepared by the master of a RNLI lifeboat, who had been involved in the rescue of many yachts in distress. Among the various points he made was the observation that virtually none of the fibreglass boats he had handled, had been provided with a strong enough point of attachment which could be used for towing. In such cases, the only solution was to take the tow line around the mast itself, as neither cleats nor windlasses were able to take the strain. The example described above would have been such a case and highlights the danger of setting off on an offshore cruise on a boat which may not even be adequate for a weekend sail. If acquiring a new boat, the builders must be informed of one's cruising plans, so that all deck fittings, chainplates, etc. are properly supported and firmly attached. If the boat is secondhand, the new owner should check all these features thoroughly so as to avoid an unpleasant surprise later on.

As well as the unfortunate skippers mentioned above, several others stressed that boatbuilders must be made to realize that it is their responsibility to provide essential safety features and they cannot expect their customers to know the details of construction that are hidden from view. If proper chainplates or strengthening the attachment of deck fittings are not standard but optional extras, this should be clearly stated in the specification, otherwise such practice amounts to irresponsible negligence.

The responsibility of boatbuilders and manufacturers of marine equipment also encompasses the after-sales service of their products; the various surveys have brought to light many instances of poor service as well as the exemplary behaviour of some manufacturers. I was told stories of equipment sent back to manufacturers and repaired free of charge although the guarantee period had lapsed, while others were unable to get faulty gear repaired at all, only weeks after it had been purchased. Obviously some manufacturers are not prepared to face up to their responsibility nor are they aware of the power and influence of the yachting grapevine. All these stories, both good and bad, are told wherever cruising folk gather and when related over VHF or amateur radio, the audience can be enormous. While in Las Palmas carrying out the Atlantic Survey, I saw on the dockside the local agent of an international electronics firm pleading with a frustrated sailor to stop broadcasting details of the shoddy treatment he had received from head office, who had refused to replace a faulty radar only recently purchased.

The long Atlantic crossing resulted in all kinds of breakages among the 100 boats taking part in the Atlantic Survey and the high rate of gear failure was indicated by the fact that 31 skippers described the breakages that occurred as more than just routine failures. Most of them appeared to have been caused by tougher than normal sailing conditions, the constant rolling motion in blustery trade winds showing up weaknesses which had not been put to such a test before.

The most frequent breakages were those of mast and boom fittings, some of which were not strong enough to stand up to the tough conditions. The main sheet attachment on the boom or the kicking strap attachment broke on four boats and in each case the skippers blamed the weakness of the gear, which had only been spot-welded onto the boom. Only temporary repairs could be effected on these boats with the exception of *Karaka* where Ronald McLaughlin was able to carry out a proper repair job when the gooseneck fitting broke on his boom as, extraordinarily, he had the necessary welding equipment on board.

Many breakages occurred to spinnaker poles, which were used extensively for poling out jibs, genoas and cruising chutes as well as spinnakers. The constant movement caused end fittings, tracks or mast attachments to break. Again it was the weakness of the fittings which received the blame, although in some cases the skippers thought the breakage might have been avoided if the pole had been fixed more firmly, with less play at its outer end. Some of the poles themselves were not strong enough and on two boats telescopic poles collapsed and could not be pulled out again. One of these unlucky skippers pointed out that maximum force is exerted on a telescopic pole when it is fully extended, yet this is also the state in which the pole is weakest, so it should not be surprising that problems occur.

Long downwind runs also took their toll on halyards and rigging. Three boats lost their jib halyards, two of which parted at the wire splice. Another halyard came down when the swivel broke at the masthead while sailing with the cruising chute. On inspection it was discovered that the stainless steel swivel had sheared because of the porosity of the metal. Substandard stainless steel fittings could have easily resulted in three boats losing their masts, if it had not been for the crew's vigilance or sheer good luck. On *Kanga*, the forestay swaged terminal failed at the masthead, the mast being held up only by the jib halyard. As a repair could not be effected at sea, one of the spare halyards was used to replace the forestay. Equally fortunate not to lose their mast were the crew of *Springer*. While peeling an orange on the foredeck, Wilhelmina Roon happened to notice a wide crack in the connecting piece between the furling gear and stemhead fitting. An emergency forestay had to be rigged, which necessitated a perilous climb to the top of the swinging mast. On *Aotearoa* one of the capshrouds was nearly lost when a chainplate attachment parted. The stainless steel rod supporting the chainplate sheered inside the boat and only the quick reaction of the crew saved the boat from being dismasted in mid-ocean. The culprit was not always stainless steel, as on *Sea Messenger* a broken bobstay was caused by a faulty link in the galvanized chain. In all four cases the skippers were convinced that the mast would have been lost if the boat had not been running before the wind at the time.

Steering gear failure was almost as common as rigging failure, also brought on by long downwind runs in which rudders were working hard all the time. On one boat the steering cables broke twice, while on another the entire steering gear was wrenched off its anchoring points because the builders had not provided an adequate backing plate for the bolts holding down the gear. Self-steering gears and automatic pilots had their share of failures, mostly caused by the gears being undersized for the work they were expected to do. Some

One step from disaster: the cracked forestay fitting of Springer.

of the less powerful autopilots were also unable to cope with continuous use in strong trade wind conditions.

Several boats blew out sails or tore them badly, although in most cases the skippers put this down to the age of the sails or to their own negligence in not having paid enough attention to chafe. Very often older sails parted along the seams when stitches gave way. Exposure to ultraviolet light causes stitching to perish and this was evident on two furling jibs which, unprotected by a UV guard, blew out shortly after leaving the Canaries. In most cases the sail repairs were carried out straight away, a few boats having sewing machines on board; while on *Duen*, the most travelled boat in the sample, Albert Fletcher used the unorthodox method of gluing on patches with contact adhesive. He stressed that he only used this method because most of his sails were over ten years old and a new row of stitches would have weakened the material even more, the needle holes acting like perforations. Some skippers suggested that self-adhesive patches are useful not only to repair a torn sail but also to strengthen older sails.

Breakages in the first two ARCs, which brought together four hundred yachts of all types and sizes, followed almost the same pattern, with halyards, booms, autopilots and sails bearing the brunt of the crossing. Chafe and the prolonged use of spinnakers and chutes caused all kinds of failures to halyards, blocks and swivels and on several occasions the only solution was to send somebody to the top of the mast to make the necessary repair or to replace the broken halyard.

Spinnaker and whisker poles broke for various reasons, but usually because they were not strong enough for the job in hand. In one instance, the pole was lost because the stainless steel wire loop for attaching the topping lift had chafed through allowing the pole to bend and break. The skipper suggested replacing the wire with a proper shackle from the beginning. Among the dozen or so poles lost during the crossing, at least three were actually dropped overboard, one cause for which the spar makers deserve no blame.

Jib furling gears also had their share of problems and on two boats the extrusion broke, rendering the gear useless for the rest of the crossing. Overall, I got the impression that some of the breakages could have been avoided if the boats had been sailed less hard and in fact some skippers agreed that they were at least partly to blame for the breakages. Ulf Lindstrom of *Merita* put it succintly when he told me in Barbados, 'We have broken more gear during this crossing than in the previous 12,000 miles of ocean sailing.'

Most skippers, however, took the breakages in their stride, even when they caused certain discomfort, for example on *Eldevika* where a broken freezer forced Jan Holvik to drink his Scotch without ice, while the only serious emergency reported in *Tai Tai*'s questionnaire was the repeated beatings suffered by the skipper at backgammon.

The winds during ARC 87 were on the whole lighter than in the previous year and most breakages during the crossing were caused by the swell and rolling rather than the force of wind. The most common breakages were again booms. Although unintentional gybes could be blamed for some of the breakages in both ARCs, many standard booms were obviously not strong enough for the kind of stress they were subjected to during the long ocean passage. Spinnaker poles did not fare any better and several yachts arrived in Barbados with damaged spars. The use of preventers would have avoided some of the breakages, as several skippers admitted that most gybes occurred when on autopilot or windvane.

From their comments on the crossing it was obvious that many skippers had not been prepared for the effect of several weeks of rolling. Their equipment was not prepared for it either, as many weak mast and pole fittings could not take the strain of the continuous rolling and broke. Chafe, particularly on halyards, was again a cause for concern. Similarly some autopilots were not able to stand up to the rigours of a 2700 mile Atlantic crossing and many a disgruntled crew arrived in Barbados having steered by hand more than they had bargained for.

The weather was not always to blame for breakages, although squalls claimed a few ripped sails. Those who had not sailed in the tropics before were often caught unawares by these mini-gales, particularly by the nocturnal variety whose approach cannot easily be detected. Apart from during squalls, which can pack in winds of up to 30 knots and occasionally more, the winds during the ARC 87 crossing very rarely exceeded 25 knots. Only 15 per cent of the yachts claimed to have experienced winds over 35 knots on the passage to Barbados and even among those who did experience strong winds, these never lasted more than one day and usually blew themselves out between four and eight hours.

Several yachts had problems with their rudders. One of them, *Tosca B*, a Dolphin 31 lost the entire rudder 80 miles off Barbados. For some unexplained reason, probably metal fatigue, the stock sheared and the rudder dropped off. The rudderless yacht was finally towed into Barbados by another yacht. Yet another boat was forced to finish the ARC steered by an emergency tiller after its steering cables had snapped.

Although there were a few emergencies that required outside help, most breakages were fixed with the means available, the ARC skippers showing a great knack for improvization. It is a talent that offshore sailors must possess if they are to survive the challenge of the sea. Several instances in ARC 87 gained my admiration for their ingenuity. Having lost his spinnaker pole, one skipper continued to run before the wind by poling out the genoa with his sailboard mast. The sailboard sail was also put to use on *Whim of Arne* following the loss of their forestay. Sailing under a jury rig of storm sail and trysail, extra speed was gained by flying the sailboard sail from the foot of the jury stayed mast.

Arne Ringdal of *Maria Two* achieved the impossible by establishing a link between Philip Benson sailing on *Tina III*, who only had VHF radio, and his wife in the United States. Arne accomplished this by making a call on his SSB radio to Norway, from where an international telephone call was placed to the USA. Then, holding the inverted telephone handset of his VHF radio, which was in contact with *Tina III*, to the handset of his SSB transceiver, he depressed one or other of the transmit buttons in a synchronized manner so that the two parties could carry on an almost normal conversation. Rather incredible, but it worked!

Just as ingenious, but rather more demanding were the attempts

A well organised workshop on Athabasca II *where most repairs can be carried out in an emergency.*

by Mark Prior of *Beam Ends* to charge his batteries after his engine had failed to start. First he took the alternator off the engine and tried to turn it with a hand drill. When this failed he tried to turn it using the back wheel of a bicycle by pedalling furiously sitting astride the bike. When this also failed he attached the alternator with a spare fan belt to the flywheel of his outboard engine, which was mounted on a bracket. To cool the outboard engine the drive unit was immersed in a water container whose top had been cut open. Meanwhile he had to hold the alternator in a sling made from plastic shopping bags to protect his hands from the heat generated. The exercise was exhausting, but succeeded and the batteries received enough charge to start the main engine.

ABANDONING SHIP

Fortunately none of the emergencies which occurred in the first two ARCs was serious enough to cause the sinking of the yacht in question and the only boat lost was that of *Bamaca* in 1987. Due to a navigational error the boat was wrecked on a reef off the Barbados coast and although one crew member swam ashore, the rest of the crew saved themselves in the liferaft. This instance shows how important it is to carry a liferaft on board. Having a liferaft is one of the basic rules of the ARC and the reason why this provision was introduced was the reluctance of some people to equip their ocean-going boat with this vital piece of equipment.

This tendency among some skippers to leave on an ocean passage without a liferaft was first investigated in the South Pacific. The matter was re-examined among the boats surveyed in the Canaries and Caribbean when in a sample of 100 yachts surveyed on both sides of the Atlantic, liferafts were carried on only 80 of them. The skippers of the 20 boats without liferafts were asked the reasons why they chose to sail without rafts and also what provisions they had made for abandoning ship. Seven stated that they had decided to leave without liferafts because they had lost confidence in them after reading reports about liferafts capsizing in heavy weather or not inflating when needed. Five skippers gave cost as their main reason, while lack of space was the main cause for the absence of a raft on another four smaller boats. Other reasons mentioned were the difficulty of having rafts regularly serviced when cruising or their inability to be steered or sailed in a certain direction, this latter reason causing some people to look for an alternative to self-inflat-

NKER DINGHY

ing [illegible] two boats with wooden dinghies, these were kept on deck with their masts and sails by their side, their skippers intending to use them as lifeboats if the yacht had to be abandoned. On another six boats without liferafts, inflatable dinghies would be used in an emergency, two of these being provided with CO_2 bottles for rapid inflation.

The solution for five of the skippers was to acquire a Tinker dinghy, which can double up as a lifeboat, but cannot be regarded a liferaft as such. These dinghies, which theoretically can be inflated as quickly as a liferaft, but also have the provision to be sailed, have acquired some popularity in recent years. Although liferafts were not examined as a separate topic in the ARC surveys, John Douglas of the catamaran *Golden Goose* attempted while in Barbados to launch his Tinker Tramp under simulated conditions of abandoning ship with the intention of sending a videotape of the proceedings back to the manufacturers as promotional material. Unfortunately the language used by his Antipodean crew while attempting, but failing, to inflate the Tinker in the advertised time, gave his video recording an 'X' certificate and I understand the tape was never sent.

Several skippers gave complete faith in their yachts as the main reason for not having a liferaft, and in three cases no provision had been made at all for abandoning ship. Two of these boats were made of steel, the third was a plywood catamaran, regarded by its owner as unsinkable.

Although the number of boats cruising without a liferaft is still in the minority (20 per cent in this sample), I consider it to be a dangerous tendency. In spite of their drawbacks, liferafts have saved many lives in recent years, some instances being mentioned in the previous section on collisions, and the few failures have been exaggerated out of all proportion. In some countries the presence of a regularly serviced liferaft is compulsory on every ocean-going yacht, but in countries where the decision to carry a liferaft is left to the skipper, the possibility must be faced that a situation might arise when the yacht has to be abandoned to save one's life. Fire could be such an occasion when even an otherwise unsinkable boat may have to be abandoned in a very short time. A self-inflating raft can make the difference between life and death.

LIFERAFT SURVEY

The seriousness of this matter prompted me to carry out a special investigation concerning liferafts and the reasons for not having them in parallel with the Atlantic Survey. The first part of the Liferaft Survey was conducted in Gran Canaria, while the skippers of 85 yachts were interviewed in several islands in the Caribbean (Barbados, St Vincent and the Grenadines). Several interesting factors came to light during those interviews. Firstly, a large number of liferafts had been acquired secondhand by their present owners, being either included with the purchase of a used boat or being a liferaft bought from a previous owner. Secondly, quite a few people were prepared to buy unsuitable liferafts for their size of boat, often far larger than necessary, because the price was right or the rafts were sold as a 'special deal'.

Although it might be tempting to buy a larger raft than required, this could turn out to be counterproductive as a liferaft which is not loaded to its designed capacity may capsize in rough weather. The occupants of a liferaft act as its ballast and a large raft which is only half full may be too light in strong winds. On the other hand, during a simulated survival test conducted in the Gulf of Mexico, it was observed that a liferaft filled to capacity rapidly became very uncomfortable as there was not enough space for all the occupants to rest properly at the same time. Bearing this in mind, the sensible solution would seem to be to have a liferaft which has two spare places above the standard crew, i.e. a six-man raft for a crew of four or an eight-man raft for a crew of six.

During the Liferaft Survey it soon became obvious that many owners had very little knowledge about the history of their liferafts; neither about any regular servicing, or lack of it, nor about features of the raft, such as whether it had a double floor or the type of emergency pack it contained. Most skippers had no idea if their rafts had a single or double floor and only a few seemed to know the reasons for having a double floor. Nor did the majority know the contents of their emergency pack or even if their liferaft contained one. The only people who were aware of the type of pack contained in their liferafts were the skippers of racing boats and French sailors. Under French regulations, ocean-going yachts must carry a liferaft equipped with the appropriate offshore pack for the projected voyage.

The main advantages of a double floor are increased strength, improved comfort and particularly in cold climates, enhanced insulation. As far as the emergency packs contained in the liferaft are concerned, the test conducted in the Gulf of Mexico mentioned previously, established that the rations provided in the standard pack would barely sustain a normal person for the nominal three days, which is the time inside which liferaft manufacturers assume a shipwrecked crew will be rescued. Every manufacturer offers the option of a more complete emergency pack, but even the most comprehensive of these is only calculated to last for a few days. Because by necessity liferafts must be compact, emergency packs cannot take up too much space and the amount of water provided is especially small. The only solution is to make provision for additional water to be available in case the boat has to be abandoned. Just as important is to supplement the emergency pack by preparing a well equipped panic bag, the contents of which are discussed on page 151.

Another factor which should be taken into consideration when making provision for abandoning ship is the likelihood of most or even all the crew members becoming seasick, even those who are not usually seasick on board a yacht. It has been recommended that every person should take some preventative medication before boarding the raft, ideally at least one hour before. Obviously this is not possible when a boat has to be abandoned rapidly, but if there is some prior indication of this possibility, each crew member should take some anti-seasickness precautions. Some liferaft manufacturers do include anti-seasickness medication in their standard pack.

Among the skippers, who were undertaking long offshore voyages without a liferaft, the usual reason given for this decision was the bad reputation acquired by liferafts. This aspect was particularly striking among American skippers, several of whom mentioned unfavourable reports they had read in the US press. The skipper of one boat, who also worked occasionally as a delivery skipper, pointed out that many delivery skippers had little faith in liferafts. His explanation was that they like to be able to rely on themselves, particularly in an emergency and sitting helplessly in a liferaft did not agree with this view. Unfortunately he did not offer an alternative, so I was forced to draw my own conclusion that even the most self-sufficient skipper ultimately might prefer to sit helplessly in a liferaft than be left swimming in the middle of the ocean.

I also observed a certain trend among charter yachts in the Caribbean, both crewed and bareboat, not to carry liferafts at all. The explanation given by the manager of one of the largest charter boat bases in the Caribbean, was that rafts were totally unnecessary. He justified this by pointing out that every one of their boats was equipped with VHF radio, towed a large fibreglass dinghy and was never supposed to be out of sight of land. For more or less the same reasons, most other boats chartering in that area do not carry liferafts either, often in order to save space on deck.

One of the difficulties mentioned again and again by liferaft owners was that regular servicing of liferafts was often a major problem outside Western Europe and North America. Once they had left home waters, many skippers had great trouble in finding a reputable service station and in most cases the liferafts ceased to be serviced altogether. Several owners complained about poor service and this may be the reason why some skippers had started inspecting and servicing liferafts themselves. As with every other specialized service, this DIY approach should not be taken too lightly and, if at all possible, the servicing should be left to those trained and equipped to carry it out.

The skippers were also asked if they had ever used a liferaft and only one skipper had ever used one in an emergency, although a few others had used one as part of a course on survival techniques. Several skippers praised the usefulness of such survival courses, at which one is trained in launching, righting and boarding a raft. Another valuable comment praised those service agents who encouraged owners to be present during the opening of rafts and actually let them pull the release lanyard to see for themselves what happened. The skipper of *Ocean Mermaid* recommended the practice of a company in Mallorca, which takes Polaroid pictures of the contents when the rafts are opened for inspection so that absent owners can judge for themselves why certain items had to be replaced.

The majority of liferafts were kept on deck, either mounted on the coachroof, aft or fore decks, or stored in a more protected place somewhere near the cockpit. Because the valise-packed rafts especially are not always fully waterproof, some people preferred to keep them in a protected, easily accessible place near the cockpit. This is certainly advisable considering the limited time one might have in which to launch the raft if the boat was badly holed and sinking rapidly.

An increasing number of production boats are equipped with special liferaft lockers in or near the cockpit. It was pointed out that in an emergency it may be difficult to lift a heavy canister out of a deep locker, particularly by somebody who is not very strong or is injured. On the Amel Mango the problem has been solved by providing a special pulley system which allows even the weakest member of the crew to launch the raft in an emergency. On boats without such special provisions a launch session should be held in port to see if everyone in the crew was able to launch the raft in case the boat had to be abandoned.

Panic bags

While discussing the question of abandoning ship, I asked the skippers, both those with and without liferafts, if they had prepared a bag or container to be grabbed if the boat had to be left in an emergency. Only about half the people had actually prepared such a panic bag and on several occasions my questions on emergency preparations prompted those who had neglected this aspect to consider putting together such a bag themselves. The question was often turned around as those interviewed tried to find out from me what other people put in their bags or what should be the most essential items to put in. From the contents of bags which had been prepared, it was obvious that what was regarded essential by some people, was expendable to others. Although undertaking a long offshore passage, many of the less experienced crews had retained the attitude of people who are within range of quick and efficient rescue services and expect to be saved in a short time. Therefore they had only concentrated on saving themselves. In contrast to this, among those with considerable offshore experience, who had given this subject a lot of thought, the main priority was to be able to look after themselves and survive for long periods without outside help.

Looking at the contents of such a great variety of bags, some containing a bare minimum, while others being able to support the crew for as long as two months, I drew up a list of the best ideas and commonest suggestions:

Food: a mixture of dry and concentrated food, not all of which has to be reconstituted with water; food in self-heating tins; chocolate; glucose.

Medicine: first aid kit; vitamins; laxatives; sunblock preparations; painkillers; anti-seasickness medication; any personal medicines.

Safety: EPIRB (Emergency Position Indicating Radio Beacon); flares (in separate waterproof container) or flare pistol; portable VHF radio, spare batteries and aerial; dye marker; torch and batteries; signalling mirror; spare sea anchor; survival handbook.

Miscellaneous: water still; knife (pocket knife with various blades); drinking cup; spoon; plastic plate(s); fishing gear; can opener; sponge; assorted plastic bags.

Personal: passports; money; paper and pencil; reading matter; playing cards; dice.

Comfort: survival suits or blankets (aluminium); spare clothing; sun hats; sunglasses; folding umbrella (can be used to shelter from rain or sun, catch rain water and even as a sail, if strong enough).

Navigation: compass; plastic sextant; almanac or navigational computer; routeing chart(s).

The above list is based on the contents of some 50 panic bags, several skippers having made valuable suggestions on this subject. Thus Jean-Charles Maurer of *Eureka*, who keeps two plastic drums with all essential survival items on his aft deck, changes the routeing

Jean-Charles Maurer of Eureka *carries two comprehensive survival containers which he inspects regularly.*

chart contained in one of them every month, to know what winds and currents to expect should he be forced to take to his liferaft. Giancarlo Damigella of *Coconasse*, who runs navigation courses for members of the Italian Offshore Cruising Club, holds a 'panic' session with the crew before each passage, assigning precise tasks to everyone. Two people are responsible for the launching of the raft, two would launch the inflatable dinghy and water containers, while the radio operator would broadcast a Mayday on the radio and activate the EPIRB. The usefulness of a portable VHF radio transmitter was mentioned by several skippers who stressed its advantages over flares in attracting the attention of a passing ship. Needless to say that if one has such a handheld VHF radio on board, its batteries should always be kept fully charged.

Most of the panic bags were in fact plastic containers, those with a wide mouth and screw top being considered the best. They must obviously float, be waterproof and should have a point of attachment and lanyard to make fast to the liferaft or dinghy. On most boats, the containers were kept close to the companionway, either under the steps or table. Also in an accessible position were a few water containers, as only rarely did the panic bag or emergency pack itself contain water. The practice of keeping a few jerrycans of water lashed on deck has much to recommend it if the boat had to be abandoned. The water containers should not be completely full so that they float if thrown overboard.

Among all the subjects I have examined in the various surveys, abandoning one's ship is the least popular topic of conversation. And yet I found that those who had given the matter serious thought were very happy to talk about their preparations, whereas those who were reluctant to confront such an eventuality and were obviously of the attitude that such things only happened to other people, had made little or no preparations. My questioning sometimes got them thinking and on several occasions I could detect a change of attitude. Most memorable was one skipper who proudly showed me how he had made his boat unsinkable by providing it with several buoyancy bags hooked up to compressed air diving tanks.

'It's all very impressive,' I said, 'but what are you going to do if you have a fire?' His face fell in disappointment, as it was an eventuality that he had never envisaged.

Most sailors are firm believers in the belts and braces philosophy. When one's own life might be involved, it may not be such a bad idea to carry also a piece of string.

JELLICLE, *STILL DANCING IN THE MOONLIGHT*

During both my voyaging and my journalistic work, I have had the privilege of meeting and talking to several outstanding sailors, but none has left his mark on me as indelibly as Mike Bailes. Arriving in Opua in New Zealand to interview skippers for the Pacific Survey, I could not have been more delighted than to see the rather elderly looking 25 ft Folkboat *Jellicle* swinging to her anchor. The last time I had spent time with Mike had been in Port Vila in Vanuatu, several years earlier, where on my arrival I had found him giving lessons in seamanship and navigation in fluent Bislama to a group of local fishermen, who were sitting in a circle around him on the dockside. Having heard snatches of Mike's fascinating life when interviewing him in Tuvalu for a previous survey, I had been determined not to miss the chance to learn more of this man and the wisdom he had to impart. So I had set the tape-recorder rolling and over a bottle of French wine, or maybe it was two, had persuaded him to tell his story.

Since the 1960s Mike has roamed the oceans in *Jellicle*, named after the T. S. Eliot cat that danced in the moonlight. *Jellicle* is simple to the point of being spartan. Mike has no use for an engine, instead preferring a sweep and full set of sails kept in tip-top condition. Below deck, amidst coils of rope, baskets and sacks of basic provisions are two bunks, a navigation table and a simple primus stove. The oldtimers like Joshua Slocum are Mike's mentors and he aims to keep his life as simple as theirs with little time for luxuries. However much money he had, he would not swap *Jellicle* for anything larger or more modern. Mike loves his small Folkboat, not only because he can sail it like a dinghy, but also because he likes to be close to the sea.

Mike's love for the sea has been with him all his life. His claim to fame that he jokingly boasts about is to be the first officer in the history of the Royal Navy to be court martialled twice, found guilty on both occasions, yet still to retire honourably as a Lieutenant Commander on a full pension. The first incident occurred when he was first officer on a submarine and involved in developing a fast turbine engine using a new fuel. His briefcase containing all the classified documents relating to the new engine disappeared from the corner where he had left it while having a few drinks with his fellow officers at a pub near the Admiralty in London. Mike and his commanding officer were found guilty of negligence, but were not punished too severely.

From fast submarines, Mike turned his attention to survival in ship's lifeboats, trying to prove that long voyages in such open boats could still be accomplished, as Captain Bligh had so aptly demonstrated. After a few short voyages sponsored by the Navy, Mike selected a crew for a transatlantic voyage. Plans were well advanced when at the last moment the top brass cancelled the voyage as being too risky. Mike accepted the decision as any good officer would and so did the crew, except for one young man who had crewed with Mike in the other lifeboat voyages. Utterly dejected and distressed by another ten years in the Navy without any adventures to brighten

Mike Bailes has sailed over 100,000 miles on his Jellicle *in the last quarter of a century.*

it, the man threatened to commit suicide. Feeling responsible for the young man's plight, Mike wrote to him advising him that it was better to leave the Navy rather than take his own life. The letter was found and Mike found himself in prison, facing yet another court martial for inciting a rating to desert. Again he was found guilty, although the board was understanding enough to realize he had acted in good faith and no punishment was exacted.

Mike however had already reached the decision that he had had enough of the Navy and when the opportunity arose two years later, he retired honourably and with a pension. He bought *Jellicle*, not much bigger than a ship's lifeboat, and set off to show that long ocean passages in such a boat were perfectly feasible.

Mike Bailes now considers the vast Pacific to be his home, for in *Jellicle* he has covered over 100,000 miles sailing back and forth to every island group south of the equator. Speaking several Pacific languages as well as fluent French, Mike is a mine of knowledge on Pacific culture and history. For several years he made his base in Tonga, running a marine school for young Tongans and commanding a local trading vessel from time to time. Bringing back forgotten skills and adding new ones to the younger generation of seafaring islanders gave him both satisfaction and a worthwhile occupation.

For the last ten years Mike has taken on as crew young Pacific islanders, teaching them the art of sailing in a practical way. One of his first crew, known to everyone as Tonga Bill, caught the bug of cruising and built his own 18-footer from secondhand timber salvaged from the Auckland docks. After sailing in the Pacific for several years, Bill set off across the Indian Ocean with the intention of circling the globe. He was last heard of in Reunion where he appeared to be about to swallow the anchor and marry a French teacher. Mike's next disciple, Pita Filitonga, was qualified enough at the age of eighteen to be the navigator on a traditional canoe sailing thousands of miles from Vanuatu to Papua New Guinea for the Pacific Festival of Arts. Pita eventually married a Sydney architect and settled in Australia. In New Zealand, Mike was sailing with his latest crew from Vanuatu, Wari Farea. Mike's 'sons' as he calls them all appear to flourish under his guidance and in 1988 he reports that he is proud godfather to three 'crew grandsons' all named after him.

The morning that I left Port Vila, I met Mike walking along the main street with a big coil of rope slung over his shoulder.

'Where are you off to?' I asked.

'Believe it or not to the prison. I have permission to give lessons on seamanship to the inmates.'

'And what is the rope for?'

'Oh, today's practical lesson is on knots and splices.'

'You had better watch they don't learn about rope ladders as it won't be the Royal Navy judging you this time,' I teased him. Meeting several years later in New Zealand, I reminded Mike how amused I had been about the idea of him teaching ropework to prisoners. His freckled face lit up in his typical grin.

'It was one of the best things I did,' he replied. Apparently one of the prisoners had been jailed for political reasons and when Independence and a change in government came, the man eventually became a Minister in the new government. With such a contact, Mike's involvement with Vanuatu increased and he again became involved in a new marine school for young sailors. The Vanuatuans regarded Mike as part of the family in the same way as he regarded his young crew as 'sons'.

Wedded both to *Jellicle* and the Pacific, Mike leaves the tropical zone every hurricane season and cruises down to the safety of New Zealand, a country that has become increasingly his home. The years have taken their toll on *Jellicle* and in June 1987 she did not make the usual trip back when winter approached but was taken out of the water in Whangarei. Six months later she was still high and dry. As Mike writes, 'After exploratory surgery, she is now being replanked on port topsides and survives on an intensive care drip of home brew and linseed oil.' He still would not swap his *Jellicle* for anything else. 'I feel towards her like the young man who at 23 (my first Folkboat) married the rather plain and ordinary girl next door and stayed happily married ever since.'

Mike Bailes is still married to *Jellicle*, and is still dancing in the moonlight.

Chapter 6

LIFE AFLOAT

Napoleon certainly did not have transatlantic sailors in mind when he said that an army marches on its stomach, but the sentiment is equally valid, for feeding the crew well is a crucial factor in running a happy boat. Meals are always a welcome interruption on a long passage and provisioning was a major preoccupation of the crews whom I interviewed in the Canaries on the eve of their transatlantic voyage. Later in the Caribbean I discussed this subject in more detail with 50 skippers who had just completed their transatlantic passage in order to see how successful their provisioning had been.

PROVISIONING

The majority of skippers were satisfied with their provisioning and none experienced any serious problems, with the exception of one boat which ran out of food before reaching Barbados. Fresh fruit and vegetables purchased in the Canaries lasted well, especially when carefully selected by hand. Cucumbers, cabbages, pumpkins and lemons were items mentioned by several crews as good buys, while hand picked green tomatoes carefully stored lasted for four weeks on one boat. The storage of fresh produce is crucial and several people recommended storing vegetables and fruit suspended in netting. A similar recommendation was that vegetables such as potatoes and onions kept better when stored in a dark place. Regular inspection and the consumption of fruit as it ripened was also advocated. By far the most popular purchase in the Canaries were oranges, which lasted extremely well and several crews regretted that they had not bought more, especially those lacking refrigeration. Many people advised that one should be generous with the fruit allowance when planning a transatlantic or other long passage.

The general selection of supplies in the Canaries for provisioning was considered adequate, but those crews who had sailed via the Cape Verde Islands pointed out that there is not such a wide selection of either fresh produce or other non-perishable goods in those islands. In both Spanish and Portuguese territories, it was suggested that rice and similar dry goods should be bought in small quantities because of the presence of weevils and moths. Storing these items in airtight plastic containers does prevent the cross-infestation of stores if any of these small beasts do appear.

Spanish matches came in for particular criticism and were regarded as highly dangerous because of the tendency of their heads to break and fly off when being struck. On one boat a matchhead had caused an unpleasant injury to a crew member's face by flying up in this way.

For making cooking easier on passage, one crew followed the practice of cooking large meals before leaving, then dividing these into smaller portions and storing them in the freezer to be re-heated as required. If one has a freezer, this is a good standby for use in rough weather, while another experienced voyager recommended carrying plenty of cans of ready-made soup in liquid form, as being the easiest, quickest and most nourishing meal to prepare in rough conditions. Another cook swore by the type of food sealed in a bag, which can be boiled in salt water to conserve water supplies. Because of the difficulty of cooking in a continually rolling boat it was also suggested that sufficient snacks and light meals be carried on longer passages. Several people were doubtful about the use of dehydrated foods, as extra water had to be carried to reconstitute them.

Arriving in the Caribbean, many skippers were disillusioned by the high price of imported food and the lack of selection compared to Europe. This applied particularly to the smaller islands, which are not so well endowed with shops. The commonest recommendation made by the skippers interviewed was that boats should stock up well in Europe on all their dried, canned and other non-perishable stores. Some even suggested that it was advisable to provision for six months or the entire stay in the Caribbean if the capacity of the boat allowed this.

In spite of the improvement in refrigeration equipment, as I shall point out later in this chapter, many voyagers still prefer to do without, mainly to avoid the daily chore of running the engine or generator to keep the freezer going. Frozen foods remained in the minority and for long term storage tinned foods continued to make up the largest proportion of the stores. Dried and freeze-dried goods are also gaining popularity and most boats carry a balanced mixture of all types of stores. In all surveys, only a small minority relied on all their stores being in the freezer, although I was told of several instances when a broken freezer in mid-ocean had left the crew almost without food for the rest of the passage. The crew of an

Australian yacht on passage from Cape Town to Rio de Janeiro, resorted to using the ruined best prime steak for bait, but the only thing they caught were sharks. It is also worth bearing in mind that some countries, the USA and Australia in particular, confiscate all frozen meats on board, so one should try and arrive there with an empty freezer. In fact, they confiscate other foodstuffs as well, such as eggs, smoked meats, and all fresh fruit and vegetables, so it may be wise to plan on arriving there with a fairly empty larder.

The usual period for which people provisioned was from three to six months, most trying to buy larger quantities in countries where certain goods were cheaper or of better quality. It is also wise to stock up with certain items which are not available everywhere, such as long life milk, tinned butter, dried eggs, etc. Nor should one forget certain luxuries or special goods which may be unobtainable in less developed countries. Last but not least, one should attempt to stock up with duty free spirits wherever these are readily available or cost little. Wine is another item which was recommended to be bought in large quantities before cruising to remoter areas as the cost of a bottle of wine in many Pacific or Caribbean islands can be prohibitive.

Baking bread

The staff of life, one's daily bread, was one aspect of provisioning which was discussed with the crews taking part in the Atlantic Survey. Bread was baked on two thirds of the boats during the Atlantic passage, varying from every day to once a week, but most usually every 2–3 days. A variety of methods were used, the majority of cooks baking the classic way in the oven using dried yeast, although one cook found soda bread an easier solution by substituting baking powder for yeast. The few who used the instant bread mixes (such as MacDougals or Granny Smith's) highly recommended this simpler method. On several boats the bread was baked in the pressure cooker, a method highly recommended by those using it, whereas several of the Scandinavian sailors used a special bread tin which goes on top of the stove and produces a bread in the shape of a ring. As microwave ovens become more common on cruising boats, an increasing number of cooks use them for baking bread. On one boat the bread was browned afterwards under the grill, while on another boat a commercially produced partly baked bread was used, which only needed 8 minutes in the oven.

From what I was told, and also based on my own not very successful experience in the field, the Lord's Prayer contains a lot of wishful thinking if applied to modern yachtsmen and yachtswomen. It is therefore not surprising that on four boats bread was baked only once during the crossing, one crew lamenting that their bread was as hard as stone and inedible: they ended up making pancakes instead. Another crew who tried various methods without any great success, suggested that it might be useful to practise baking before leaving home if one lacked experience in that direction.

In fact on one third of the boats no attempt at all was made at baking bread. Those with freezers often kept bread in the freezer, one boat having 100 loaves in a large deep freeze. Others carried long lasting bread, such as German black bread, which is available in the Canaries. One crew recommended painting freshly baked bread with wine vinegar, sealing it with cling film and putting it in plastic bags. Treated this way they found it lasted 12 days and claimed the vinegar could not be tasted. The rest of the crews solved the daily bread problem with a different style menu, either by making scones or by replacing bread with biscuits, crispbread or hard tack.

Water

Most boats taking part in the Atlantic Survey left the Canaries with full tanks and a few additional jerrycans on deck which could be taken off the boat in an emergency. The average amount of water

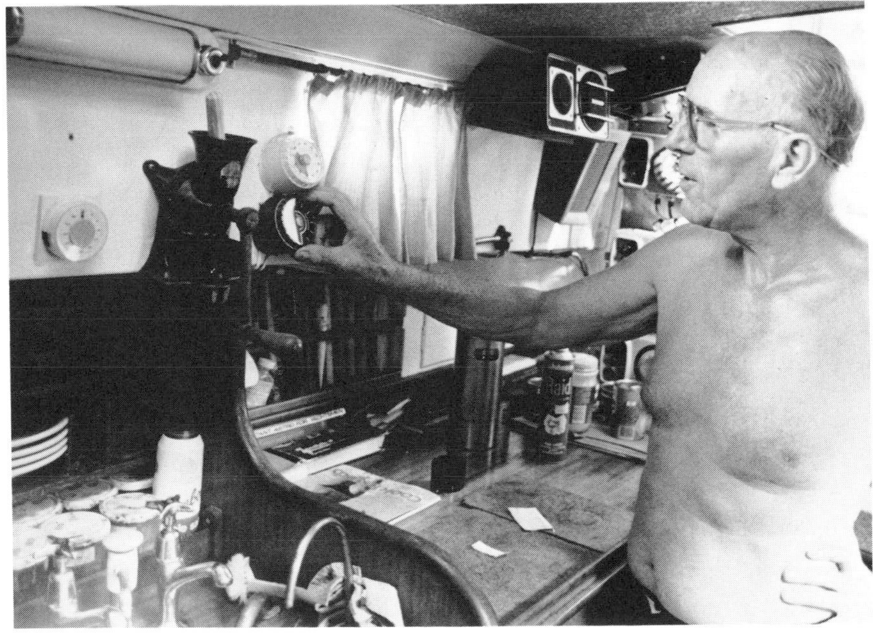

Keeping an eye on water consumption is essential on long passages and Clifford Fitch of Dolcelle *invented a water meter which gives him an instant reading.*

carried was 40 gallons (183 litres) per person. The consumption of water averaged out at 22 gallons (98 litres) per person, which is very close to a daily consumption of one gallon or 4.5 litres per person per day. On five boats the consumption was much higher and exceeded 45 gallons (200 litres) per person, whereas on 11 boats less than 10 gallons (45 litres) were used by each crew member. Invariably more water was used on boats equipped with showers and pressurized water systems, while on the three boats that ran out of water, the average personal consumption was 33 gallons (150 litres), which was more than the skippers had imagined the crew would consume.

The least water used was 4.5 gallons (20 litres) by a couple who consumed one litre of fresh orange juice every day, but admittedly did not wash in fresh water at all during the entire passage! A low consumption of water usually occurred on boats where people drank liquids in other forms, such as beer or fruit juices.

The average consumption of water was lower on the boats taking part in the ARC, and in ARC 87 an average of 18 gallons (81 litres) of water per person was consumed during the crossing. This figure is slightly lower than the average consumption in the Atlantic Survey, but to be safe when provisioning for an offshore passage one should allow a minimum of between half and one gallon (2.25 to 4.5 litres) of water per person per day. These are absolute minima, yet there seem to be skippers who are unable to plan their provisions and in ARC 87 I was concerned to see three boats arrive in Barbados completely out of water, one of them also out of food. Light winds had made their passages longer than they had estimated, but if any emergency had occurred the crews would have been in real trouble. Most skippers, however, prefer to make the crossing with full tanks and in ARC 86 an average of 63 gallons (283 litres) of water per person was carried on each yacht.

Another valuable tip given by ARC participants may well be valid in other parts of the world as well as Las Palmas. As the taste of the water was not the best, many skippers also bought several of the large plastic bottles of drinking water available from all supermarkets. This suggestion, as well as the practice of taking a few additional jerrycans of water, is highly recommended as it is a mistake to have all drinking water in only one tank in case it becomes contaminated while on passage.

Fresh water capacity varied widely on all the boats surveyed, although most boats designed for cruising had a minimum capacity of 100 gallons, usually in one tank, which may not be the best solution for the reasons mentioned above. Either to supplement the existing capacity or to provide an alternative source of water, several boats had been fitted with additional collapsible tanks. Usually these were smaller production boats whose fresh water capacity was considered too small for an extended cruise by their skippers.

Among the boats taking part in the Equipment Survey during ARC 87, the average water capacity in permanently installed tanks was 105 gallons, which was considered adequate by most skippers. Nevertheless, several boats carried additional jerrycans on deck, mostly on boats with smaller than average built-in tanks. In some cases the jerrycans were kept on deck as part of the skipper's preparations in case of abandoning ship.

One way to stop worrying about water consumption is to equip the boat with a watermaker, but the number of cruising boats who do this is still relatively small. In the Atlantic Survey only one boat had a watermaker, whereas in the ARC their proportion had increased to about five per cent of the total, the boats having them being usually the larger more expensive ones. Their owners' comments were invariably favourable, most of these boats arriving in Barbados with full water tanks. A few skippers mentioned the high consumption of electricity, but this did not seem to be too big a problem as all boats who had watermakers also had inboard diesel generators which provided their energy needs.

In line with the general trend to electrify everything on board, an increasing number of boats have a pressurized water system, which on many production boats is now standard. From a mere 12 per cent of the boats equipped with the system in the Pacific Survey, their proportion had increased to over 30 per cent in the Atlantic and Equipment Surveys. However, several skippers pointed out that they preferred to pump water manually (or pedal operated if fitted with a foot pump) while on passage and only revert to the pressure system where there was plenty of water available.

Hot water and showers are also becoming more common and the proportion of boats having them has more than doubled compared to the earlier surveys. In most cases the hot water is provided by a calorifier connected to the cooling system of the main engine. Usually the hot water tank is also fitted with an electric immersion heater, which can be used when the boat is hooked up to shore power in a marina. Independent water heaters, usually operated by bottled gas, were used by only a small number of boats.

Several boats had portable deck showers, often used in conjunction with special water bags. These black plastic bags have a capacity of approximately two gallons and when left in the sun provide a most efficient way to heat up water. Hooked to the boom they make an excellent hot water shower over the cockpit, while on one boat the hot water was poured into a large insecticide sprayer mounted in the shower room, an ingenious way of providing a pressurized hot shower without electricity.

Refrigeration

Although the number of boats having refrigeration is steadily increasing, some skippers still doubt its real usefulness on a cruising boat. Most people questioned in the Equipment Survey agreed on the usefulness of a refrigerator, but were less inclined to give their approval to freezers. It is probably significant that many of those who were against freezers had been cruising for longer periods and had reached their decision either because they had learnt to live without freezers or because they had lost faith in their reliability. In all of the various surveys I have carried out, there have been quite a noticeable number of boats where the freezer had broken down and was often put to use for other purposes.

In the Atlantic Survey nearly half the boats had a refrigerator, although only about two thirds of these were in use during the crossing, the remainder being switched off to save electricity. Asked to rate the usefulness of their refrigerators, seven owners considered them very useful, ten quite useful and only four had doubts about their usefulness, although they all stressed that even if not essential, a fridge can make life very pleasant and a cool drink is greatly appreciated on a hot day in the tropics. It was also pointed out that a fridge can be particularly useful to keep butter or margarine chilled or to preserve the contents of tins or milk cartons after opening.

In spite of the advantages of a fridge to keep things fresh during a passage, they are usually much more in use while in port especially when there is shore power available. On several boats fridges had been installed independent of the main energy supply by hooking them up either to solar panels or wind generators.

On the nine boats that had freezers, seven were kept in operation, which is not surprising as four of their owners considered freezers to be very useful on cruising boats, two quite useful and only one regarded a freezer a non-essential luxury. Several skippers stressed the usefulness of freezers on a long passage both to preserve food and to store freshly caught fish which cannot be consumed all at once. The main drawback of a freezer is that it consumes a lot of energy and the engine, or a separate generator, has to be run about once a day to keep the freezer going. In some instances the insufficient insulation provided by the boat builders was criticized by owners who felt that this aspect has not been given the attention it deserves.

Thermal bags can provide a hot shower without the need for a complicated installation.

COOKING FUEL

In spite of many people's continuing dislike of having gas on board, propane or butane appear to be firmly established as the favourite cooking fuels. Seventy per cent of the boats in the Atlantic Survey had gas cookers, while in the Equipment Survey their proportion had increased to nearly ninety per cent. In the former survey the majority were still using the larger domestic type propane or butane bottles and only one third were equipped with the smaller Camping Gaz type containers. On twenty-eight per cent of the boats the cooking was done by paraffin (kerosene) and one boat used methylated spirit. In the Equipment Survey paraffin was to be found on less than seven per cent of the boats and three per cent were cooking by electricity.

Although the ratio between gas and paraffin cookers is increasingly growing in favour of the former, an interesting development is the proliferation of Camping Gaz cookers on cruising boats. This type of container is indeed easier to buy or refill in Europe, particularly in the Mediterranean. Until recently, Camping Gaz was almost unheard of outside of Europe but the containers are now accepted at filling stations in the Caribbean and even in some of the Pacific islands.

The difficulty of obtaining cooking fuel was investigated both among the boats interviewed in the Canaries and those surveyed in the Caribbean. As far as ordinary gas bottles were concerned, most crews had no real problem filling them either in the Mediterranean or the Canaries, although the valve fittings vary between countries. Some difficulties were encountered by boats equipped with non-European type containers. Unfortunately there is no international standard for the valve fittings and because of this some cautious skippers carry the necessary adapters, as most filling stations do not have them, being only equipped to service their own types, which sometimes vary even within the same country. Even less problems with filling non-standard bottles were encountered by ARC participants which may mean that most filling stations in places frequented by yachts have learnt to cope with the various types of tanks that land on their door step.

Some cautious skippers using less common tanks also carried spare Camping Gaz cookers in case they could not have their ordinary tanks refilled. The spare cookers were mostly of the single burner type that screws directly onto the container and are an excellent standby if the main supply runs out. Two skippers had converted their cookers to run on either propane or Camping Gaz, while one singlehander used his small single burner Camping Gaz cooker for the entire Atlantic crossing after his paraffin cooker got repeatedly clogged by the poor quality paraffin purchased in Spain. The problem of finding clean paraffin was mentioned by several skippers on both sides of the Atlantic, the most praised paraffin being that purchased from the DESA refinery in Tenerife. Methylated spirit appears to be even more difficult to find, especially outside Portugal and Spain, where it often has to be purchased in pharmacies.

The British type Calor gas bottles are difficult to fill in some Caribbean islands and in other parts of the world it is often a matter of pleading with the manager of the filling station who may be persuaded to allow the bottle to be filled by some unorthodox method if the right adapter is not available. This is a problem shared by Camping Gaz bottles which in some countries have to be filled with propane. In the case of the larger type bottles, the switching over from butane to propane is not a recommended practice and can lead to unexpected problems. Propane gas is normally used in tropical countries and can damage burners designed for use with butane gas. The burners tend to burn out and have to be replaced more frequently. When changing from butane to propane, it is recommended to also change the regulator or at least have its rating checked. Another suggestion, made by three skippers who had their Camping Gaz containers refilled in the Canaries, was to check their weight on the premises as often they are not filled properly. Two of these skippers ran out of gas during the Atlantic crossing and one crew had only cold meals for the last week before landfall, except some tinned soup which they managed to heat up on the engine – not the most efficient way of cooking a meal at sea!

Engine fuel

The amount of fuel carried by the boats in the various surveys varied in accordance with their needs and cruising area, although the majority left on longer passages with full tanks. In the Atlantic Survey, the average amount carried was 107 gallons (484 litres), but this included four boats with reserves of over 200 gallons each. The average reserve of the smaller consumers worked out at a more reasonable 68 gallons (306 litres). In a similar way, the general fuel consumption during the Atlantic crossing averaged out at 35 gallons

(158 litres) per boat for the entire sample, or even less, at 25 gallons (113 litres) per boat, if the four largest consumers were not included. In most cases the amount carried was considered adequate by the skippers, only three boats stopping to refuel in the Cape Verde Islands, two because they motored for a week after leaving the Canaries due to lack of wind, the third being a motorsailer that used its engine on all offshore passages when the speed fell below 4 knots.

Although the average fuel consumption seems high for an ocean crossing in the trade winds, on most boats less fuel was used for propulsion than for charging the batteries. This was shown by the fact that on several boats fuel consumption was conspicuously lower, either because they did not possess autopilots, satnavs or freezers, or because other charging sources were used. In most cases, more fuel was used to run the engine for battery charging purposes. This is particularly true in the ARC, in which skippers had to declare the number of hours the engine was used for propulsion which makes an assessment of the actual use of the engine much easier. Although most boats leave for the crossing with full tanks, most of the fuel is still there by the time they reach the Caribbean. However, the practice of leaving with full tanks on a long passage is highly recommended as the engine may have to be used for long periods in an emergency, such as a broken mast or a medical emergency which necessitates a speedy landfall.

For these reasons, fuel capacity and range under power were examined in the Cruising Survey. The average fuel capacity was 90 gallons per boat, although several skippers took extra fuel in jerrycans for longer passages or when cruising in areas where diesel fuel was not readily available. The average range under power when motoring under calm conditions was 750 miles per boat or an average consumption of 0.4 gallons per hour. Asked about the minimum amount of fuel to be carried, some skippers suggested that when setting off on a long passage, one ought to have enough fuel to be able to motor between one quarter and one third of the intended distance should there be a serious emergency.

Ideal Boat Survey

The galley and on board comforts were examined closely in the Ideal Boat Survey and the skippers were asked to rate the importance of various features as they had done with instrumentation. Although opinions were divided on many aspects, microwave ovens were far from being considered a necessity on board a boat, nor did many skippers consider a second head to be essential. Most cruisers would like to have a refrigerator if possible, but a freezer seemed less important. Many admitted that a pressurized water system would make life more pleasant, as would a shower, but the need for running hot water depended very much on the cruising area. Several skippers suggested that the question of both shower and hot water can be easily solved in warm countries by hanging one of the specially designed black plastic shower bags in the rigging.

The difficulty of obtaining fresh water in some places has prompted many cruisers to become self-sufficient in this respect, either by using an awning to catch rainwater or by acquiring a watermaker. The advantage of the latter was mentioned in several questionnaires. Failing that, most skippers agreed that a cruising boat must carry an adequate reserve of water. Each skipper indicated an optimum water capacity for their ideal boat, the average being 125 gallons (560 litres).

The most popular cooking fuel continues to be gas (LPG), which was chosen by 138 skippers, the rest preferring paraffin (17), diesel (2), spirits (1) and electricity (2). A few more would have chosen electric cookers if generation of electricity was easier at sea. As this is a matter of such concern to the modern sailor, the skippers were asked to specify what means of generating electricity they would install on their ideal cruising boat. Although the majority (90) would be quite happy to continue relying on the main engine to charge the batteries, other means using renewable sources of energy would also be used. Solar panels (72) and wind generators (69) were the most popular, while a hydro or towing generator would be fitted on 12 ideal boats. A generator coupled to the free wheeling propeller shaft was considered by several skippers as a more efficient arrangement than the towing type. In many instances two and even three different means of generating electricity were indicated, each one being used for maximum efficiency, a frequently suggested method being that of using a shaft or towing generator while at sea and a wind generator in port.

There is little doubt that using the main engine to charge the batteries is a costly exercise nor is it very efficient, particularly as most skippers had chosen powerful diesel engines to drive their ideal boat. Probably with this in mind, most skippers indicated the need for an adequate fuel capacity which on the majority of boats ranged from 60 to 120 gallons, and averaged 110 gallons.

Finances

There is nothing that can spoil the joy of cruising more than the lack of funds. Many a dream voyage comes to a sad end because of an empty kitty and in most cases this is not caused by an unforeseen emergency or huge repair bill, but by leaving home without adequate reserves in the hope that things will work out somehow. Sometimes they do, but more often they do not and a drop in the currency exchange rate or a higher than allowed for cost of cruising can spell the end of a voyage.

The cost of cruising has been examined in several surveys undertaken in the past ten years, but in order to obtain a better idea of the actual costs involved, as part of the Communications Survey conducted during ARC 86, participants were asked to list their expenditure separately. This expenditure included insurance premiums, repair and maintenance, and running expenses.

The average insurance premium paid by the skippers was £951 (US$1617). In most cases the premium amounted to slightly over one per cent of the capital value of the vessel, although premiums tended to be proportionally higher for the less expensive boats. Many boats had to pay an additional premium for the Atlantic crossing and in some cases the skippers decided because of this to cancel the insurance altogether, as they did not consider the risks involved in the crossing itself to warrant the extra expenditure, which amounted to between 25 and 50 per cent of the annual premium.

Just over two thirds (69 per cent) of the boats were insured and there were various reasons, not all of them financial, why the remaining 31 per cent were uninsured. In some cases the boats were uninsurable as they did not have the required minimum of three experienced crew for the Atlantic crossing. This is a relatively new stipulation made by most insurance companies and it has hit hardest those experienced couples who have been cruising together for years. Some cruising couples were forced to take on additional crew for the crossing while others preferred to cross without an insurance, but intended to renew their policies in the Caribbean. Sometimes the renewal of a lapsed policy can lead to complications as some insurance companies insist that the vessel is resurveyed before renewal, probably to make sure that it actually got there. Some insurance companies, however, are prepared to revalidate the policy on receiving a formal letter from the owner stating that the boat had completed the ocean passage safely and was engaged now in cruising.

In the Communications Survey, 107 yachts gave precise figures concerning their running expenses and maintenance costs. The annual running expenses came to an average £1863 (US$3167) per boat, which was made up mostly of fuel and mooring charges. An approximate figure of £5 per day (roughly US$10) is close to what I regard as the absolute minimum to be allowed for a cruising itinerary which includes some time to be spent in marinas as well as one haul-out per year.

Excluding the above costs, the annual repair and maintenance budget of these ARC participants was on average £1145 (US$1946) per boat, which varied from a modest £150 (US$250) on a small boat to an impressive £10,000 (US$17,000) on a large yacht engaged in chartering. Although in most cases the maintenance costs bore a direct relation to the size of boat, they seemed to be also related to the owner's style of living as many of the skippers on lower budgets often carried out their own repairs.

Although one would expect newer boats to have lower repair bills, in fact this was seldom the case and almost all new yachts in the ARC fleet had a lot of things go wrong during their first year. The lowest maintenance budgets were those of yachts between three and five years old, either because the owners had had time to fix everything slowly or had learnt to live with their faulty equipment. One of the ARC's successes is the pre-start jumble sale in Las Palmas at which disgruntled skippers try to unload onto someone else their useless bits and pieces.

Looking at the cost of yacht repair over the last decade, it would appear that in real terms the cost has risen out of proportion to inflation and other factors. With the increase in the number of cruising yachts, in many foreign ports local engineers regard yachtsmen as a soft touch, especially when they are called to a job in a marina. Therefore it is sometimes better to dismantle the faulty equipment and take it to a repair shop, rather than call the engineer to the yacht.

Overall, maintenance budgets were relatively higher on the less expensive boats mainly because of the higher value of the equipment in relation to the capital cost of the vessel. The annual maintenance budget varied between 1½ and 2 per cent of the actual value of most yachts rising to as much as 5 per cent on boats valued at £20,000 (US$34,000) or less.

The only costs that do not appear to have risen in real terms are living expenses and the good news is that one can cruise in some comfort for comparatively less than one needed a decade ago. With the exception of a few countries, the rise in the cost of food has not kept pace with inflation; international flights are also relatively cheaper as are other expenses, such as postage, telephone charges, car rental and even fuel. As lifestyles and individual requirements vary so widely it is impossible to make an accurate assessment of cruising costs generally. However, based on the figures provided by the ARC as well as the results of previous surveys, I would suggest an annual allowance of approximately £3000 (US$5000) per person for a cruising budget in the North Atlantic. Many ARC participants cruised successfully on considerably less and just as many managed to spend a lot more. Like the trade winds which rarely blow at the *average* force 4, when dealing with money averages usually mean different things to different people.

ANTIFOULING

One item which must be allowed for in the annual budget of any cruising boat is a regular haul-out and bottom paint. How regular can depend on both the availability of hauling-out facilities in the ports en route and the financial state of the cruising budget. Generally I noticed that the longer a boat is away from home base, the longer the periods become between haul-outs. In the Atlantic Survey this subject was looked at in depth and although the state of antifouling paint was examined both among the boats surveyed in the Canaries and those surveyed in the Caribbean, a more meaningful assessment could be made only after the completion of the transatlantic voyage.

Among the 50 boats in the latter sample, seven had been hauled out in the Canaries where they were freshly antifouled. An additional five crews scrubbed the bottoms of their boats prior to the passage, while the remaining 38 boats left the Canaries with bottoms described by their skippers as ranging from perfectly clean to badly fouled. Most boats arrived on the other side in more or less the same condition, although seven skippers described the state of their antifouling paint as having gone from bad to very bad. Five among them agreed that they should have put on a fresh coat of antifouling paint before leaving the Canaries.

Looking more closely at these boats, the effect of a fouled bottom on their performance became immediately obvious. Although their average length was 40 ft, they had taken an average of almost 25 days to cross the Atlantic, which was three days longer than the average time taken by other boats of similar length. The poor state of their bottoms was due to the fact that the last time they had been painted had been six months earlier. The average time since antifouling took place for the 43 boats which had not been painted in the Canaries was 4½ months, which coincided with the average time since those boats had left their home ports.

Most skippers did not seem to be too concerned about the state of their antifouling paint, expecting at least six months of good service between applications. In most cases this was perhaps too optimistic as most boats had arrived in the Canaries from Western or Northern Europe, the transition from cold to warm waters being often very sudden. The paints that fared best under these conditions were of the self-polishing copolymer type, which is a combination of resin and biocide in a soluble matrix. Being fully soluble the coating will deplete gradually to expose fresh biocide and thus become increasingly smoother. Because of this, it may be necessary to apply new paint more frequently and although hauling out in the Canaries is not always easy, in the Caribbean it can be even more difficult. Recent environmental pressures have resulted in the development of new copper-based, controlled solubility copolymer antifoulings. These are far less harmful to the marine environment and are supposed to be just as effective as the earlier brands, which contained banned components such as tri-organo-tin.

Practically all the boats arrived in the Caribbean with an array of goose barnacles under their sterns and along the water line, generally in those areas in which the water is aerated. Neither antifouling nor ordinary boot topping paints seem to bother these creatures and the most effective way to get rid of them is to scrub them off. The crew of *Duen* performed this operation while becalmed in mid-Atlantic, when the entire hull was scrubbed with Brillo pads showing the skipper's attention to the care of a wooden hull in the tropics.

Among the ARC yachts, the average time since the last antifouling job was four months, which is a relatively short time by cruising boat standards. However, as far as the ARC boats were concerned, there were two good reasons for this good state of their bottoms. One was the fact that the majority had only left their home ports a few months earlier to join the ARC fleet in Las Palmas. The other factor was the wish of most owners to do well in the ARC and therefore only a few were prepared to face a 2700 mile long Atlantic crossing with a fouled bottom.

FIREARMS

Regulations concerning firearms vary enormously from country to country and their presence on board a cruising boat can cause certain difficulties because of the formalities involved. In some countries firearms are bonded on board, but more often they are removed for the duration of the boat's sojourn in a particular port or even country. The return of the firearms on the eve of departure can sometimes lead to complications and it is advisable to make the necessary arrangements in this respect when surrendering the weapons on arrival.

Among 100 skippers questioned on the subject, 38 had such firearms on board and many of them were in two minds about the advisability of carrying a gun while cruising. All skippers taking part in the survey, both those with guns and those without, were asked their opinion on this subject and were encouraged to comment and make suggestions. The majority of skippers were firmly against the idea, and this included both those who had a gun and those who did not. Only eleven skippers considered firearms to be essential for their protection. Six skippers, who were reluctant to carry arms, stressed nevertheless that their possession might be justified in certain parts of the world, even if not in the South Pacific, where the interviews took place. For some skippers who did not wish to carry guns, the solution to this problem was to avoid areas with a bad reputation. In the Pacific Survey, 21 skippers mentioned Colombia as one of the areas which they had deliberately avoided, while others had kept away from various places in Central America, the Caribbean and the Bahamas.

Several owners described their guns as a deterrent and not an offensive weapon. The most unexpected condemnation of guns on boats came from André Fily, a retired officer in the French Gendarmerie, who refused to have guns on board his *Stereden Vor* as he considered them to be more trouble than they were worth. Because of the various disadvantages of having firearms on board, several people had acquired tear gas spray containers which were regarded as an acceptable alternative for self-defence. As Willy Zech, the skipper of *Spirit of Cockpit*, saw the problem, 'It's far better to have a potential robber crying his eyes out in the cockpit, than to discover you have shot dead the cousin of the local police chief.'

Similar feelings were expressed by the skippers interviewed in the Atlantic, among whom the proportion of yachts equipped with guns was considerably lower. Less than one fifth (18 per cent) of the boats taking part in the Atlantic Survey had firearms on board, which is similar to the number of ARC boats carrying guns. It was pointed out on several occasions when firearms were discussed, that it was foolish not to declare the guns when clearing into a country just to avoid a few formalities, as the complications can indeed be severe if the authorities discover that guns have been hidden.

PETS

Similar considerations apply to pets and indeed there are a few countries where importing a pet illegally is considered no lesser crime than trying to hide a gun from customs. Regulations concerning cruising pets are extremely stringent in some countries and this is the main reason why the number of boats with pets has decreased over the years. Compared to 13 boats with pets on board in the Cruising Survey, only five in a sample of fifty boats surveyed five years later had animals on board. To have or not to have a pet is a difficult question and anyone considering having a pet should think very carefully before setting off on a long voyage.

The subject was examined in two surveys, in which three quarters of those interviewed rated the idea of having a pet on board a cruising boat with a resounding zero. Many of those interviewed pointed out that although they were fond of animals, they considered it cruel to keep an animal in the confined space of a sailing boat. Ilse Gieseking of *Lou V* admitted that having a dog with them during their voyage around the world had been a major mistake, mainly because their freedom of movement had been severely restricted in many countries because of the dog. In some ports they were not even allowed to come alongside a dock, while in others they were frequently inspected by health officials who wished to make sure that the dog had not been taken ashore.

FAREWELL TO DUEN

The satisfaction of a completed transatlantic passage behind them, dozens of boats swung gently at anchor in Carlisle Bay on Barbados. All shapes and sizes, the flags of many nations fluttering, my eye was immediately caught by the varnished hull and graceful lines of a large boat of classic beauty. My heart skipped a beat as I recognized *Duen*, which I had last seen five years previously on the other side of the world in Sydney, Australia.

Hijacking a passing dinghy, in no time at all I was on board and embracing Dottie and Albert Fletcher. Tripping over our words, we tried to cover all that had happened in the intervening years and describe the thousands of miles that had flowed under our keels. All cruising people will know that special joy that is felt by meeting old friends in unexpected places, the warmth that comes from memories of shared anchorages and the common love of the freedom of the seas. Among the many cruising people I have met, the Fletchers and their distinctive *Duen* have been among the most remarkable. With the easy-going attitude and spontaneity that characterizes them, Dottie and Albert immediately suggested I join them for a cruise in the Grenadines and over several pleasant evenings, they recounted the story of the transformation of *Duen* from a shabby fishing boat to a graceful sailing lady.

In the early 1970s in California, Dottie and Albert enjoyed a comfortable easy life, they had everything they wanted except one thing – adventure. Working as a truckster, plying the highways of California and Nevada with his rig, Albert spent his spare time restoring old boats, although what really fascinated him was bringing their defunct engines back to life. Reflecting this interest in engines, the Fletchers cruised up and down the Californian coast in a small motor boat, until one day their eyes fell on a Colin Archer double ender cruising out of Seattle. They suddenly realized that the solidly crafted vessel was exactly the kind of boat their dreams were made of, and that nothing else could be more suitable for the world voyage they were planning. The change of style from power to sail must have been dormant in Albert's genes, for his family hailed from Maine and had a long association with sail during the now bygone era, owning several Grand Banks schooners. Albert's great grandmother had also been a unique character for that era, captain of her own lumber schooner, trading the East Coast with timber.

It took the Fletchers some time to discover where the Colin Archer boat, which had taken their fancy, originated from but as soon as they found out they packed their bags and set off for Norway. In a small Norwegian fishing port their long search came to an end when they caught sight of *Duen*, condemned to rot away beside scores of other fishing vessels, whose owners had been encouraged to quit the sea by government incentives. Strongly built in 1939, *Duen* was one of the last boats built before the outbreak of war and the 50 ft hull exemplified the best in Norwegian craftsmanship. Albert looked beyond the rusting fishing gear on deck and saw a solid, well maintained hull, whose double ended traditional lines, built for the demanding conditions of her home waters, promised the makings of a sea-kindly cruising boat.

Powered by an ancient one-cylinder Rapp engine, sporting a large wheelhouse and no sailing gear, *Duen* belied her Norwegian name of 'Dove' and was obviously in no state to cruise anywhere. Albert and Dottie decided to make their base in Norway, working from dawn to dusk tearing out all equipment and completely gutting *Duen*'s interior. The strength of the hull was impressive; her 9-by-9 inch frames were only seven inches apart, the two inch pitch pine planking being held together by four double sets of stringers. During the freezing winter months they worked on the interior and when the weather turned warmer, they turned their attention to the spars and rigging. Initially, *Duen* was rigged as a gaff ketch with two stubby masts. This short rig, evolved for the rough North Sea, suited the Fletchers' lack of experience in handling such a heavy vessel on their own. Step by step, *Duen* slowly turned into the cruising boat they had dreamed of, and after eighteen months of hard work, at last they were ready to set sail.

They learned to sail *Duen* as they went along, coast-hopping southwards in search of warmer weather, before the onset of the next winter. After exploring the Mediterranean and now confident both in their vessel and their seamanship, Dottie and Albert embarked on their first ocean crossing. Their slow transatlantic passage and the subsequent leisurely cruise in the Caribbean reinforced their initial impression that they had indeed got themselves a comfortable and sea-kindly boat, but also at times an infuriatingly slow one. A radical solution was called for, so on the beach at Bequia, *Duen* underwent a complete metamorphosis. The most painful decision for Albert was to get rid of the ancient engine, aptly nicknamed

Rapp the Monster, which had to be started with a compressed air bottle and hardly qualified as a cruising auxiliary. Every hour on the hour, seventeen points had to be oiled, twelve grease cups turned and five wicks filled – a time consuming and unpleasant job at sea in a hot, smelly engine room. The Monster was duly banished and replaced with a modern diesel. The tall pilot house went the same way as Rapp to save both weight and windage. With more space on deck, the boom and gaff could be lengthened, the sail area being also increased with the addition of a topmast. All the new spars were adzed by Albert himself on the beach with the help of some Bequians, who regarded the burly Californian as one of their own. How true this was, I saw when we sailed *Duen* into Bequia twelve years after her first visit and the locals, who seldom take more than a passing interest in visiting sailors, greeted Albert like a long lost

A boat from a bygone era, Duen *is put through her paces on a short passage in the Caribbean.*

brother. A man who fashioned his own spars was obviously a man to the liking of these descendants of the Bedford whalers of yesteryear.

During her fourteen-year circumnavigation, *Duen* was to go through several more transformations as Albert was forever searching to improve the rig and performance, while still keeping the boat within traditional lines. By countless trials and no lack of errors, he searched for perfection, finally declaring himself satisfied with her present rig which sets some 2400 sq ft of canvas with the full complement of topsail and jibs. It is a picture to behold, when this distinguished lady of uncertain years gets moving with a bone in her mouth and spray flying, romping along at 10 knots and overtaking fibreglass youngsters that could be her grandchildren.

Maintaining such a large wooden boat requires a lot of hard work, but Albert never shirked the task. 'Keeping *Duen* in tip top condition not only protects our investment, but also our lives,' observed Dottie. It was not all hard work, however, as the Fletchers knew very well how to enjoy themselves. For fourteen years they roamed the oceans of the world, spending several years in the South Pacific, enjoying the adventure they had set off to find. Often their children and, later, grandchildren sailed with them; they also took on crew, usually young people who wanted to learn how to sail a traditional vessel, whose topsails had to be set by hand perched precariously on the crosstrees. The atmosphere on board *Duen* was always relaxed and happy, centering around Dottie with her infectious sense of humour and constant laughter. A typical example of how they can turn even the frustrations of sailing into pleasure is when they were completely becalmed in mid-Atlantic during their last crossing. Down came the sails, out came the musical instruments and they played the night away, Albert singing to guitar, Dottie strumming the ukelele, son Toby on the bongos and the rest of the crew on whatever they could find.

In the same way that Albert was remembered in Bequia after twelve years, so the Fletchers are remembered in countless places around the world. Describing himself a compulsive tool collector, Albert has fitted out *Duen* with a complete workshop, which has enabled him to carry out repairs in many remote islands and villages, whether on other cruising boats or more usually repairing an islander's defunct outboard engine so he could go fishing again. *Duen* has left a wake of goodwill everywhere she has sailed, unsung ambassador for the American flag she flies. Children of the 1960s, an era when people hoped enough love might change the world, Dottie and Albert have remained true to this philosophy, their kindness and humanity being genuine. Still today they refuse to be changed by a materialistic world. This was borne out while we were in Bequia, when the Fletchers took the painful decision to sell *Duen*. The adventure had come to an end; it might have been easy to carry on gently cruising with a perfect boat, but they both felt the time was ripe to do something else and look for new challenges. But after such a long love affair, they wanted to be sure *Duen* was going to be sailed to the full and not end up as a toy in a marina. True to their idealism and principles, Dottie and Albert turned down a substantially higher offer from a wealthy Swiss sailor who had fallen in love with *Duen* at first sight, preferring to sell her to a Canadian foundation which will give underprivileged teenagers a chance to learn how to sail. Leaving the boat they had lovingly created and which had carried them safely over 100,000 miles of ocean was painful; but the separation was softened by the fact that under her new owners and with Toby Fletcher in the crew, *Duen*'s first assignment was to grace Operation Sail in New York on July 4.

Chapter 7

THE HUMAN FACTOR

During a long ocean passage neither repair facilities nor rescue services are near at hand; therefore a crew must be prepared to deal themselves with unforeseen breakages and emergencies. Because this is a major concern for many sailors, in the final section of my interviews with the fifty skippers taking part in the Atlantic Survey, who had just completed a transatlantic crossing, I examined the problems, breakages and emergencies they had encountered. I also questioned them about the fulfilment of their expectations and psychological problems encountered during the long time spent confined on a small boat. These discussions brought to light many interesting observations regarding crew. After being taken aside several times by either skipper or crew to discuss this aspect more privately, I decided to follow up this most important topic, often by letting my taperecorder run, rather than interrupt or make notes.

Equipment failure and breakages are discussed elsewhere in the book, for in this chapter I want to concentrate on that most important piece of equipment, the human machine. The best words of wisdom on this topic I received from a doctor who sailed on *Candide* in the TRANSARC from Antigua to Bermuda. Dr Steenstra remarked that before going offshore, many skippers endeavour to learn everything they can about the working of the various pieces of equipment on board and how to repair them, but often neglect to find out about their most important item of equipment, which is their own body. When something goes wrong, often they do not know what to do, basically because they have little idea how the human machine functions.

In fact, the situation is not quite that bad, as among the hundred crews questioned in the Pacific, on half the boats at least one person and often more than one, had taken a first aid course before leaving. On quite a few boats at least one member of the crew had the necessary knowledge from their profession in the medical fields, whether it be as doctor, nurse, dentist or pharmacist.

First aid courses, however, rarely include psychological training and one of the subjects I tried to investigate was the effect of living in a confined space during an ocean passage, which in this survey took on average three weeks. The frankness with which my questions were answered both by the skippers and their crew gave me an insight into the psychological side of life aboard, an aspect often ignored when the beauty of cruising is discussed.

Although problems of some sort were reported on 14 out of the 50 boats, in most cases these were described as not serious but merely the normal tensions to be expected when people are confined in a small space. Looking at these 14 boats and their crews more closely, it was interesting to note that in all cases where clashes of personality were reported, none of these were among members of the same family, but all were among crew unrelated to each other. Almost without exception, on boats where previously unknown people were taken on as crew for the Atlantic crossing the atmosphere on board was tense, both skipper and crew seeing only the other person's faults and never their own. In contrast to this, the atmosphere was visibly more harmonious on boats crewed by people who had been sailing for a long time together, whether they were related or not. A similar congenial atmosphere was also found on boats with large crews, who had a strong motivation to sail together, such as *Asterias*, on which seven members of the Silesian Yacht Club in Poland had obtained permission from the authorities to make a six-month Atlantic voyage. Another apparently happy ship was the square rigged *Svanhild*, on which a group of young Norwegian teachers had pooled their savings for a voyage around the world.

Crew satisfaction is greater when decisions are taken jointly, the crew of Protan *decide on their route in the Caribbean.*

Crew size

The number of people in the crew may well play a part in both the boredom and the tension factor on a long voyage. According to the statistics of yachts clearing into the Whangarei area of New Zealand in 1987, by far the majority (41 per cent) were crewed by just two people, 20 per cent had three and 13 per cent had a crew of four. The remaining boats were spread over the whole range from singlehanders to a crew of 13. The average number of crew per boat worked out at 2.9.

In contrast, in the Atlantic Survey, the average crew size worked out at nearly four per boat. In fact the average number of permanent crew was just over two, but more than half the boats had doubled their crew just for the transatlantic crossing. On the majority of boats (60 per cent) the permanent crew was made up of members of the same family, in most cases by couples. On seven boats these were accompanied by a total of 15 children of varying ages, from babies to teenagers. Quite unique was one boat where two young children were making the crossing with their grandparents, who were delivering both boat and grandchildren to the parents in Martinique. There were also older children sailing with their parents, some in their twenties, some even older, up to a father in his sixties who was helping his son sail his newly acquired boat to the USA. The majority of the crews were related in one way or another, although in three cases wives had decided to fly to the Caribbean to join their husbands as they did not like long passages.

One unusual crew was that of the French yacht *Jeloa*. Five recently graduated young people, unable to find suitable jobs in France, had got together and decided to make an Atlantic circuit with a purpose. They persuaded a friend to lend them his yacht for a year, then approached several producers of nautical equipment or materials to give them a floating franchise. Their route took them to West Africa, Brazil, French Guyana, the Caribbean, Bermuda and the Azores, where they tried to get local traders interested in importing various goods, ranging from foulweather gear and wetsuits to sailboards.

Similar to the Atlantic Survey, in ARC 87, the average number of crew per yacht was four, only 22 per cent of the boats being crewed by two people, 21 per cent by three and the largest category, 25 per cent being crewed by four. The year before in ARC 1986 a larger proportion (30 per cent) were crewed by only two people.

The higher number of crew per boat in the transatlantic events as compared to those cruising in the Pacific may be due to several factors, partly because the event has a competitive element and air links make it comparatively easy for friends and guests to join the boat. The recent stipulation of insurance companies that for trans-ocean passages a crew must comprise at least three people, has forced many couples to take on extra crew. The accessibility of the North Atlantic circuit to both Europe and the United States is also a factor, as is the increased number of large boats and offshore sailing schools crossing this ocean regularly with a proportionally larger size of crew.

The make-up of the crews in the various surveys remains very much the same mixture of young and old, male and female. In the ARC approximately 80 per cent of the boats have at least one woman on board, while in 1986 there were 34 children under 16 years old, and 23 skippers over 60. In ARC 87 there were slightly less of each: 25 under-sixteens and 15 skippers over 60, but three skippers over 70. The number of older people among the crew was correspondingly greater with half a dozen over-70s taking part in the event – showing that age is no barrier to enjoyment on yachts. In fact, several of the younger crews in the ARC were quite astonished to be outperformed by people more than twice their age, whom they had dismissed as 'old codgers'. On the sea, experience and endurance sometimes matter more than physical strength. In general, the older experienced people who had done a lot of sailing had far fewer problems coping with the length of time of a trans-ocean passage.

On passage

The long passage across the Atlantic, which a few of those interviewed described as boring, had different effects on people, a few complaining of what can best be described as 'cabin fever' after about ten days at sea. The situation was exacerbated at the time of the survey by rougher than usual weather, which forced crews to spend longer periods inside their boats. In such conditions the availability of a separate cabin made a great difference, as the lack of privacy was the main cause of irritation on all the boats where tempers flared. The lack of a personal cabin was deplored even on boats crewed by the same family and one teenage girl complained bitterly about having no choice except to share a cabin with her younger brother. The lack of space often seemed worse than in port because many people slept longer than normal during the passage. The commonest ways of trying to overcome the monotony of the voyage was by playing games, listening to music, reading or fishing.

Loneliness can be just as frustrating as living too close to other people and one singlehander, who had a particularly slow crossing, described the pain of being alone for so long. His most depressing moment happened at Christmas when he opened his only bottle of wine which he had kept for this occasion, but found it had gone sour.

The atmosphere was noticeably lacking in friction on boats where the crew took an active interest in sailing the boat as efficiently as possible, changing sails more often or sometimes steering by hand. Not surprisingly, these were also the yachts which made faster crossings. Several skippers of such boats remarked that this pleasant atmosphere often deteriorated in port, when there was less to do, the crew squabbling over the dinghy and the lack of space becoming more irritating than when the crew were on watch at sea and rarely meeting each other.

Some of these aspects were re-examined during the ARC, particularly the boredom factor which can create problems during a long ocean passage. Undoubtedly the fact that the ARC is treated like a race by some skippers takes care of the boredom factor by keeping the crew on their toes to put in a good performance. Even among skippers who were not driven by the competitive spirit, the ARC added a new dimension to the crossing and there were far less

When in port, the decks of Birlinn Chlann Roanuill *are littered with sleeping bags as the large crew find their privacy under the stars.*

complaints about boredom than one would have expected. The weather always plays an important part in the passage and the late arrival of the trade winds in 1987 found many crews frustrated by their unexpectedly slow progress. Tim Aitken of *Airwave* found that several days of running under spinnaker in light winds became terribly boring. The 126 ft *Gloria* was so effortless to sail under these conditions that boredom was kept at bay by watching videos. According to owner Mikael Krafft, the only problem encountered was the daily debate among the crew as to which film to watch.

Taking on Crew

Finding crew for the transatlantic passage did not appear to be a problem for skippers; on the contrary, it is a voyage that attracts many enthusiasts. Most of the crewing arrangements had been made well ahead of time and in most cases crew joined the boats by flying out to the Canaries. In Las Palmas there were plenty of itinerants looking for a passage, although few of them struck lucky, probably because of the unconventional appearance of some of these marine hitchhikers. All of the charter boats being delivered to the Caribbean for business were crewed by unpaid hands, with the exception of the skippers, among whom several had been doing this shuttle service for years. There were also some boats on which the crew had paid for the passage, often this being part of a navigation or sail training scheme run by yacht clubs and sailing schools.

Since carrying out the Atlantic Survey, dealing with the ARC and other sailing events has taught me a lot about the subject of crewing. I am continuously approached by people who are looking for a crewing position and unfortunately few of them can be placed because there are many more people in their situation than skippers looking for crew. Looking at the problem from the point of view of the crew, the first thing that should be stressed is that there are not many skippers who are prepared to pick up crew from the dock and therefore it is better, cheaper and less time consuming to try and make any arrangements beforehand. This can be done either through advertisements in the classified section of the yachting press or by joining one or more of the crew registers run by clubs, associations or specialized agencies.

Another aspect which must be borne in mind is that by and large the days when crew were welcome aboard without any financial contribution are gone and most owners expect the crew to at least cover the cost of his or her food. In fact, many people cruising on a tight budget try and supplement their meagre funds by taking on additional crew, who are expected to make a reasonable contribution both towards their own upkeep and that of the ship. Although it cannot be described as chartering, the difference is not that great and unless the conditions are spelt out clearly at the beginning and both parties know exactly what to expect, either the crew or the owner will end up disappointed. One area in which it is still possible to find crewing positions with relative ease is on board charter boats being delivered to another base at the end of the sailing season. Some of the larger yachts employ permanent crew, but this is a job and the crew are expected to work hard for their money.

Looking at this subject from the point of view of the skipper it does not take long to understand why so many crew find it almost impossible to find a yacht to take them. Perhaps the main problem is that some would-be crew have somehow got the wrong idea and expect a naive yacht owner to offer them a cheap holiday. Many of them are not willing to pay their way and by their appearance give the impression that even if they were willing, they could not afford to. In fact appearance is what turns most skippers off and I am not at all surprised that some of the characters I see drifting around ports like Gibraltar or Las Palmas are never taken on.

Skippers should be aware of the problems they can encounter by taking on crew without careful consideration and without knowing the person. Half an hour's conversation on the dock before leaving on a voyage of several weeks is not long enough to make an assessment of suitability. This also applies in reverse, as many crew only discover in the middle of the ocean why a particular skipper had never managed to keep his crew. The main points to be considered are the obligations assumed by the owner towards a crew member, such as liability in case of injury, death or some other unforeseen occurrence. The skipper is also legally responsible to repatriate his crew should this become necessary and to the crew's place of residence not the port where he or she was taken on. This is the reason why some skippers insist that their crew are in possession of a valid return ticket to their country of origin from the intended port of destination. If a ticket is not available, some skippers play it safe by holding the equivalent sum of money in bond until the crew leaves the yacht. Some skippers go even further by drawing up a formal contract which spells out both their obligations and those of the crew and which both sign in front of an independent witness.

Countless stories have come to my knowledge during the last

few years, but perhaps the best example is that of the skipper who was forced by the immigration authorities in Barbados to repatriate his crew to Ghana. The skipper had picked up the man in Las Palmas more because he felt sorry for him than actual need. Shortly after arriving in Barbados, the crew demanded to be repatriated and the skipper had no choice but to send him via scheduled airlines to Accra, an exercise which cost him about 2000 dollars.

In spite of the horror stories that buzz around the cruising grapevine, I am constantly amazed at the number of people who are still willing to take on crew on the spur of the moment only hours before an ocean passage. It happens every year in the ARC and I can usually guess what the outcome was from the speed with which the owner and crew part company virtually minutes after they dock in Barbados. One such skipper suggested to others who may be faced by the same situation to think very carefully before taking on somebody they do not know for a long passage. Having two young children on board, he and his wife decided to take on another couple so as to have some extra help during the crossing. The problem was not that the crew did not get on with the owners, but that the couple themselves did not get on with each other and fought and quarrelled all the way across. The situation got so bad that the skipper decided to put into the Cape Verde Islands to rid himself of his quarrelling crew, but strong winds made this impossible. He warned others to be very careful about taking on crew for a passage during which it

There is always a solution if one does not have one's own cabin and wishes to get away from an older sister.

would be impossible to stop en route to change crew. The advice is equally valid for crew as there are probably just as many cases of crew being taken on by a difficult skipper, so prospective crew would be well advised not to get on a yacht with a skipper they do not know. This question of clash of personalities must be considered very seriously as it can lead to grave consequences, even murder in rare cases.

As a general rule, from the cases I have encountered during the last few years, skippers appear to have been most content with crews who have a fair amount of sailing experience behind them, preferably including a longer passage. Ultimately the atmosphere on board is set by the personality of the skipper and in contrast to the problems I have mentioned, I have also seen many boats where people have come and gone, yet were always welded into a happy crew by the talent and character of the owners. There are many contented skippers and crew out there.

Expectations

The above examples were not given with the intention to be alarmist but only to point out some problems that could and should be avoided. The joy of cruising can often be marred by subjective factors and it is usually lack of experience which leads people into such situations. Cruising is for most people a long nurtured dream come true and I am happy to report that from my experience, the number of happy and contented people far outnumbers those who regret their decision to go cruising. The Atlantic Survey provided the opportunity to probe deeper into this subject and the conclusions I was able to draw, were later supplemented with observations made during the ARC.

Crossing the Atlantic is for most sailors a unique experience and the profound sense of achievement felt by those who have successfully completed such a voyage is entirely justified. For many of those interviewed this had been their first major offshore passage, so I rounded off each interview by asking the crew, not just the skipper, if the transatlantic passage had lived up to their expectations. In nine cases this question was irrelevant as the crews had already undertaken long ocean passages or were in the middle of a world cruise. Perhaps because the weather that year had been slightly rougher than usual and the trade winds more boisterous than expected, a surprisingly large number of skippers (15) stated without hesitation that the crossing had not lived up to their expectations and in fact had been worse. A more positive reaction came from 11 skippers who stressed that the passage had been better than expected, fewer problems had been encountered and they felt a satisfaction both with themselves and their boats. To these should be added several skippers who mentioned the great sense of achievement they felt after their first long offshore passage, even if the crossing itself had not always lived up to their expectations. Another three skippers admitted that the passage had gone well, but they were not eager to repeat the experience in the immediate future.

Looking more closely at the various reasons for dissatisfaction, the most often mentioned cause was that the crossing had been more uncomfortable than expected. It was clear that an unusual cross swell had spoilt the passage for many. A few people also complained about the boredom of being cooped up in a small space for three weeks or more and this was particularly noticeable on boats which had suffered some friction among the crew, usually those who had taken on additional crew for the passage. However, complaints were also made by short handed crews who found watch keeping and interrupted nights very tiring. On the other hand, on boats with larger crews who were actively sailing their boats, people seemed to get more satisfaction out of the Atlantic crossing. The least complaints were voiced by the singlehanders, only one of whom admitted being rather lonely at Christmas, when he saw his slow passage stretch into a fifth week.

In a few instances the disappointment expressed by the skippers reflected their annoyance with some writers, who had led them to believe that the Atlantic crossing would be all blue skies, fluffy clouds, steady 15 knot trade winds and flying fish waiting on deck for breakfast. In some cases this frustration was also due to their own lack of experience, which had led them either to choose an unsuitable boat or to prepare and provision inadequately, several crews complaining about the poor diet, one actually running out of food a few days before landfall.

Lack of sailing experience and its effect on the crew was particularly noticeable in the case of two fathers who admitted being extremely worried about their responsibilities towards their families. One of them arrived in the Caribbean mentally and physically exhausted having stayed awake for the last few nights due to his apprehension of the impending landfall. The wind had been very strong and because of his limited knowledge of celestial navigation he had to put all his faith in satellite navigation, not being able to check if the instrument was indeed accurate. Under these conditions it was not surprising that his greatest satisfaction was not the crossing itself but his safe landfall on Barbados, the position of which was finally revealed by the strong loom from the airport lights.

Equally frank about his disillusionment was another skipper sailing with his family, who admitted that he had been looking for peace at sea, but the only thing he had found was apprehension. He was worried about high following seas and his obvious inability to cope with an emergency should it arise. He was therefore determined to give up the voyage at the earliest opportunity. This was a painful realization for someone who had dreamt for thirty years about such a voyage, but had never considered the practicalities of this dream. It was ironic that his wife, who admitted having been reluctantly dragged along on the voyage because of *her husband*'s dream, had come to love the cruising life and was very reluctant to give it up.

Those who approached life at sea with a positive attitude were usually the most satisfied, as were those willing to learn from their own mistakes and not surrender at the first difficulty. The same conclusion was drawn when the results of the ARC Survey were examined and in most instances the main reason for the enjoyment to be tempered by a certain disappointment was a lack of preparation, both mental and practical.

Looking more closely at the preparations for the voyage, even if it had been planned well ahead, the actual preparations did not seem to have taken all that long, the average length of time being five months. In many cases the time spent on preparation had been much shorter, on one third of the boats lasting less than two months. Many skippers had therefore left home only partially prepared, planning to get things done en route before the crossing proper. In fact several of them discovered that this was not as easy as they had thought and regretted not having done the necessary jobs when facilities were easily available. As in previous surveys, I was told the same stories of the difficulties in repairing electronic equipment, getting liferafts serviced or boats antifouled in ports en route.

Seasickness

Seasickness is an ongoing problem, which affects both the physical and mental state and a surprisingly high number of voyagers suffer from it to a lesser or greater extent, the proportion of women apparently being higher than men. Over one third of the boats in the Pacific Survey had at least one person suffering from seasickness among the crew. In the majority of cases the worst bouts of seasickness occurred during the first days at sea after a long spell in port. Several children also complained about it, although as they did not have to play a part in the sailing of the boat, they usually just lay down until they felt better. Most of those suffering only occasionally from seasickness took no drugs and had obviously learnt to live with this disability.

The matter was looked at again during the Atlantic Survey, although the ocean conditions prevailing during the time when the crews were interviewed made their transatlantic crossing rather different from most years in that many people reported an uncomfortable cross swell. In spite of this, it was again noticeable that most people took a very relaxed attitude to the problem of seasickness, not being too bothered if they were actually sick. As the passage started after everyone had done some sailing, most people who suffered from seasickness had come to terms with their condition. The commonest problem was a queasiness at the beginning of the passage until people found their sea legs. Most of those who were prone to seasickness prepared for this by taking some medication before leaving port.

Scopolamine patches and stugeron were the two most popular medications used, although several people complained that stugeron made them drowsy. A radically different method was tried out by the crew of the Swiss yacht *Deles* who used a device which emits a high frequency signal. Two pads are placed close behind the ears and kept on for two minutes while the person is lying down. The crew assured me that bouts of seasickness were easily prevented by this method which had absolutely no side effects. Yet another apparently successful remedy for some are wrist bands, which keep pressure on a certain point on the wrist. However, as seasickness seems to affect people in different ways, remedies which work well on some people have no effect on others.

A severe bout of seasickness struck a strapping young fellow taking part in ARC 87. He was so sick that he was on the verge of going into a coma and his concerned skipper, worried that the young man's life might be at risk if he continued the voyage, made a detour to the Cape Verde Islands from where the sick crew returned home by aeroplane. Another person who also suffered from seasickness very severely took tranquillisers as well as other medication in order to go to sleep.

Several people, although admitting that they got queasy from time to time, stated that this did not interfere with their sailing. One diabetic sailor pointed out that diabetics have to be particularly careful not to vomit, as this can upset the balance of insulin in the body, but as far as she was concerned this condition was no reason to prevent her from cruising. Useful advice came from another lady who had become pregnant after unknowingly disgorging her daily contraceptive pills in bouts of seasickness.

Medical emergencies

The list of medical emergencies that have been recounted to me during the various surveys is so long and varied that I could fill a whole book with them. Fortunately most of them were not serious and were dealt with quickly and efficiently with the means available on board. In this chapter I have included only those examples of some relevance to others and the main emphasis is on the more recent emergencies reported in the Atlantic and ARC Surveys.

Among the boats taking part in the Atlantic Survey, the constant rolling and fairly rough sailing conditions caused several injuries, although the number of serious emergencies was relatively small. Even so, some of the injuries could well have been avoided with a little more care.

Bernhard Witt of *Kiwitt* caught his right hand in the mainsheet block, which ripped off both skin and flesh and left a deep wound. As the boat was only some 100 miles north of the Cape Verde Islands, it was decided to go there for treatment, but bad weather hindered their progress so much that they eventually carried on across the Atlantic. The wound was thoroughly washed, disinfected and butterfly plasters were used to hold the skin together. A complete course of antibiotics was also taken to prevent infection and after one week the wound had almost healed. Antibiotics also came to the help of singlehander John Gregory of *Tahaki* who developed a serious infection following a scratch obtained while swimming in Las Palmas harbour shortly before his departure.

A most frustrating accident occurred to Gunnar Tornqvist of *Vagabond*, while taking in the spinnaker pole. The pole broke its mast end fitting, slipped out of his hands and fell on deck. It bounced once, hit the deck again and Gunnar tried to grab it, but just missed the pole as it vaulted over the lifelines and was gone. Expressing his frustration at losing the pole, Gunnar stamped his foot hard on deck, hit a ventilator and cracked a bone in his heel. The foot had to be bound up and for several weeks he could hardly walk. Also while working on the foredeck, a spinnaker pole hit Waltraud Bittner of *Lorebella* on the cheek. Fortunately the cheekbone was not broken and the swelling was kept down with bags of ice. Yet another injury sustained on the foredeck was to Marlies Grossmann of *Hol Di Ran*, who tried to haul up a bucket of sea water while sailing along at over 6 knots. The strong pull exerted by the heavy bucket injured her back and she was laid up for several days in great pain, relieved by the muscle relaxant Norgesic.

The seriousness of a mid-ocean emergency which cannot be dealt with by the crew alone was highlighted by the following two cases. The crew of *Pentreath of Rock* became very concerned when Janet Bookock's pupils became very dilated for no apparent reason. They tried to contact passing ships on VHF, but all their calls remained unanswered. Having no choice, they continued towards Barbados and gradually Janet's condition improved, but the anxiety felt over an unknown medical problem marred their passage. The crew of *Gypsy Dane* had more luck in drawing attention to themselves when Fiona Long developed high fever and abdominal pains shortly after leaving the Canaries bound for St Lucia. A Soviet vessel, returning from a research trip to the Antarctic, was raised on VHF, but because of the swell, the yacht could not be brought alongside the larger vessel. The Russians sent across their ship's launch with an interpreter and a doctor, who insisted that Fiona be transferred to the ship's hospital and taken back to the Canaries as appendicitis was suspected. Although making a special detour, the Russian vessel did not receive permission to stop in the Canaries and the patient had to be transferred to a pilot launch off Las Palmas to be taken to the local hospital, where a serious kidney infection was diagnosed.

Ake Sundström of *Kalea II* was extremely fortunate in that his accident happened on arrival in Barbados. Trying to free a jammed hatch with a knife, the blade broke off and punctured his eye. He was rushed to the local hospital with a collapsed eyeball. Luckily there happened to be a visiting eye surgeon present, who operated immediately and saved his eye. I was extremely pleased to meet Ake in Bermuda two years later and to see that his eye had completely healed. His accident reminded me of a similar eye injury sustained by a sailor on a boat moored near ours in Whangarei. He was taken to the casualty department of the local hospital where the doctor took him by surprise when he exclaimed, 'You must be off one of the yachts in the harbour.'

'Yes,' replied our neighbour, 'but how did you know?'

'Because only yachties come to us with stupid accidents like this,' said the surgeon and proceeded to patch him up.

There is undoubtedly a lesson to be learnt from the remark made by the Kiwi doctor and looking at the various injuries reported in the first two ARCs, I am the first to agree that many were caused by carelessness. At the top of the list are injuries caused by booms, usually knocks on the head. It has been calculated that a yacht rolls about one hundred thousand times during the average Atlantic crossing, so it may not be so surprising that having missed it on 99,999 occasions one of the crew will eventually rear his head at the wrong moment and put it on a collision course with the swinging boom. More culpable was the oversight of one skipper who managed to avoid the menace throughout the crossing, but knocked himself out cold when he stood up to his full height in the cockpit shortly after arriving in Barbados, having forgotten that the boom was now resting over the cockpit.

Most boom injuries however, were caused during gybes, either deliberate or not, such as a serious whiplash injury sustained by Courtenay Bollay on *Snow Goose* who was struck by the main sheet in the head and chest and was still showing the black and blue signs of her painful injury one week later. Also struck by the boom was one of the crew on *Silver Apple*, whose skipper Tony van Hee described the incident in cryptic terms on the Rally Declaration. 'Blow to the head by boom. Hard head! Patient survived.'

Undoubtedly the simplest way to avoid the menace of the swinging boom is to use a preventer. Although most people use a handy billy to hold the boom in place, a better system is to lead the preventer all the way forward, through a block and back to the cockpit, from where it can be easily handled during a controlled gybe. An efficient method is to have a preventer, preferably made of wire, permanently attached to the outer end of the boom, its fore end being cleated to the underside of the boom near the gooseneck fitting when not in use. This means that even with the mainsheet fully paid out, the preventer can be handled in safety, as a line can be attached to its free end without having to lean overboard. The line is then taken forward, where it can be cleated, or led back to the cockpit through a block. If one needs to gybe, the line is disengaged from the preventer and another one is set up on the other side.

The only time when preventers can be counterproductive is when the sails have to be handled quickly in an emergency, either to take avoiding action if on a collision course with another vessel, or if hit by an unexpected squall. Such squalls can be particularly dangerous in the tropics and although their approach can be detected in daytime, on dark nights they can strike without warning. As the wind can rapidly rise to 30 or even 40 knots, the best way to cope with such squalls is to shorten sail, furling or dropping the sails if possible, or at least easing the sheets. The latter may not be easy with a well prevented boom, so if squalls are anticipated, a close eye should be kept on the weather or else the risk taken of sailing without a prevented boom. As unintentional gybes, which usually occurred while the boat was on autopilot or selfsteering, were blamed for most of the accidents involving booms, it is a matter that obviously merits some attention.

Burns are another common accident and the most serious in ARC 86 was sustained by Werner Stumpe of *Antaia* who scalded himself with a pot of boiling water which caused severe second degree burns to his chest. Fortunately he had special burn ointment available, but even so the wound took a very long time to heal and the skin had not fully regenerated one year later.

A bad fall by one of the crew who slipped on the genoa winch forced skipper Mike Hindmarsh of *Palaemon* to return to Las Palmas where the injury was stitched up in hospital. Had the accident happened further offshore, it could have been very difficult to deal with it with the means available on board. *Katrina* also had to return to Tenerife to obtain the proper medication for a crew who suffered an insulin reaction and had been treated with the only dose of Glucogen on board.

There were several more cases of minor surgery, such as a cut palm which had to be stitched on *Gimlet*, but as there were two doctors among the crew the patient received all the care he needed. Yet another bad gash and concussion was sustained by Puja Graham on *Lionheart* when she missed her handhold as the boat rolled and fell six feet backwards, hitting the back of her skull hard. Her husband Henry received advice over the amateur radio, shaved the area around the one inch gash and stitched the wound together. The potential seriousness of this injury was shown by the fact that the concussion was still bothering Puja with headaches and dizziness when she arrived in Barbados.

FIRST AID

The fact that virtually all the emergencies described above were treated on board shows the importance of carrying a well stocked medicine chest and also to have at least some basic knowledge of first aid. Both in the ARC and the Atlantic Surveys most crews possessed at least the basic principles of first aid and on all boats there was a handbook giving instructions on the treatment of injuries and other kinds of medical emergencies.

In the Pacific Survey at least one person on half of the boats had taken a first aid course. The same degree of preparedness was seen in the medical supplies carried on board. On 40 boats in the sample of 100, the medicine chest was described as comprehensive, on 54 it was described as adequate and only six skippers thought they only had the minimum. Obviously for ocean voyaging the medicine chest should contain a wider variety of medicines than for coastal cruising. People with ongoing medical conditions must make sure that they carry enough supplies of their regular treatment or other drugs that they might require. A basic list for an extended cruise away from immediate medical facilities should include the following:

Cotton wool
Waterproof adhesive dressings in various sizes
Butterfly plasters which pull a cut together
Sterilized lint
Bandages
Crepe bandages for sprains
Special sterile dressings for burns
Scissors, forceps, safety pins
Thermometer
Disposable syringes and needles
Sterile needles with sutures for stitching
Skin disinfectant e.g. cetrimide, chlorhexidine or iodine tincture
Local anaesthetic to allow cleaning and stitching of a major wound
Specific local anaesthetic drops for removing foreign bodies from the eye
Drops and ointments for eye infections, e.g. chloramphenicol
Ear drops for bacterial ear infections
Antibacterial cream e.g. fusidic acid, neomycin sulphate, silver sulphadiazine for infected burns or ulcers
Antibiotic powder or spray e.g. neomycin sulphate. These are better than creams under moist tropical conditions
Antihistamine cream to relieve insect bites, stings or sunburn
Antiseasickness tablets or patches

Antihistamine anti-allergic tablets for allergies to food, insect bites, jelly fish or coral stings, etc

Antibiotics. Two broad spectrum antibiotics should be carried in case one is ineffective or there is sensitivity.
– a penicillin e.g. ampicillin or amoxycillin (available in a syrup for children)
– tetracycline (not recommended for under 12 years or pregnant women. Large doses can suppress appendicitis)

Analgesic – for minor pain, paracetamol or aspirin (the latter is also anti-inflammatory)
– for more severe pain, pentazocine

Sulphonamide antibacterial for urinary-tract infections

Laxative

Antidiarrhoeal tablets (or kaolin mixture for children)

Sleeping tablets, useful for helping someone in severe pain to go to sleep

Promethazine elixir, such as phenergan, useful as a sedative for a sick child and also for allergic conditions, nausea, etc.

Antifungal preparations for athletes foot and other fungal infections

Insect repellant

Sun screen lotion

Antimalarial tablets for prophylactic use

In the above list generic not proprietary names have been given for all medicines.

Medical advice should be sought as to which antibiotics to take as some people are sensitive to penicillin and like all powerful drugs, antibiotics should not be taken lightly. Taking the wrong antibiotic can hinder the correct diagnosis of an infection and sometimes make the condition worse. It is advisable to carry disposable syringes and needles in case one needs to have an injection in countries which do not use disposables, as the risk of a serious infection, hepatitis or AIDS, from improperly sterilized or shared needles and syringes is considerable. Especially when sailing to more out of the way places, it is wise to check what immunizations may be required, such as yellow fever for countries in South America. Failure to have the required certificate can result in having to have the immunization on the spot, one crew reporting from Brazil recently that the same needle was used for them all, when they had to have their yellow fever vaccinations at the local dispensary.

When setting up the medicine chest for a longer cruise, it is advisable to consult one's own doctor, the best person to give advice on what to take. Most doctors will also prescribe certain drugs, which are on the restricted list, once the reason has been explained.

Regulations regarding drugs vary enormously from country to country and some customs officials confiscate certain drugs, such as strong painkillers like morphine. In several countries however, the laws are very relaxed, and many drugs that normally are only available on prescription, such as antibiotics, can be bought over the counter. Many skippers use this opportunity to stock up their medicine chest or replace drugs which have passed their expiry date. Some doctors among the skippers interviewed stressed the importance of renewing medicines regularly, especially antibiotics, as their effectiveness decreases with age and storage in tropical conditions. Nevertheless most antibiotics can still be used after the expiry date although the dosage might have to be increased.

The danger of using antibiotics without proper advice was highlighted by the case of Mac Macauley, the skipper of *Acheta*, who was taken severely ill while the boat was anchored near a remote island 70 miles off the coast of Mexico. His symptoms were described over the amateur radio and he was advised to take the antibiotic tetracycline. In spite of this, Mac got steadily worse and finally his wife June decided to sail the boat to the mainland on her own, where a doctor diagnosed hepatitis and prescribed the proper treatment. It turned out they had been given the wrong advice, as the strong antibiotic tetracycline should not be used where liver or kidney ailments are suspected.

Health dangers worldwide

There is no doubt that life at sea is healthier than sitting behind a desk, prey to all the viruses that waft along the office heating or air-conditioning ducts. While infectious diseases might be rare on sailing boats and the commonest problems are usually of an accidental nature, such as knocks, gashes or broken bones, there are several less obvious health dangers lurking even in beautiful tropical anchorages, waiting to strike the unwary sailor.

Malaria

The most sinister of these is the scourge of malaria, which has resurged dramatically in the last few years, spreading into areas, from which it had previously been eradicated. One of the main reasons for this is that most strains of the disease have become resistant to the anti-malarial drugs in use. Also the worldwide increase in travel has spread the disease, as travellers with infected blood are bitten by mosquitos in malaria-free areas, so passing on the parasite. It is estimated that there are more than 350 million cases of malaria every year with about one million fatalities, mainly in young children.

Malaria is caused by a parasite, which is transferred into the blood when a person is bitten by the *Anopheles* mosquito, which feeds mainly at dusk. Mild symptoms resemble a common cold, but more serious cases involve high fever, destruction of blood cells, loss of weight, and can lead to coma and death. There are several varieties of the parasite, some being more virulent than others, as well as varying in their resistance to drugs. Particularly lethal is the *Plasmodium falciparum* strain, which affects blood vessels in the brain and causes the deadly cerebral malaria.

The danger of contracting malaria is not when sailing offshore because of the limit to the mosquito's flight, but more when at anchor close inshore in a malarial area. The perfect protected anchorage in still waters is ironically the most likely place where one could be bitten by a malaria carrying mosquito. The first obvious precaution is to avoid being bitten and repellant lotions, sprays, slow burning coils and various other devices for repulsing mosquitos are recommended for those cruising in vulnerable areas. The type of device that emits a high pitched noise does not appear to be effective. Simple screens, either detachable or permanent, can be fitted across opening hatches or doors, or alternatively mosquito netting can be hung across bunks or hatches. Some hatches are now made with insect screens as standard. In the tropics however, part of the pleasure of cruising is to sit in the open cockpit on a warm evening and on such occasions in malarial areas as much of the body as possible should be covered up with long sleeved shirts and long trousers or skirts, which is not always pleasant when it is very hot.

The malarial parasite does need a hot climate to survive and the countries where malaria poses a risk reflect this, as they are spread out in a broad band across the tropical regions of the world (Map 2). All of Central America from Mexico through Belize, Honduras and Costa Rica to the Panama Canal are affected and South America as far south as Peru and Brazil. The north coast of South America, including Guyana, Venezuela and Panama, is one of the high risk areas of drug resistant strains. The islands of the Caribbean are free

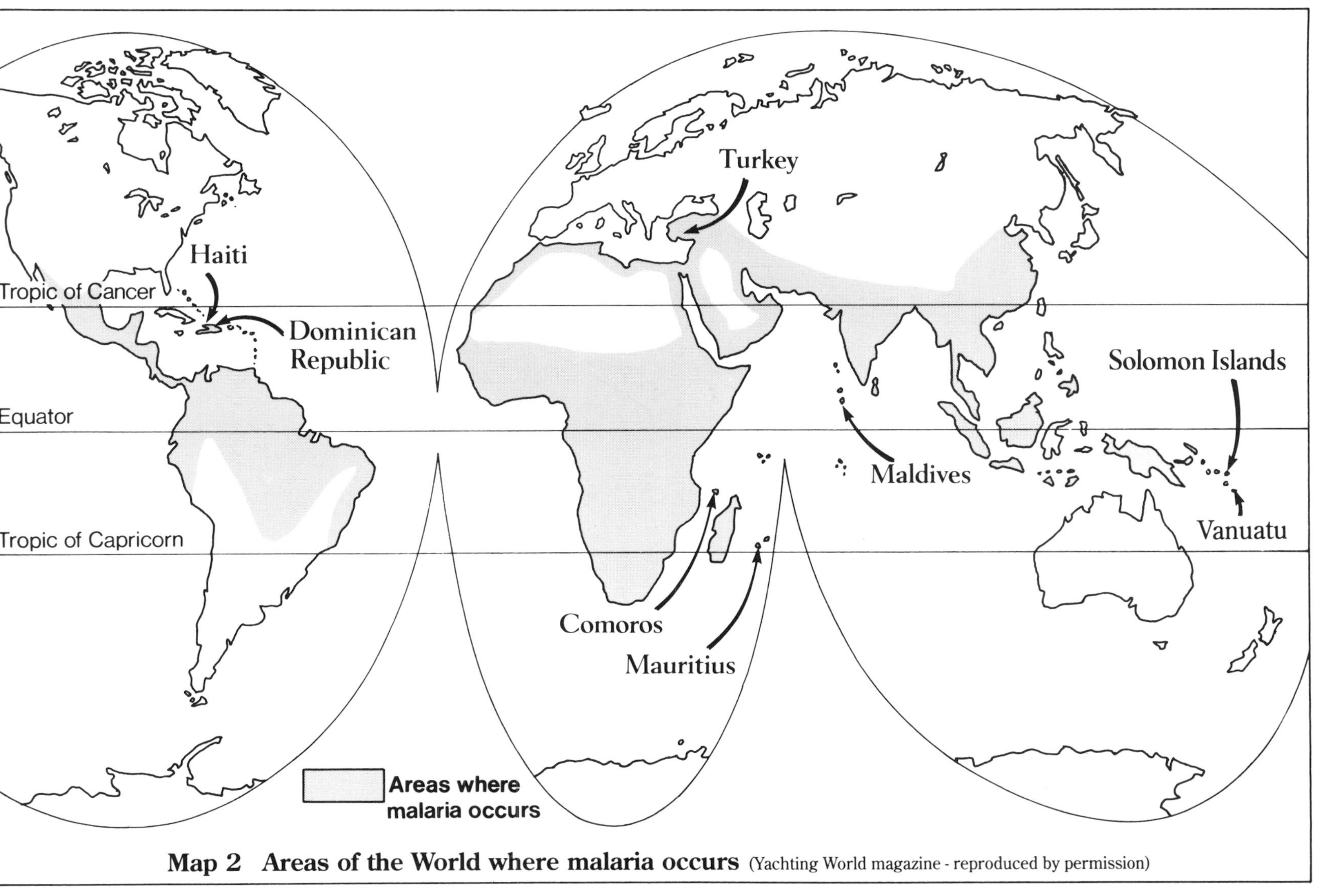

Map 2 Areas of the World where malaria occurs (Yachting World magazine - reproduced by permission)

of malaria, except for Haiti and the Dominican Republic. Almost all African countries bear some risk and Senegal, Gambia and Guinea are increasingly popular destinations for yachts where precautions should be taken. The Cape Verde Islands have also had cases of malaria reported. Aden, Djibouti and lands bordering the Red Sea come in the malarial zone, although they are not such a high risk area as Kenya and neighbouring East African states where drug resistant strains occur.

The Mediterranean is relatively malaria free, although it is recommended to take anti-malarial precautions in Turkey, Egypt, Morocco and Algeria. In the Indian Ocean, malaria is not reported in the Seychelles, but the Maldives, Sri Lanka, Comoro Islands, Madagascar and Mauritius are all in the malaria belt. Most of South East Asia, including Indonesia, Thailand, Philippines and Malaysia, has drug resistant strains, although Singapore is notably free due to stringent precautions taken by the government. The South Pacific is another clear area except for the western section from Vanuatu to the Solomons and Papua New Guinea, where malaria has had a particularly virulent impact in recent years. It was reported that most of the 30 yachts spending the cyclone season in the Solomon Islands recently had one or more members of the crew afflicted, in one case this proving to be fatal.

As a rule towns and cities are less likely to harbour the mosquito than rural areas, but it is just the more remote anchorages that yachtsmen often seek out while cruising. The time of year, wet or dry season, can also affect the situation. When cruising in any of the areas specified above, anti-malarial tablets should be started at least one week beforehand, taken during the entire cruise and for up to one month after leaving the area. It is vital to take these prophylactic drugs for the entire recommended period to ensure that any malaria parasites which enter the bloodstream are destroyed. Advice on which drug to take for a particular area should be obtained from a doctor or local health centre. Chloroquine has been widely used in the past and is effective in most cases, but this is the drug to which the parasite has become resistant. Amodiaquine has serious side effects affecting the bone marrow, which have caused a few deaths and is no longer recommended. A new drug, mefloquine, which promises to be effective against the chloroquine resistant strains, is used in some areas, but as it is still under trial, medical opinion is divided on its use. It tends to be kept for treatment only. In brief, the first choice is to take chloroquine weekly with proguanil daily as this combination has minimal side effects. In resistant areas, such as

Central and South America, South East Asia, Oceania and East Africa, pyrimethamine tablets should be taken weekly together with chloroquine.

As malaria is such a large worldwide health problem, research is being carried out in several centres to develop a vaccine, but although some progress has been made, there is not yet a vaccine available for the general public. Advice on the current situation and which anti-malarials to take for different areas can be obtained from local Health offices in most countries.

Health protection

Information about which other precautions, vaccinations and immunizations are required for various parts of the world can also be obtained from Public Health offices. Yellow fever is another mosquito-borne disease which fortunately can be vaccinated against, although this can only be done at special vaccination centres. The certificate is valid for ten years and at the moment is required mainly in South America and Africa. Countries where sailors may be required to be vaccinated are Brazil, Panama, Senegal and Gambia. It is also recommended for Venezuela, Guyana and French Guiana.

Vaccinations should be kept up to date against polio and typhoid fever when travelling outside of Europe, North America, Australia or New Zealand. Scrupulous care should also be taken over food, drink and hygiene outside of these areas to avoid not only the risk of polio or typhoid, but also infectious hepatitis. A massive worldwide programme of polio vaccination is underway at the moment aiming to eradicate the disease in the same way as smallpox was eradicated.

In any part of the world tetanus is a risk from a wound or open injury, especially in areas where medical facilities are not readily available. A booster vaccination should be had every five years to protect against this. Not only to avoid tetanus, but as a general precaution against infection, especially in tropical areas, all scratches and cuts, however small, should be washed and disinfected thoroughly, for they can become infected at lightning speed in warm moist conditions. Many of those sailing for longer periods in tropical waters have had problems with these kind of infected cuts and sores, leading sometimes to tropical ulcers. The infection is usually due to the *staphylococcus* bacteria, which is very difficult to eradicate once it is in the bloodstream, necessitating internal antibiotic treatment.

Ciguatera

Another danger that those sailing in tropical waters are becoming aware of is that of *ciguatera.* This type of fish poisoning has been regarded as rather a mystery since it was first described by Columbus, for over 400 species of fish have been incriminated at one time or another, a species being toxic in one area but not in another, even within the same lagoon. Although more is now known about *ciguatera* and its causes, there is still no reliable test for discovering if a fish is poisonous or not, except in the laboratory, nor is there a simple treatment or cure. This is the essence of the problem and has led to a wide variety of local remedies and ways of testing fish, most of which are not reliable.

Not everyone eating ciguatoxic fish has the same symptoms, although vomiting or diarrhoea usually occur within a few hours. The characteristic symptoms of *ciguatera* are tingling around the mouth and prickling in the fingers and toes. An alteration of sensations can make plain water taste like soda and a shower feel like a barrage of tiny electric shocks. In many cases the patient is left very weak and full recovery can be slow, taking weeks or even months. If the poisoning is severe, muscular paralysis and convulsions can occur, leading occasionally to death from respiratory paralysis. The only treatment is to relieve the symptoms, such as anti-histamines for the itching. A promising therapy is the intravenous injection of calcium glutonate with Vitamins B6 and B12, which appear to act by restricting the increased passage of sodium into body cells, which is the current explanation of how the toxin acts at cell level.

The culprit causing *ciguatera* was tracked down by the team led by Dr Raymond Bagnis, head of the Medical Oceanographic Research Unit in Tahiti, and identified as a tiny unicellular plant similar to an algae. Normally only a few of these microscopic plants live on a coral reef, but under certain circumstances their numbers can multiply dramatically. The fish which graze on these algae then introduce the toxin into the food chain. The toxin does not affect the fish itself, but accumulates in its flesh. When a predatory fish, such as a snapper, grouper or barracuda swallows one of the grazing fish, it acquires in one bite the toxicity that the smaller fish had spent a lifetime accumulating.

For the last 20 years all cases of *ciguatera* in French Polynesia have been carefully recorded and Dr Bagnis has drawn some interesting conclusions. In every major outbreak, some disturbance or damage had occurred to the coral reef in the preceding year or two, either as a result of a natural occurrence such as a cyclone or bad storm, or by man's interference as in blasting a pass, dumping metallic or other polluting debris, or building quays and break-waters. Apparently the toxic micro-algae likes to breed on newly exposed coral surfaces and so man interferes with the reef at his peril.

Cases of *ciguatera* have occurred in almost all areas where there are coral reefs in the Pacific and Indian Oceans and in the Carib-bean. Steep-to islands and coasts lacking reefs are generally free of toxic fish and fish caught by trolling offshore are normally safe to eat. In French Polynesia there has been an increase in the number of outbreaks in the last 25 years, significantly in the Marquesas, some atolls of the Tuamotus and the Gambier Islands. Other Pacific islands have also reported cases, although these have not been studied systematically.

In the Caribbean, CAREC (Caribbean Epidemiology Centre), based in Trinidad, also started a regional surveillance programme, although mild cases often go unreported. Cases have been reported over the years from most islands in the Caribbean, most commonly in the northern section from Puerto Rico to Montserrat, including the Virgin Islands, Anguilla, St Maarten, St Barts, St Kitts and Nevis, Antigua and Barbuda. Cases have also been reported repeatedly from Jamaica, the Bahamas and Florida. Although trolling in the open ocean is usually safe, the banks between Antigua and the Virgin Islands have shown a high incidence of ciguatoxic fish, particularly Anguilla Bank, Redonda and Saba. South of Guadeloupe, reports of *ciguatera* poisoning are rare and almost unknown in the large central islands of Guadeloupe, Dominica, St Lucia, Martinique and St Vin-cent. There have been occasional reports from the Grenadines and Barbados.

There is some evidence of a seasonal build up in the Caribbean with more cases reported between April and October. Outbreaks of poisoning were reported from 6 months to 2 years after Hurricane David devastated Dominica and after Hurricane Allen in Puerto Rico. Similarly it can be expected to find outbreaks in the wake of Hurricane Gilbert (1988).

The most common species of fish to be implicated in *ciguatera* poisoning are the larger predatory fish, such as red snapper, grouper, amberjack and barracuda. All oversized fish should certainly be treated with caution. Dr Boyd-Scobie of CAREC advises yachtsmen, who want to fish, to listen carefully to what local fishermen have to say about dangerous areas or sections of a reef, but not to trust the local tests for toxicity, whether it be with silver coins or the absence of flies! Poisonous fish are usually confined to certain areas, so that once the areas are known, fish from them can be avoided. Nevertheless large numbers of fish are not poisonous and it seems a shame not to enjoy a fresh tasty dinner while cruising. Risks can be minimized by gutting a fish as soon as it is caught and never eating the head, flesh close to the head, the roe, liver or other viscera, as the toxin concentrates in these parts. As the toxicity is directly related to the amount eaten, it pays to eat moderate portions of fish from unknown areas. Another method is to eat a very small amount for lunch and if no ill effects are felt, to serve the rest for dinner.

Several crews I spoke to, most of them in the South Pacific, had suffered from *ciguatera* intoxication, some of them being left sensitive and unable to eat any fish without a recurrence of the symptoms. One of these, a doctor, admitted that he should have known better than to eat moray eel, which is one of the species most likely to be toxic. Many yachtsmen cruising the South Pacific have been affected by this type of fish poisoning, only a few being badly intoxicated, although there was at least one fatal case in French Polynesia.

Meningitis

Seafood has also been implicated in cases of *eosonophilic meningitis*, a very debilitating disease which affected some yachtsmen in Fiji and caused the death of a girl on a cruising boat. This infection, which is characterized by a severe throbbing headache, nausea and vomiting, is caused by the larvae of the rat lung worm. This parasite has a complicated life cycle, involving several larvae stages which pass through intermediate hosts such as snails, slugs, freshwater prawns, land crabs and fish. The larvae can be ingested by man either by eating raw sea food or raw vegetables, which have been contaminated by slugs or snails. The larvae invade the central nervous system, causing the symptoms described above and more rarely fever, mental confusion, convulsions and impairment of vision. The majority of people do recover completely, but this can take several months and there is no specific treatment. The disease was largely found in South East Asia, notably Thailand, but in recent years the rat population of several Pacific countries have become infected with the worm. Cases have been reported from Australia, Papua New Guinea, Western and American Samoa, Tonga and Fiji. The obvious precautionary measures are to ensure that all salad and other vegetables eaten raw are well washed and to avoid raw sea food in these areas. In restaurants where one cannot be sure how food is prepared, it is wise to avoid salads and raw foods.

Botulism

The old adage about washing fruit and salads is well known and has been advice given to travellers for many years. Bacteria, yeasts and moulds are present all the time in food, but need the right conditions to multiply or produce the toxins which cause various types of food poisoning. There is a danger of this on board boats, particularly those lacking refrigeration, because the conditions of humidity and temperature are often perfect for bacterial growth. Partly cooking a dish at home and then transporting it to the boat for a weekend sail, although time saving, can be perilous. The use of pressure cookers on boats is widespread and undoubtedly they are of value in reducing both cooking time and the consumption of cooking fuel. However, there is a false security in regarding pressure cookers as a method of sterilization and using them for bottling or canning. The practice of making a stew for several days, eating some, then bringing the cooker up to full pressure and letting it cool without removing the lid, does not guarantee that all organisms and toxins will be destroyed. A vacuum is not retained in the cooker, and air does flow back in through the same vents through which it escaped.

Bottling or canning foods must be done correctly because of the danger of *Clostridium botulinum*, which produces one of the most poisonous substances known to man. *Clostridium botulinum* is present in minute quantities in many foods but flourishes in a lack of air, which is why if it is not destroyed, it can multiply in the conditions inside a bottle or can. It produces a lethal toxin, even small quantities of which can cause death from botulism. Although the practice of canning using a pressure cooker has become popular on boats and has been described in various books and articles, both the Ministry of Agriculture, Fisheries and Food in England, and pressure cooker manufacturers themselves, advise strongly against canning meat, poultry or vegetables using this method. To guarantee the destruction of all *Cl. botulinum* spores, a temperature of 121°C (250°F) must be maintained for a considerable time. Reaching this high temperature, above the boiling point of water, is achieved by supressing the escape of steam and building up pressure inside the pot. However domestic pressure cookers have no gauge to indicate if this temperature is reached and maintained for the correct time.

Food can be canned using special pressure canners, which are fitted with a gauge to monitor pressure and are of a heavier construction material. If a canner is used the manufacturer's instructions should always be followed precisely to ensure the correct pressure and temperature are maintained for the specified time.

Cl. botulinum is sensitive to acid conditions and so does not grow in more acid foods, such as most fruits, which can be canned or bottled successfully using an ordinary pressure cooker. Vacuum sealed jars should be used to prevent the growth of other organisms after canning. Lemon juice can be added to borderline products such as tomatoes to increase their acidity, but most vegetables are not acid enough and should not be canned. Home bottled tomatoes which were not acidic enough have been blamed for several outbreaks of botulism in the United States.

Fortunately botulism is extremely rare, but general food poisoning has often struck people on boats. One way to avoid this is to keep the galley very clean and to inspect foodstuffs carefully, rejecting any that are suspect. Tins and cans which show signs of damage, such as bulging, dents on the side seam, seepage, foam or fizz on opening, or other danger signals, should be thrown out.

If this chapter resembles a catalogue of horrors that lay in wait for the unwary sailor, it is only meant to draw attention to potential hazards which are easily overlooked. With care and attention, all these health traps can be avoided or minimalized.

A TRUE VIKING

After interviewing hundreds of skippers over some ten years, it does not take me long to sense the atmosphere on a boat when I step aboard. For all the boats where tension between the crew prevails, there are many more 'happy ships', where it is a pleasure to sit and while away the time in conversation. Almost always the scene is set by the personality of the skipper or owner, such as Kit Greene, whose beautiful old Rhodes classic yacht *Maruffa* was sadly lost in New Zealand. Kit generated a quiet serenity and the exceptional atmosphere on board *Maruffa* remained the same even when the young crew members changed here and there.

I had a similar feeling when I first stepped on board *Her Ladyship* in Las Palmas harbour before the first ARC. At first glance the spick and span 49 foot Hallberg Rassy looked like a standard production boat with blond stalwart young Norwegians busy on her deck. Only a folded wheelchair in the corner of the cockpit gave any clue to the exceptional man who is her skipper.

Ernst Torp has been a racing man all his life, sailing in many three-quarter ton races, including for the Norwegian team in the 1975 Admiral's Cup. As well as sailing, Ernst had been involved with

The happy atmosphere which prevails on board Her Ladyship *is entirely due to Ernst Torp's positive attitude to everything.*

the Royal Norwegian Yacht Club and the Norwegian Yachting Association, producing their racing programs on computer. The onset of multiple sclerosis put an end to his serious racing career, although he has been fighting the disease gamely for over fifteen years. However, Ernst is not one to be daunted or confined to his wheelchair a minute longer than necessary. No longer able to race he decided to go cruising, not in spite of his handicap but because of it, determined to keep sailing, see more of the world and enjoy himself while he still could. The ARC caught his imagination with the idea of being able to be competitive again. Even if the ARC was a 'fun' race, Ernst was determined to put in a good performance and assembled a crew of friends and relations.

There are few special arrangements on *Her Ladyship* except wider steps down from the cockpit, extra grab rails and hand holds. Ernst was able to cope with most aspects of sailing the boat including handling sheets in the cockpit, steering and the navigation. He is also a keen amateur radio operator. There was no doubt who is the captain on board this ship. It is only the foredeck work that he has to leave to the younger members of the crew.

Down below *Her Ladyship* revealed what was then an unusual feature on a cruising boat, but one which I am sure we will see plenty more of, a compact computer system. Computing is both Ernst Torp's profession and his passion, and he has computerized almost everything on board *Her Ladyship*, from crew lists to the budget and kitty. He has also devised a special cruising program similar to a ship's log, which stores details of previous passages and projections for future ones. Ernst Torp has his own software company in Norway, which among many other things has developed sailing programs for yacht clubs and associations. Even while cruising he follows his profession by writing articles for computer magazines.

It was inevitable of course, but Ernst took the ARC organization in hand and soon was producing updated lists of the boats, sorted by length, class, country or however we wanted them. Even on the morning of the start, while others were doing their last minute provisioning, Ernst was busy at his computer, entering late ARC arrivals and deleting those who had not shown up.

Ernst's racing experience stood him in good stead as he took *Her Ladyship* across the Atlantic in a very creditable 16 days and 8 hours to be the seventh boat to arrive in Barbados out of a fleet of over 200, an excellent performance by any standards. He reckoned he could have made it even faster if he had kept a more northerly course as did another Norwegian boat *Aquarion*, a 42 footer that beat *Her Lady-*

ship by 21 hours. Keeping radio contact with *Aquarion*, which had as navigator an airline pilot with a keen nose for the weather, Ernst had chickened out of staying north as *Aquarion* did during the last week and had dipped down on a more southerly route, which he later regretted.

Ernst was joined in the Caribbean by his wife Brit and their daughter. Although enjoying sailing, Brit had been unable to take time off from the physiotherapy clinic she runs at Puerto Rico on Gran Canaria. After the ARC Race, the Torps cruised in the Caribbean and then sailed back to Norway to deliver *Her Ladyship* to Ernst's brother, who owns a half share in the boat and sails in the summer months off the Norwegian coast.

It had been because of Brit's clinic on Gran Canaria that Ernst had originally sailed to the Canaries and then taken the decision to cross the Atlantic with the ARC. The following year I was not too surprised to see *Her Ladyship* again tied up in Las Palmas and to receive Ernst's entry form for ARC 87. This time Brit had organized her life so that she could sail with Ernst, but light winds and a more relaxed attitude meant that they did not manage to improve on their time across the Atlantic. 'We cruised across quite leisurely,' commented Ernst when arriving in Barbados the second time to quite a welcome from local sailors who knew him from the year before.

A leisurely cruise for Ernst meant sailing *Her Ladyship* back to Norway the following May, so completing two Atlantic circuits in two years, a total of some 20,000 miles, something that could put many a younger or fitter sailor to shame. His future plans always depend on the state of his health and for the autumn of 1988 he planned to cruise *only* the 3000 miles from Norway to the Canaries and not across the Atlantic, but with Ernst's character and determination one never knows.

Despite his health problems, Ernst always appears cheerful and willing to play a full part in everything, even the ARC fancy dress competition, where Ernst wheeled his way at the head of a huge dragon made up of his crew. I do not know if Ernst has anything to do with it, but his boat is getting a reputation as a matchmaker, as following the first ARC, his daughter married a Barbadian participant and now lives on the island. The following year romance blossomed between one of his crew and a Canadian ARC skipper, which ended up with a wedding in Norway and guests flying in from all over the world. The pleasant atmosphere aboard *Her Ladyship* undoubtedly has something special going for it.

At the ARC 1987 prizegiving, Ernst Torp was presented with a special 'Spirit of ARC' award for his outstanding performances and for embodying the spirit of the event. He received a standing ovation from the audience for the exceptional sailor that he is and responded in typical fashion by standing up unaided to receive his prize, showing what man is capable of when he puts mind over matter.

Chapter 8

HOW MUCH OF A MACHO WORLD?

The large increase in the number of sailing boats in recent years has brought an unprecedented degree of female participation into yachting, mostly in cruising, but also in racing. However, this new state of affairs has not necessarily resulted in a significant change of attitudes. Some men appear reluctant to relinquish their dominant position on the boat, while many women accept without complaint the passive role assigned to them. Nevertheless, change is in the air and particularly among those involved in long distance cruising. Various aspects of female participation were examined in the Pacific Survey and this was backed up by observations made during the first ARC.

I had first looked at cruising from the women's point of view by interviewing forty seawives in 1979. Five years later in the survey conducted among 50 long distance cruising boats in the South Pacific, I again had a chance to reappraise how much women participated in cruising life, from decision making to washing dishes. The most important factor which I was hoping to find out was whether the majority of women were still cast in a passive role, an attitude that I regard as counterproductive and potentially dangerous in an emergency when the women might have to take over running the boat.

All the fifty yachts surveyed in various ports from Tahiti to Auckland were undertaking a long cruise and only five did not normally have a woman in the crew. On the remaining boats, forty women were questioned on all aspects of cruising with the main emphasis on their own role and responsibilities on board. All of them were willing to talk about their lives, describing both good and bad experiences, and many of their observations were clearly directed at other women who may be considering taking up such a life.

All the women interviewed were undertaking long voyages, many of them having been away from their homes for several years, so I tried to find out how many of them had been interested in sailing before the start of their present cruise. Twenty-five women stated that they had shown an interest in sailing before leaving, a few of them having sailed since childhood. The remaining fifteen had not been interested in sailing before, some having actually met their partners en route after these men had already left home and started cruising. These latter were among the ten mixed nationality couples cruising together.

Although more than half the women had been interested in sailing during their previous land based existence, in many cases the interest had been superficial and only six stated that the decision to go cruising had been entirely their idea. On almost half the boats (18), the decision had been taken jointly by the partners on a fifty-fifty basis. Two women said that they had been slightly more eager to go than their partners, while five admitted that it had been the man's idea, although they had made their own decision to go along. Nine women admitted that they had taken a very small part or no part at all in the decision making process. Of these nine women, seven found cruising had lived up to their expectations or even exceeded them. The other two women gave a qualified response, admitting some very low as well as high moments. For one of them the long ocean passages remained a traumatic experience, although she readily agreed that cruising life was easier in many respects than she had expected. Marianne Twisdale of *Pelagic II* felt very strongly that 'women should never agree to go cruising just to please someone else, but only if they really want to do it.' This valuable suggestion is borne out by the fact that over half the women taking part in this survey had played a positive role in the decision to go cruising.

Jolanthe van de Weg of Jonathan *takes a full share in all decision making. Her freelance journalistic work brings a useful contribution to the cruising kitty.*

The pleasant side of cruising life was shown by the general level of satisfaction expressed by those interviewed. Nineteen of the seawives stated that cruising had lived up to their expectations, while a further sixteen were very positive in stressing that they enjoyed this kind of life far more than they had imagined. Only three women found that cruising had not lived up to their expectations and was in fact worse. Ironically one of these dissatisfied women had been one of those who had been keener to leave than her husband. In another of these dissatisfied cases, I was struck by the tension between husband and wife and the vehemence with which the wife described her utter dislike of life afloat. Saskia Whitehead of *Cornelia*, who was among the women for whom cruising was much better than she had imagined, was distressed to see miserable women on boats and had this advice. 'If the idea of cruising doesn't attract you, don't even contemplate it.'

Labour division

As in the earlier Cruising Survey, when it came to discussing labour division among cruising partners, I found the seawives well in control of the galley, with twenty-seven among the forty women interviewed doing virtually all the cooking. Only one woman did no cooking at all, another one very little, whereas the remaining eleven had some help from other members of the crew and cooked from fifty to eighty per cent of the time.

No woman got away without doing some washing of dishes, although four admitted that they did as little as from ten to thirty per cent. On twenty boats the women did all the washing up, while on a further twelve this chore was shared equally by all. Several women emphasized how important it was not to get stuck in the galley and that much more enjoyment could be got out of the cruising life by taking more interest in sailing the boat and navigation. As Margaret Pickering of *Keegenoo* advised, 'Don't exchange one kitchen for another, but share in all the boatwork. You get more out of cruising that way.'

Some division of labour was obviously dictated by the difference in physical strength of the crew, one of the main reasons why the women on fifteen boats never touched the anchor. However, on another seven boats women claimed to do all the anchor work. It was interesting to note that all these boats had anchor windlasses, often of the electrical type. On boats with stalwart sons as well as skippers, the mothers rarely did any of the heavy work, while on fourteen boats the anchor work, like many other aspects of cruising life, was shared fifty-fifty.

Steering in and out of port was also shared equally on ten boats, while labour division was set rigidly on another ten boats whose skippers never entrusted the helm to their mates. On thirteen boats however, the women were nearly always at the helm, while the rest of the women estimated that they took the helm from ten to thirty per cent of the time. Overall, wives did more time at the helm than at the anchor, which appears to me the most reasonable arrangement for a shorthanded crew where one member is physically stronger than the other. This view was best expressed by that doyenne of seawives, Susan Hiscock, who was interviewed on *Wanderer IV* in the Cruising Survey. 'Coming into congested ports for instance, the wife should be at the helm and the man at the lines and fending off. Yet often the husbands try to make themselves look superior. It is only vanity on their part. They want to be seen to be in control.'

Compared to the previous survey, the women in the Pacific Survey were much more in evidence on deck, with only five women doing no sail changing at all, although when it came to reefing, their contribution was as limited as before. Concerning actual sail handling, two women estimated that they did 75 per cent, nine 50 per cent, and a further twelve 33 per cent, the rest doing even less, down to a minimum of 5 per cent.

Navigation appeared to have remained predominantly a male occupation, on seventeen boats the women never doing any navigation at all. Three women were the navigator on board their boats, reflecting a slight shift towards more female participation since the same issue was investigated five years earlier. Ten women told me that they did from a third to half the navigation on a regular basis, with a further ten doing less or specifying coastal navigation only. On three of these boats the crew had a routine where the skipper took the sextant sights and the mate did the calculations. On one boat, both skipper and mate did astronavigation in parallel and compared results, while another wife said that this parallel routine was applied on their boat when sailing in dangerous areas.

DEALING WITH EMERGENCIES

Many of the women were able to navigate even if they did not normally do so, as emerged from the next section of the interview, which tried to assess the way in which women could cope alone in an emergency situation if the skipper had been incapacitated.

Thirty-one out of the forty women interviewed were confident that they could navigate to a port by traditional astronavigation methods, should such an action become necessary while they were sailing offshore. Three more said they could do it using the satnav they had on board, although they would not be able to navigate using a sextant. One woman was uncertain and only five said they could not attempt any offshore navigation. This was the most marked difference compared to five years previously when out of a similar number of women interviewed, seventeen had not been able to do any offshore navigation whatsoever. It is true that the number of boats equipped with satellite navigation had increased considerably in the intervening period and this fact more than anything else gave women the necessary confidence to deal with a possible emergency.

No such marked differences were noted in the other aspects of dealing with an emergency situation when women would have to do everything on their own. Exactly the same majority as in the previous survey (38) said that they would be able to sail their boats singlehanded, only two women admitting that they were unable to do so. The majority could also deal with the anchor and chain (34) and bring the dinghy aboard. Several women said that they would have a struggle doing these jobs, but were convinced that in an emergency they could summon the strength from somewhere. Three of the women who could not raise the anchor, specifically mentioning that it was too heavy, were sailing on boats equipped with mechanical windlasses, every one of which had been rated very low by their skippers in a different part of the survey. It would certainly be to every skipper's advantage to make sure that all essential equipment on his boat can be handled by the weakest member of the crew.

Altogether thirty-five of the women thought that they would be able to put to sea alone from an anchorage, dealing with all aspects of getting underway, some specifying that they could probably only do it in reasonable weather conditions. Those who could not bring their tenders or ground tackle on board would not hesitate to leave them behind in an emergency. Once underway, twenty-six of the women on the thirty boats having self-steering gear knew how to adjust them to steer their boats, while on the nineteen boats having an automatic pilot, only three did not know how to set it. One seawife sailing on a boat without either self-steering or autopilot said that if she was forced to manage on her own she would attempt to arrange the boat to steer itself by trimming the sails.

Just as in the previous survey, the engine remained a mystery to most women, twenty-seven saying that they could not cope with the simplest repair, such as bleeding the air out of the fuel system, probably the most obvious reason for diesel engine failure. There was however a higher number of women (9) who were confident enough to tackle the engine in an emergency. Maria van Zelderen, an experienced circumnavigator on *White Pointer*, pointed out that if the engine was broken she would concentrate on sailing the boat efficiently and not waste time trying to repair the engine, perhaps emulating her neighbour moored alongside, Cristina Plantier of *Madame Bertrand*, for whom this question was irrelevant as she sailed on an engineless boat.

All these hypothetical questions were easily answered by June Macauley of *Acheta*, who had had the experience of doing all these things in just such an emergency and had to sail their boat single-handed after her husband Mac was struck down with a severe case of hepatitis. This incident emphasizes the advice given to other seawives by Pascale Fecamp of *Kalabush*. 'It is a priority for a woman to be able to sail the boat alone.' Later on I discovered that one of the women interviewed in the first survey, Liz MacDonald of *Horizon*, had similarly had to cope on her own under emergency conditions. Her husband Bruce developed blood poisoning from an infected knee and was completely immobilized in his bunk in a serious condition. This happened while the MacDonalds were on passage from Australia to Indonesia. With great trepidation Liz took over the role of captain and navigator as well as trying to nurse Bruce, and after two days of little sleep, she managed to bring *Horizon* in to anchor in the port of Kupang on the island of Timor. As Liz asked herself, 'Why did it have to happen when we were approaching Indonesia of all places? Why not New Zealand or Australia?' Her dealings with all the paperwork and officials on arrival in a country where women did not do that kind of thing, she found just as traumatic as bringing her boat safely into port. As these examples show, the possibility of the skipper becoming incapacitated while on passage is real and one never knows where and when an emergency may strike. It therefore pays all skippers to delegate responsibility to their crews and ensure that they know how to sail and navigate the boat in their absence.

LIFE AFLOAT

It was interesting to hear that few of the sailing women missed the comforts of life ashore, especially those cruising on boats equipped with hot water or a shower. An abundance of fresh water on tap, a shower or a hot bath were commonly cited as the items missed most. Only seven women really missed their shore comforts and a further six did occasionally, twenty-seven stating categorically that they never missed such things. It was noticeable in many cases that the longer a woman had been cruising, the simpler her life style had become. 'One must be prepared to do the domestic chores as one would have done them fifty or a hundred years ago, such as washing laundry by hand in a bucket,' said Marika Hantel who was sailing around the world with her husband and two young children on eighty year old *Pytheas*. 'If one is not prepared to give up the shore comforts, it's better not to go at all.'

Doing away with some of the machinery of modern living does not necessarily mean that all these women led spartan lives. Many yachts were equipped with a freezer or refrigerator and a few even had small washing machines. The galley on some yachts does not differ all that much from a kitchen ashore, being equipped with electric mixers or liquidizers, while even microwave ovens are not such a rarity on yachts any more.

During the interviews, the importance of having a good relationship with one's partner was stressed by many women. 'One should never start off on such a voyage unless you already get on well with each other ashore,' advised Irmtraud Klein of *Haubaut*. Another wife admitted that cruising had been an eye opener and she now realized that she had hardly known her husband before. Spending twenty-four hours in such close proximity obviously has an effect on any relationship and one woman observed cynically that life afloat is very good at pulling people apart. Another woman commented that the passive role played by some women in the initial decision to cruise can lead to problems later on, endangering not just the continuation of the voyage but the relationship itself.

On the positive side however, it must be stressed that in most cases cruising life had brought people closer together. The couples who had been cruising for a long time, or had done a lot of sailing together before the voyage, had a noticeably harmonious relationship. This closeness was also shown by the fact that half the women interviewed felt more dependent on their partner than they did ashore, only two women saying that they had become more independent than previously. For thirteen women their degree of dependence on their partner had not changed, while another five could not answer this question as they had never lived with their partner on dry land. Several women pointed out that life at sea was different, in that both partners are dependent on each other to a much higher degree than ashore, and have to work as a team. 'As it is us against the elements, we both depend on each other more,' said Betty Eastman of *Con Tina*.

Suggestions

To round off the interview, I asked each woman if she had any specific advice or suggestions for other women who may contemplate setting off on the high seas. Apart from general advice, many women also gave hints from their own experience on ways of making life aboard more enjoyable.

Several women thought one should have as many comforts as possible, such as a small washing machine. One wife advised others to take along practical books on such subjects as preserving food and cooking with tropical ingredients. Several women stressed the importance of women having their own interests and hobbies, especially those which had a relevance to the sailing life, such as diving, shell collecting, painting, photography or amateur radio. Some women used the opportunity that cruising offered to pursue special interests, such as one woman who studied the history and political life of the countries she visited, while another enjoyed learning languages. Several women played musical instruments and one had a special interest in astronomy – indeed, her boat was the only one on which star sights were taken regularly as part of the navigation routine.

In advising potential seawives, many women suggested that those who intend to go cruising should try and find out all they could beforehand. 'Read lots of cruising books before you leave to get an idea of what to expect,' advised Sylvia Beaurivage of *Drummer*. Several women suggested that it was a good idea to go as crew on another boat to see what sailing offshore was all about. 'Charter for at least two weeks and make an offshore passage of several days,' suggested Elizabeth Veuve of *Penelope*, who meant this advice for both men and women contemplating a lengthy cruise. As cruising is so different to life ashore, many women pointed out that one had to approach it with a positive attitude and not leave with too many preconceived ideas. Yet another suggestion was to live on board for a while before setting off, as most couples had never lived in such close proximity before.

Dana Nicholson of *Spray*, who was strongly in favour of more female participation in sailing matters and had organized a female racing team in Antigua, stressed that, 'Above all, women must believe in themselves. It is the only way of counteracting male chauvinism at sea.' This view was shared by Cristina Plantier of *Madame Bertrand*. 'Don't accept a passive role and believe that things are too difficult, but take an active interest in everything. There should be no difference between men and women on board a cruising boat.' In the end, the role of women on their boats boiled down to their own mental attitude and the attitudes of the men sailing with them. Illa Gieseking of *Lou IV*, who has sailed all her life and has been an equal partner for thirty years with husband Herbert on their various *Lou*s, has never been in doubt about the cruising life. When I asked her for suggestions she declined with a smile, saying that if she did divulge how beautiful the life was, everyone would set off and crowd the oceans.

Like many of the women interviewed in these two surveys in the Pacific, Illa found it difficult to settle back ashore and has since returned to sea in their new *Lou V*. She is not the only one among those who contributed to the earlier surveys to have departed on a new voyage, often in a new boat, joining the ranks of women with an outstanding record of ocean cruising.

Women in the ARC

Remarkably less difference between the sexes was noticeable a few years later in the first ARC, in which 80 per cent of the boats had women on board. Just over a quarter of the boats in that event (52) were crewed by a couple on their own. That the female half of the crew contributed fully to sailing their boats was brought home by the fact that two out of the first three boats to arrive in Barbados were crewed by just two people.

My own seawife Gwenda, who takes an interest in these matters, interviewed many of the women taking part in ARC 86 and has contributed to this section. The increased involvement of women in sailing is something that I am keen to promote and no more so than on my own boat. Gwenda has played an active role in the designing stage of our new *La Aventura*, incorporating many of the features that are mentioned in this chapter. It is up to women to make sure that boats are designed with them in mind.

The third boat to arrive in Barbados in ARC 86 was *Albatros* and Vera Schmidt had played a full part alongside Manfred Kerstan in bringing their 61 foot Swan across the Atlantic in 14 days to win the Prime Minister's Trophy. Many other women wondered how Vera could manage a boat of that size so easily, but in fact with all sails furling hydraulically, Vera found it easier than their previous smaller boat, a 48 footer on which they had spent five years circumnavigating the world. The development of furling gear in recent years has undoubtedly been a boon for women sailors, as are self-tailing winches, allowing not only women, but anyone with less muscle power to be more involved with sail handling.

Determined to put in a fast passage, Vera and Manfred had handsteered almost all of the 2700 miles across the Atlantic. By day they steered one hour each, but at night kept four hour watches, two hours steering and two hours on autopilot. The autopilot was also switched on at mealtimes so they could enjoy their meals together. Their disdain for the autopilot stemmed not only from their desire to sail the boat more efficiently, but also because of the heavy electricity consumption of this equipment.

Although basically a standard production boat, *Albatros* is home for Vera, so she has incorporated a few extra features for her comfort, such as a built-in sauna. For Vera, sailing hard does not mean that the comforts of life have to be sacrificed.

The ARC, although a fun rally, uncovered a competitive streak in quite a few cruising women. Marcia Davock, author of the *Cruising Guide to Tahiti and the Society Islands*, who had been sailing the

Noelle Corbett of Sweet Dreams *shares with Gwenda the impressions of her singlehanded voyage.*

oceans for seven years with husband Mugs on their Rhodes 41 *Shearwater*, also admitted to having often handsteered during the ARC to improve their performance. 'The greatest surprise was how my comfortable cruising style evolved into a finely honed, sail-it-to-the-edge attitude,' said Marcia. She admitted that she learnt more about sailing *Shearwater* in one Atlantic crossing than in the previous 30,000 miles she had sailed on her. Bettering their expected time for the passage by two days and with almost no breakages, Marcia believes that advances in the boating industry have made it possible for a shorthanded crew to sail with more comfort, style, safety and at faster speeds than ever before.

Shearwater treated the ARC timekeepers to one of the most exciting finishes of the rally, the 20 year old boat crossing the line just one minute ahead of Alice and Howard Wright in their 30 year old, 40 foot *Ziggurat.* The two boats had been having a private duel ever since contact via the ham radio made them realize how close they were. Alice was a newly qualified radio amateur operator and very enthusiastic about its place on a boat. She is of the opinion that if the woman does not do the navigation, it is very good instead to take over the responsibility for the radio. Although sailing all her life and a veteran of several Newport to Bermuda races, Alice only studied for her amateur licence prior to the Wrights' departure on a longer cruise, of which the ARC was part. She passed her test just two days before leaving the United States, having immersed herself in the morse code all the time, even listening to tapes in the car while driving. Alice was enjoying her radio contacts not only for the safety factor, but also to relieve the boredom that sometimes sets in on a long ocean passage. The radio was also used to get messages to her family back home. During the ARC, Alice plotted on a chart all the positions of other yachts checking in to the amateur net, which she felt pushed her and Howard to make the effort to sail harder when they saw other boats making better progress.

In total agreement with Alice was Janet Murphy, an old friend from the same yacht club, who also sailed in the ARC on *Apogee.* Janet was also the amateur radio operator of *Apogee*, leaving the navigation to partner George. Louise Tapsell, on the other hand, is normally the navigator on her Trapper 500 *Whim of Arne.* In the four years that Louise and her husband Gordon had been sailing in the Mediterranean, they usually shared all the boat work equally. For the ARC they decided it would be more interesting if Louise was the official skipper. So on the Atlantic crossing, Louise not only navigated but took all the decisions, such as which route to take. Louise believes quite strongly that both partners in a shorthanded crew should be able to do everything, so as to be able to cope in an emergency. To prove her point, she has taken her RYA Yachtmaster certificate and is quite capable of dealing with anything on board, including simple engine repairs if necessary. She thinks that women have a capacity for endurance greater than men, especially where the day to day sailing of the boat is concerned.

The Tapsells did experience an emergency during their Atlantic crossing which could have cost them their mast. The bottom fitting of their jib furling system broke, bringing down the forestay and unrolling the sail. As skipper, Louise sent Gordon to the top of the mast to replace the forestay with a halyard. As the jib furling gear could no longer be used, they sailed on slowly with a small storm jib and trysail. Trying to gain more speed to reach Barbados by Christmas Eve, Louise jury rigged the sailboard sail, which she tied to the mast. It gave an extra half knot, but that was not quite enough and *Whim of Arne* only arrived on Christmas morning.

Louise was not the only female skipper in the event and one of the others, Noelle Corbett of *Sweet Dreams*, attracted much more attention. Normally cruising with husband Jim, on the eve of the start, Noelle decided she would like to try and singlehand in the ARC. 'It is something I had always wanted to do and at that moment it felt right, both within myself and with the boat.' Having sailed *Sweet Dreams*, a Moody 33, for four years in the Red Sea and Mediterranean, Noelle felt confident about her boat, knowing 'every creak and groan, what the boat could do and couldn't do.' Jim Corbett, who found a crewing passage on another ARC boat, encouraged her and his full support was a great help.

Noelle found singlehanding very tiring at the beginning as she tried to sleep in the day and keep watch at night. Her biggest problem was when the spinnaker wrapped itself around the forestay and she had to go up the mast to unravel it. Slowly she worked out the best combination of sails with which both she and the self-steering could cope best. She found it quite frustrating having to rethink the normal ways of doing everything to be done by just one person. In fact Noelle was not quite alone, as she had kept her dog Joe with her. Having Joe to be concerned about stopped her thinking too much about herself and so she experienced no real down moments or loneliness.

Noelle's determination to sail *Sweet Dreams* well brought its own reward, as she beat the nine male singlehanders in the ARC to carry off the singlehander's trophy. Having acquired a taste for racing,

Noelle went on to acquire a light displacement boat, *Outrageous*, in which she competed in the 1988 Carlsberg Singlehanded Transatlantic Race from Plymouth to Newport. She certainly demonstrates what can be done by women if they are determined enough.

Most of the women mentioned so far were experienced sailors with several years of sailing and other ocean passages behind them. However, also sailing in the ARC were several women for whom this was their first ocean passage. Several of them admitted that they would not have taken part if it had not been for the sense of security engendered by the event. According to Lorris Chrisope, 'It put my family at ease, my mother had qualms about our crossing the Atlantic, but being in an event like the ARC reassured her. It was an extra security factor.'

Apart from some sailing on the Great Lakes, Lorris was a complete novice when she and Ron bought their 37 foot Nauticat *Camelot* while working in England. Gradually the plan evolved to sail *Camelot* home to the United States. After a quick cruise around the Mediterranean, in which the Chrisopes had little chance to meet other cruising people, Lorris found the atmosphere in Las Palmas very supportive. 'I found out that other people had the same problems as me and that there were solutions to them. The tips and suggestions made both by the organizers and other cruising people were invaluable.' When Ron was hospitalized in Las Palmas with a serious leg infection the week before the start, Lorris became very depressed, worrying that there might be a recurrence of the infection while they were at sea. For this reason, at the last minute they decided to take on another couple as crew. The presence of another woman on the boat also encouraged Lorris and she found the passage less boring and tiring than when they had sailed alone. In Barbados she arrived a far more confident sailor, sure about her own style of cruising and also with the sense of having accomplished something.

The example of Lorris confirmed an observation that I had made on several occasions in the past, that women often seem to gain support from meeting other women in similar circumstances, and maybe more so than men, feel the need to communicate with others. Taking crew for long passages may be one solution for those who are inexperienced or worried about coping on their own.

Another novice who had sailed little before the ARC was Paula Swan, sailing with Nigel Lennard on the 30 foot catamaran *Guzzledown*, the two of them sailing alone and not taking on extra crew. Paula also found that the atmosphere in Las Palmas helped her, both meeting other novices as well as those who had done

Atlantic crossings before. Not only did it give her confidence, but also helped in practical matters, such as calculating the amount of stores and what were good things to buy when provisioning. When she heard someone else refer to his wife as the 'baggage' he carried on board, her spirits lifted. There were other women out there just as bad as she was. Sailing with a very experienced sailor and navigator as Nigel was, Paula was extremely tense during the crossing. Aware of her own inexperience, she was frightened she might do something wrong, especially when it was her turn on watch. In fact she did not do anything wrong and *Guzzledown* arrived safely in Barbados with a good enough time to win a prize.

Anne Tiemann of *Antares II* was another woman who admitted to being apprehensive before setting off, mainly because the Tiemanns had two small children of 4 and 1½ sailing with them. With night watches split between her and husband Olaf, she found occupying the children all day extremely tiring. Many women faced with this problem do take on extra crew for a long passage, as did Tina Moss on *Jenny M*, who sailed with her three children. Although the children were older (13, 12 and 10) and so were more able to amuse themselves, Tina found the crossing much easier with crew as she did not have to do the sail handling that she normally did, as well as keeping everyone fed with proper cooked meals.

Conclusions

From the number of children who now sail with their parents, both coastal and offshore, it is obvious that the situation will continue to change, with more and more women having sailing experience from childhood. It has become increasingly clear in succeeding ARCs that women are playing a fuller role in sailing, as daughters sail with fathers, mothers with sons as well as with friends and partners. From speaking to many of these women it is evident that some consider it a priority to see that certain features are incorporated on their boats to suit their requirements, whether at the designing, building, buying stage or in modifying their existing boat later on.

First and foremost is the ease of handling, such as installing winches powerful enough for the sails to be handled by female muscle, or even to winch the man up the mast if necessary. Self-tailing winches are also easier to use as they can be operated with two hands. The difference in physical size and strength between male and female cannot be denied or ignored, but women have already proved that they can sail singlehanded around the world or participate in major ocean races, so there is no reason why a family cruising boat should not be able to be handled by the woman in the crew. It is also a matter of safety for all the crew.

A divided sail plan with smaller sails, whether it is a cutter, ketch, staysail ketch or yawl, might well be more suitable for family cruising, than expecting a woman to be able to handle the huge sails on a tall masted sloop. Jib furling gear is well worth considering for its ease of handling, as is any other aid which can help the weaker sex. Even if the woman does not normally plan to handle the sails, she may have to do this in an emergency.

Another feature to consider is the anchor and particularly the type of windlass fitted. Even if the anchor work is normally done by the man, that does not mean that the anchor will decide to drag only when the man is on board. An electric windlass is another piece of equipment much favoured by women. From the surveys as well as the ARC it is apparent that on many boats the women spend as much if not more time at the helm than men. For cruising couples, the most sensible procedure when entering or leaving a port, is for the woman to be at the helm, freeing the stronger male to jump around throwing lines, fending off, dealing with the anchor, giving directions or whatever else needs doing. It not only makes sense, but is more efficient. Therefore it is worth paying attention to the steering position and the visibility from it. It is surprising how many boats have been apparently designed by tall men with tall men in mind, where it is difficult for a smaller woman to have an unrestricted view over the cabin top towards the bow.

Although women are participating more in sailing, on most boats the galley remains very much their domain. For this reason the galley should come in for critical attention. It is not necessarily an advantage for it to be spacious, often the more compact and snug the better. A lot will depend on people's own requirements, whether one will be only making small snacks at sea or attempting a full scale dinner for guests in port. If anything more than basic cooking is envisaged the cooker should have at least two burners and preferably an oven too. The sink and cooker should be conveniently close to each other and it should be easy to serve from the galley to the table or wherever one will be eating.

Moving up on deck, the aspect of deck safety should be considered, especially if planning to sail with children. Points to look for are sufficiently wide side decks, a lack of things to trip over, grab rails on the coachroof, sturdy pulpits, pushpits and strong lifelines, all features that provide something solid to hold onto when moving around the deck and lessen the risk of falling overboard. If the boat has a high freeboard, it might be difficult for a smaller woman to get on and off from a dinghy, and quite dangerous if carrying or helping a small child. A ladder built on the stern or a transom platform are both factors that make boarding safer. A transom platform is also useful for swimming from and can be a safety factor for anyone falling overboard, making it easier to get back on board.

Having been interested for many years in the level of female participation and speaking to so many women involved in cruising has made me realize just how much women have contributed to many of the outstanding voyages that have been made in small boats. However, just as in life ashore, in order for their contribution to be recognized, women have to be more assertive, make their voices heard and not accept to be cast in a secondary role. Admittedly they have to overcome a certain amount of prejudice in what is still a male dominated world, both ashore and afloat. There are even still a few yacht clubs where a lady member cannot enjoy the same rights as her male counterparts. How deep some of these preconceived ideas are was brought home to me during ARC 88, in which several yachts had female skippers. One of them, Patricia Beard, an experienced sailor and owner of *Blue Cornflower*, was told by her insurance company that as the boat had a female and not a male skipper, a minimum of three experienced crew apart from the skipper would be required for the Atlantic crossing, not two as usually stipulated, otherwise they would not insure her. I cannot think of a better example of male chauvinism than this request from an insurance company based in a country that is governed by a female Prime Minister and ruled by a Queen.

Chapter 9

THE STORY OF ARC

Every year as the cruising season in the Mediterranean and Western Europe draws to a close, hundreds of boats prepare to leave on the long transatlantic voyage to the Caribbean. A popular point of departure is Las Palmas in the Canary Islands, where provisioning is good and the steady north east trade winds of the winter months are not far away.

Following on from the cruising surveys I had undertaken in other parts of the world, in November 1985 I went to the Canaries to interview a sample of 50 skippers about their preparations and expectations for this major ocean passage, the result of which was the Atlantic Survey. The atmosphere in Las Palmas during the final days of preparation was full of excitement, although a trace of apprehension crept into the voices of some skippers, as they wondered what awaited them on the long and often lonely passage. The

Grandstand view for the Naval escort at the start of ARC 87.

warm camaraderie among all the voyagers crossed lines of nationality, income or age, as they shared the same hopes and fears, joys and problems. It was not difficult to transpose myself backwards in time to when I had been in a similar position, setting off on my first long ocean passage with the responsibility of two young children on board. Moored next to us in the Canaries had been a French family in a similar situation and the friendship we struck up as we both prepared for the Atlantic crossing remained wherever our sailing tracks met and we are still close friends today.

It was this atmosphere in Las Palmas among the cruising boats that gave me the idea of organizing a friendly fun race across the Atlantic, as a way of maintaining the links between boats and the friendships made in port, as well as being a way of relieving some of the monotony of a long passage. Although one of the thoughts behind the event was to add some zest to the long passage, another consideration was to increase safety and confidence, especially among those making their first long ocean passage.

Having been at the start of many major ocean races from the OSTAR to the Whitbread, I have seen the enormous changes that have taken place over the years, as boats have become more and more high-tech racing machines, light years away from normal cruising boats. The difference has grown to be equivalent to that between Formula 1 racing cars and the family saloon, even reflected in the name Formula 40 for the racing multihulls. In the same way that few keen drivers can ever hope to enter a Grand Prix, so ocean racing has become so professional and expensive that few ordinary sailors can hope to take part in these events.

I wanted to create an event that returned to the amateur spirit of early ocean races, such as the singlehanded race now known as the Carlsberg STAR, but which had first started as a bet between friends. In recent years, ocean racing has come under increasing commercial pressures, so that the fleet of competing boats often look like floating billboards plastered with advertisements. To avoid these pressures and to try and ensure that only genuine cruising boats entered the event it was decided not to allow any sponsorship of individual boats or advertising by the competitors. However, sponsorship of the race itself was not precluded, and support from interested organizations and companies was welcomed, as long as they were prepared to accept the amateur nature of the race. In that way it was hoped that all competitors would benefit equally.

The name ARC, an acronym for Atlantic Race for Cruisers, was chosen because it also represented the idea of an arc bending across the Atlantic Ocean. Las Palmas de Gran Canaria was the most convenient place for the start because of its good provisioning and capacious harbour, while Barbados was the logical landfall from which the participants could start a Caribbean cruise. That the time was ripe for such an event became apparent as soon as the idea was launched and hundreds of enquiries began flooding in from all parts of the world. I had envisaged interesting maybe fifty boats, but four months before the start over 250 yachts had registered and the list of entries had to be closed. Although the race had been thought of with boats that were planning to cross the Atlantic anyway in mind, it soon became apparent that some people were entering just to be in the race itself, especially those with faster production boats or elderly racing boats, hoping for a victory they could not achieve in other races. It also nudged a few, who had been leisurely pottering around the Mediterranean for several years, to take the plunge across the pond. Making the start in the Canary Islands also ensured that everyone had sailed a decent distance offshore and that boats and crews were more tested than if they had been leaving from a mainland port. Eventually 209 yachts from 24 nations lined up for the start in Las Palmas on Saturday 29 November 1986, making the ARC the largest transocean race ever staged and earning it a place in the *Guinness Book of Records*.

AN ARC ACROSS THE ATLANTIC

For many of the participants, the atmosphere of the event had begun long before the start in Las Palmas, as they had sailed down from Northern Europe, the English Channel, the Mediterranean and even from the east coast of the United States, meeting other competitors in anchorages and marinas along the way. By the time they reached Gran Canaria, many already knew each other, and if not, soon did in the congenial atmosphere of Las Palmas. Fiestas, folklore concerts and fireworks were just some of the entertainments put on by the municipal council of Las Palmas, which helped to coalesce the ARC participants into one large family. The fun spirit was set going by a dinghy race in the harbour as well as a fancy dress competition, which showed the ingenuity of some participants in improvizing original costumes out of the gear carried on board.

Amidst the parties and gaity, a certain tenseness pervaded the atmosphere as crews prepared their boats for the long ocean passage, working hard to ensure all equipment and gear was in good working order, checking and repairing sails, buying and storing provisions for the weeks ahead. The less experienced and first-timers found encouragement and advice from those who had crossed before or who had sailed across other oceans.

It was a moving moment when the Barbados flag was hoisted by special permission on the Spanish naval ship *Villa de Bilbao* and the President of the Canary Islands, Señor Jeronimo Saavedra gave the signal for the start. As the yachts jostled for best positions along the mile long start line it was evident that the racing bug had already bitten many of the cruisers, most of whom had never taken part in a race before. The bay of Las Palmas filled with hundreds of sails sparkling in the sunshine as the boats fanned out and sped on their way.

One of the main aims of this race for cruising boats was to bring all the boats and crews safely across from one side of the Atlantic to the other without the tragic losses that have marred some other ocean races. From the 209 yachts from 24 nations that entered the race, four withdrew and returned to Las Palmas shortly after the start, while one skipper decided halfway across to abandon the race and make for another destination. No serious mishap occurred among the 204 yachts that completed the course, which was undoubtedly the most satisfying achievement.

Although promoted as a fun race across the Atlantic, the fun was very much restricted to the time spent in port and the safety aspect was taken very seriously both by organizers and participants alike. One of the few rules stipulated that every yacht must be in the possession of an EPIRB (Emergency Position Indicating Radio Beacon) and liferaft. Many participants were thus forced to either buy this equipment or have their existing ones serviced. In several instances the batteries on the EPIRBs were found to have run down long before the expiry date, while two liferafts were discovered on inspection to be in such bad condition, that the owners decided to replace them with new ones.

As many people appeared to have joined the ARC for the feeling of security it provided, it was decided to operate a VHF emergency net during the race. All participants were requested to listen to Channel 16 at two specified times morning and evening. The idea was that if anyone had a serious emergency, for which outside assistance was necessary, a message could be relayed by VHF until a yacht was reached that was equipped with long range radio and could pass it on to the outside world. Although a few emergencies did occur, these were dealt with promptly within the fleet, usually by consultation with one of several doctors who were sailing in the ARC.

The VHF net was doubled up by a more far ranging net run by the forty amateur radio operators sailing in the ARC. As well as keeping in contact with several amateur radio nets, Peter Rodenburgh of *Blyss II* and Zeke Holland on *Ace of Hearts* ran an informal net for all the boats heading west, which likening to the cattle drives of the past, they called the Rawhide Net. This net was a great success and provided enjoyment for many of the participants as well as adding to the overall safety.

These amateur operators kept in touch not only with each other, but also with the Transatlantic Maritime Mobile Net, which provides a daily weather forecast and also keeps track of yachts that check in. The Rawhide Net also kept contact with several radio amateurs in Barbados, who were thus able to predict the arrival of these yachts with great accuracy. SSB marine radio operators also kept in touch with each other by means of an informal net.

Although the safety aspect was uppermost in the minds of the organizers, it was also hoped the ARC would give an added interest to the long passage. The dormant competitive spirit aroused among the cruising fraternity had certainly been underestimated, as it soon became clear that many people were taking the fun race very seriously indeed.

However, no one was able to predict the arrival of the first yacht in Barbados and many were taken by surprise when the 53 ft trimaran *Running Cloud* crossed the finishing line at 0600 on Saturday 13 December, 13 days and 22 hours after the start. As the only trimaran in this mostly downwind race, *Running Cloud*'s fast passage was to be expected and it helped underline the excellent times put in by the next two arrivals. Only five hours later, the line was crossed by Michael Gluck's *Moonshadow*, a Deerfoot 62 designed mainly as a comfortable cruising yacht. *Moonshadow*'s achievement was almost overshadowed by that of *Albatros*, when the 61 ft yacht sailed in at midnight the same day to the welcoming cold rum punch that awaited all arrivals. Circumnavigators Manfred Kerstan and Vera Schmidt undoubtedly had the experience to sail the mighty Swan on their own, but it also took a lot of stamina as they chose to handsteer *Albatros* most of the way across; their victory on handicap in Class A and Prime Minister's Trophy was fully deserved.

By Sunday noon, the whole of Barbados had warmed up to the event and a steel band had been provided by the Board of Tourism to welcome the arrivals in a special area of the port, which had been set aside especially for the ARC. A huge shed had been cleared of containers, which were then used to block off the entire area from the rest of the harbour. The Barbados Port Authority had arranged a reception area in which all facilities were provided for the ARC yachts: customs, immigration and health officers, bank, telephone, tourist information, bar, restaurant, mail delivery, showers, toilets and plenty of fresh water on the dock. Everything possible was done to welcome the participants and Mount Gay Distilleries had someone on hand day and night to greet the crews with cold rum punches and a presentation pack which included even more Mount Gay rum.

The fourth boat to arrive and first in Class B to cross the finishing line was Tim Aitken's Centurion 47 *Airwave*. Although recording excellent fast passages, the first four boats had all been expected to do well, but it took everyone by surprise when Pål Stiansen sailed the 41 ft *Aquarion* into Bridgetown only 19 minutes after *Airwave* to complete the crossing in 15 days 11 hours. Pål had made the decision to take the more northerly great circle route instead of sailing south to pick up the trade winds and his gamble had paid off. After 15 days, the arrivals started accelerating, nine boats completing the passage in 16 days, fourteen in 17 days and twenty-two in 18 days. The order of arrivals however continued to surprise everyone, with small boats and shorthanded crews often arriving before much larger boats with bigger crews. Outstanding were Stuart Feinblatt who sailed his 33 ft *Desire* across the line in 17 days to take line honours in Class E and Erkki Lempiainen, who also took the great circle route to astonish everyone by bringing his 26 ft *Alfa* across the Atlantic in 18 days.

As the number of arrivals gained momentum, the group of local sailing enthusiasts keeping watch 24 hours a day off the finishing line were treated to some exciting finishes. The most spectacular finale was between two well matched boats, *Oyster Lady* and *Roter Baron*. For the last 50 miles they had engaged in a nailbiting duel which continued right up to the end, when *Roter Baron* sailed across the finishing line only a few feet and two seconds before *Oyster Lady*. The following day 41 ft *Shearwater* and 40 ft *Ziggurat*, both 20 year old boats crewed by couples on their own, provided another exciting finish, Marcia and Moore Davock sailing *Shearwater* over the line only one minute ahead of Alice and Howard Wright's *Ziggurat*.

Marcia and Moore, who have been cruising for seven years and had already crossed the Pacific and Indian Oceans, were among those long term cruisers who admitted that they had put in a much greater effort because they were in a race than they would normally have done on an ocean passage. The fast average times achieved by most participants showed that cruising people know how to race their boats when the opportunity is offered them. Compared to the times recorded by the 50 boats in the Atlantic Survey who crossed along the same route at the same time the year before and in almost identical conditions, the average times for boats of the same size were three to four days less in the ARC. Some boats however just carried on cruising in their normal style, which accounted for the slower passages made by some boats. This was reflected in the number of blown out sails and broken spinnaker poles among the early arrivals and the lack of gear breakdown among those who took their time. Fortunately there were few mishaps and no dismastings, although booms were broken on four boats. The only boat to request assistance was *Blue Trout*, a 50 year old wooden boat which was taking on water and had engine problems. Fortunately another boat, not in the race, stood by until *Blue Trout* came safely in.

To cope with the problem of trying to match heavy displacement boats some 50 years old with the latest cruiser-racers off the production line, a special cruising handicap was devised, attempting to keep to the simplest of parameters and not to involve too many complicated measurements, yet to take into account all the factors that can affect cruising performances. A time correction factor was worked out for each boat and the elapsed time of each arrival was multiplied by this factor. As with all handicaps it attracted some criticism, usually from those who felt they have been penalized too heavily. It did become apparent though that the cruising boats who received prizes in their classes on handicap had all put in excellent times for their particular boat.

The 43 ft *Flamingo* sailed in to Barbados in 19 days 11 hours, an excellent time for a heavy ketch displacing 17 tons. For several days until the final results were calculated it looked as if she was going to carry off the overall prize on handicap. Eventually Hanspeter von Allmann, Renate Busch and one year old Veronika had to settle for second place overall, but had the satisfaction of winning their class and the Barbados Port Authority Trophy. Hanspeter and Renate were the kind of people that the ARC has been designed for. Cruising for two years in the Mediterranean on their previous 33 foot boat, the arrival of Veronika forced them to move up in size to accommodate all the extra gear demanded by a baby. They bought the 12 year old *Flamingo* in 1985 and for one year cruised the Atlantic coast of Europe before making their way to the Canaries to join in the ARC.

The eventual winner of the ARC on handicap was the Finnish yacht *Molla III*, also sailed by a family crew. Kari Hynninen, an electrician from Helsinki, had fitted out the 30 foot hull himself and was making a circuit of the North Atlantic with his wife Mariella and eight year old son Toni.

A rather unexpected excitement was provided by the large number of whales sighted during the crossing. Several yachts reported meeting with large pods of whales, while two boats *Molla III* and *Summer Wind* actually hit whales, although without damage to the boats. The triple keeled steel *Summer Wind* wounded the whale they hit, which distressed Lyn and David Charles considerably as they had only recently joined the Greenpeace campaign to save whales. For both crews it was a frightening experience, as other whales approached them after the incident and they both started their engines, which eventually persuaded the whales to leave them alone.

A lucky escape was also had by Choy Choy, one of two cats sailing on *Lionheart.* Curled up in the folds of the genoa, Choy was unnoticed by Henry Graham one black night as he hoisted the sail. Hearing a plop in the water, it took a moment for him to realize that Choy had been catapulted overboard into the dark water. The Grahams quickly dropped sails and motored back on a reciprocal course, although not very confident that they would find Choy. After motoring for about 15 minutes calling her name, they heard Choy shrieking and homed in towards her cries. Eventually they managed to make out a small bump on the surface and as they closed in, Choy swam towards the boat and clung to the self-steering paddle until Henry managed to fish her out with a fishing net. At the prize giving ceremony in Barbados, Choy Choy received a special prize for the most heroic cat, a dinner of two flying fish.

The greatest attraction of the ARC however, was not the prizes but the framework it provided for people to meet each other and socialize, regardless of age, language, financial means or sailing experience. The docksides in Las Palmas and Bridgetown became a concrete example of what cruising is all about, as crews made friends not only among fellow participants but also among local people. The reception extended to the ARC fleet both in Gran Canaria and Barbados greatly contributed to the friendly atmosphere as local authorities, yacht clubs and people generally went out of their way to make the visitors welcome. A prime example of Barbadian hospitality was given by Alison and Bill Hoad who invited all 24 children who had taken part in the ARC to a Christmas party in their home, complete with Santa Claus and presents for everyone.

Apart from the cruising families, more than three quarters of the ARC boats had women on board and the high level of female participation was unprecedented for an ocean race. This female presence was felt especially in the social side of the event, which was accentuated by many of the participants' friends and families flying into the Caribbean for Christmas in the sunshine.

A better finale to the first ARC could not have been anticipated as the last of the 204 yachts sailed into Bridgetown less than one hour before the presentation party on 1 January, bringing the ARC to a successful close. Not even the first arrival received such an impressive reception as David Shipton who spent 33 days singlehanding his 24 ft *Dunkers* the 2700 miles from Gran Canaria and found most of the participants assembled in Barbados to greet him.

The fun aspect of the ARC was evident at the prize giving ceremony when the merits of some boats and crews were recognized that had nothing to do with speed. The most appreciated prizes were those awarded to people like Chuck Hoffman of *Schussboomer*, for being the most helpful skipper, and to Ernst Torp, the skipper of *Her Ladyship*, for his help in computerizing the ARC lists in Las Palmas.

There were many other prizes which reflected the not so serious side of this amateur race. The prolonged cheers at the end of the prize giving ceremony when participants were reminded that the ARC had tried to be a true reflection of the Olympic spirit showed that this aim had been achieved against all odds. It was symbolic that the only Spanish competitor, Jorge Brosa of *Ave Phoenix*, flew the Olympic flag, not only because he came from Barcelona, venue of the Olympic Games in 1992, but also because he was a firm believer in the Olympic principle, that taking part is more important than winning.

By the end of the presentation party, it was clear that ARC had become one huge family and the memories that most participants carried away with them as they sailed on was not only of a keenly fought ocean race, but also of the good time they had and the many new friendships made. Almost all the boats kept their blue and yellow race pennants flying high, so as to easily recognize fellow ARC participants. The ARC atmosphere carried on wherever they sailed, both in the Caribbean and beyond.

SECOND TIME AROUND

As the yachts started gathering in Las Palmas for the second ARC, there was a certain apprehension in the air. Could that special atmosphere of the first fun race for cruisers ever be recaptured? Would the lessons learned and suggestions made by participants in the first ARC make for an easier smoother time? What new problems might loom ahead in dealing with the crews of nearly 200 yachts?

The first visible result of the success of ARC 86 had been an improvement in the facilities in Las Palmas, a benefit for all yachtsmen using the port, not only during the ARC. More pontoons, showers, hot water and telephones had been laid on and the harbour area cleaned up, shrubs and trees planted. This time the authorities *believed* me when I said that 200 yachts were coming. A comprehensive list of repair facilities was on hand and following press coverage of the first event, several marine manufacturers had sent personnel to service or repair their equipment prior to the start. With excellent provisioning in the city, Las Palmas de Gran Canaria is undoubtedly the best place from which to prepare for an Atlantic crossing.

As the port started filling up, the individualistic nature of cruising folk soon became apparent. Big and small, old and new, almost every type of boat was on display, from old gaff schooners to sleek

A cool welcome for Jorge Brosa of Ave Phoenix*, the sole Spanish participant in the first ARC.*

new cruiser-racers. The smallest boat was the 24 ft *Augsy*, normally sailed by Peter Augsdorfer on one of the large lakes near Munich in Southern Germany. At the other end of the spectrum was Mikael Krafft's *Gloria*, a 126-foot schooner built a couple of years earlier in the style of the luxury yachts of yesteryear. Built over seventy years ago was the classic Norwegian ketch *Tirrenia*, while not quite so old, but well known was the Nicholson 38 *Cohoe IV*, which once belonged to that doyen of small boat voyagers, Adlard Coles, and which is depicted in his classic book *Heavy Weather Sailing*. However, the vast majority of the boats were standard production boats in the middle of the range.

The variety of boats was matched by the variety of people from 25 different nationalities. Again there was a large female participation and on the sole Indian boat *Jaykus III*, Ujwalla Rai, always immaculate in her sari, showed all the women how graceful a lady can be while boarding from a dinghy or clambering across rafted boats. Nearly 30 boats were crewed by a couple on their own and 25 children under 16 accompanied their parents on other boats, the youngest being 8 month old Philip Wheeler on *Admiral's Lady*. Philip's father had increased the Wheeler family for the crossing by taking along his brother and sister as additional crew. The family nature of the event was evident on many boats where adult members of the family joined as crew. George Fraizer sailed *Tuppence* alone with his daughter Katherine as Philip Benson on *Tina III* did with son Matthew. Ian Maiden took along his two daughters among the crew on *Fanfare*, while Marshall King skippered *Seareign* for his mother Heather and on board *Idefix* William Matthieu sailed with his son-in-law. No skipper as yet has joined the ARC sailing with his mother-in-law, but the day will surely come.

The fact that most cruisers taking part had family and friends for crew meant that there were a lot of disappointed would-be crew members hanging around the harbour in Las Palmas hoping to find a berth. A few people did take on extra crew at the last minute, but this did not always work out, some skippers finding out that it is not easy to get on with someone you do not know when you are at sea for such a long time.

In Las Palmas the atmosphere slowly started to coalesce as a series of pot luck dinners for each class brought people together. Liz Hermann of *Halcyon* rounded up SSCA members for a get together, while Anita and Tom Kintz threw a Thanksgiving party for the American contingent on the wide decks of their catamaran *Sundsvalla*. The dozen boats that had participated in the Canary

Islands Rally around all seven islands, which took place prior to the ARC, took over one of the pontoons and showed what the atmosphere of international camaraderie was all about. Karsten Witt, the skipper of *Gunvør*, making his debut at the children's knot making competition, showed talent as a compère and was immediately co-opted for the fancy dress competition and whenever a Master of Ceremonies was needed. The town of Las Palmas provided folk dancing shows, marching bands and a carnival atmosphere. It seemed difficult to think about the serious business of sailing.

It soon became clear, however, that many of the participants were taking the ARC very seriously indeed. In an attempt to make it clear that the ARC was something different and not just another ocean race, the name was changed from the Atlantic Race to Atlantic Rally for Cruisers. This change was made on the suggestion of many participants in the first ARC, who felt that Rally best described the atmosphere of the event and who were afraid that because of its success the event would go the way of other ocean races, which have ended up by being dominated by commercial interests. The change of name seems to have been too subtle for some, for the controversy between those who wished to race and those who only came along for the fun of it continued unabated. It is almost impossible to satisfy both factions. Nevertheless, the ARC has also shown that an increasing number of cruising sailors want to make faster passages and are no longer content to plod along at a respectable 4 or 5 knots. The average time taken to cross the Atlantic has been getting less over the years and even non-racing minded ARC participants have shown what a difference it can make if a yacht is sailed efficiently. Cruising does not mean that one should lie back and not make any effort to sail one's boat as efficiently and quickly as possible.

As a result of the detailed questionnaire filled in by participants in the 1986 event, as well as changing the name from race to rally, it was decided to have two starts in 1987, so as to give smaller boats a better chance to reach Barbados before Christmas. Fifty-six yachts under 35 ft LOA therefore left Las Palmas de Gran Canaria on Wednesday 25 November with the 134 larger yachts starting on Saturday 28 November. The early start gave the smaller boats not only the advantage of three days but, as it turned out, more favourable weather conditions with many small boats recording relatively better passage times than larger yachts. The Saturday starters met with strong winds and rough weather at the beginning which the smaller boats escaped.

Unusual weather conditions prevailed in the North Atlantic

during the latter months of 1987, which affected the weather all the way down to the equator and the NE trade winds which normally are found south of latitude 20 °N during the winter months were absent in December. Instead participants had to contend with light winds and several days of calms.

While light winds disappointed those all out for a fast crossing, others were happy to enjoy a more comfortable and pleasant passage than they had expected. It also reduced the number of boats arriving in Barbados with broken spars, blown out sails and other equipment failure.

The light conditions favoured the lighter displacement boats and those not loaded down with the gear that those cruising for longer periods carry with them. It was no surprise when only 12 days and 23 hours after having left Las Palmas, the light 45 ft trimaran *Rusty Pelican* arrived in Bridgetown to a rum punch welcome by the Minister of Tourism and Sport, the Hon. Wesley Hall, thus winning Class O, the open class which had been created for yachts that did not fit into the main ARC event. Line honours in the ARC went to Herbert Dahm's 72 ft monohull *Inspiration* who took 14 days and 15 hours to complete the 2700 mile course.

The second yacht to cross the line to an enthusiastic welcome was one of the early starters, *Bruggadung*, a 32 ft locally designed and built boat flying the Barbados flag. *Bruggadung*'s participation in the ARC had focused the attention of the entire island population on the event and both local radio and the press published daily reports on her progress. From an event regarded previously by many Barbadians as an outside phenomenon, the ARC was suddenly transformed into a national event. After *Bruggadung*, but in real time two days faster, the next arrival was Herbert Dahm's *Inspiration*.

Inspiration would have arrived sooner had her owner not insisted that she complete the entire crossing without using the engine. In line with the rally philosophy of the ARC, no engine restrictions were imposed in 1987 and the choice to sail or use the engine when the wind dropped was left entirely to each skipper. Although this decision was disputed by some skippers, who felt that they were put at an unfair disadvantage by their motorsailing colleagues, the overall results did not bear this out and some of the fastest passages were recorded by those who had *sailed* their boats most efficiently. In spite of the fact that in December 1987 winds were much lighter than usual, many yachts recorded fast passages, the first 75 yachts making the crossing in three weeks or less. Nor were these only the larger boats, as a fair number were participants in Class E, sailing boats under 35 ft. Perhaps the most remarkable performance was that of *Kobold*, a Nantucket 32 laden with stores and cruising gear that took only 18 days 17 hours for the crossing. Also in Class E was the overall winner of the ARC on handicap, *Silent Running*, a Freedom 33 skippered by Mark Bromhead who crossed in 19 days 14 hours.

For many sailors however, sufficient reward for their crossing was not winning a prize but a safe arrival and a welcoming rum punch provided by Mount Gay. Although Barbados lacks a marina, a section of the commercial harbour in Bridgetown had been made available for the ARC as in the previous year and facilities such as a bank, travel agent, laundry service as well as two bars, one providing light meals, were laid on in a large shed normally used for container storage. A large Christmas tree reminded the crews of the season and on several evenings steel bands, a jazz band or discos provided musical entertainment for the arriving yachts.

While early arrivals celebrated, many were still at sea slowed down by the light winds. In spite of a recommendation that enough water and provisions be carried to cope with any possible emergency, several skippers banked on a faster passage or underestimated the amount they consumed. At least three yachts arrived in Barbados without water and several others arrived with both food and water at a critical level, while on one of the yachts running out of water, the crew also had had nothing to eat for two days. On this boat this was due entirely to fear of adding more weight than necessary, a racing mentality not welcomed in the ARC. In the other instances it was either lack of experience or, in one case, a leaking water tank. All participants had been advised by the organizers to victual for a passage which could take as long as four weeks, or even more in an emergency such as a dismasting or some other serious breakage. Fortunately none of these boats had any serious problems to delay them any further.

One such emergency that did delay a boat was *Tosca B*'s loss of the rudder. About 100 miles from Barbados, Ray Murton noticed a complete lack of response from the steering. The tiller was moving from side to side without the slightest resistance from the rudder, which felt as if it did not exist. On inspection he found that this was true. For some unknown reason the rudder stock had sheered and the spade rudder of the Dolphin 31 had simply fallen off.

Realizing that they had a serious emergency on their hands, Ray put out a call on the VHF radio, which was immediately picked up by *Maria Two*, another ARC yacht which happened to be in the vicinity and fortunately had long range radio. While *Maria Two* alerted race control in Barbados, another two ARC yachts, *Sundsvalla* and *Sunbeam Chaser*, stood by the stricken yacht in case they were needed. In the meantime, Ray and Valerie Murton had managed to improvize a jury rudder which allowed them to steer a roughly NW'ly course, which unfortunately was slowly taking them away from Barbados. In the end *Tosca B* was towed in by *Beachcomber*, a large motorsailer on its way to Martinique, whose Swiss skipper Karl Sauder decided to make a detour to help a fellow sailor in need. The *Tosca B* incident showed the value of this feature of the ARC, which helps yachts with only VHF radio to reach the outside world when necessary.

Unfortunately some disasters cannot be avoided whatever safety measures are in force. Due to a navigational error, the 33 ft *Bamaca* hit a reef off the east coast of Barbados and although the crew got ashore safely, the boat was lost. This incident dampened the festive spirit, but reminded everyone of the perils of the ocean and that one can only relax when safely in port.

As the small boats started from Las Palmas three days before the rest of the fleet, many of the larger yachts were overtaking smaller yachts all the way to Barbados. The skipper of one large yacht equipped with a powerful radar was surprised to find that several small yachts he passed in visual range did not show up on his radar. Calling up the skippers on VHF he was surprised that some admitted to having dismantled their radar reflector as they considered it unnecessary during the Atlantic crossing while others didn't have a reflector at all. Following my own observations during the Canary Islands rally when boats without properly mounted radar reflectors failed to give a clear signal on an advanced Navy radar, it was decided to introduce a new rule making a correctly mounted radar reflector compulsory.

One of the ongoing problems of organizing the ARC is to reconcile and satisfy the different kinds of cruising people, those who come along to race and to win and those who come along for the fun and the safety in numbers. It is a problem that can never be resolved completely satisfactorily. The explanation for most of the controversy but also the reason for its continuing success is that people join the ARC for various reasons. Some do so for the safety provided by a large number of yachts crossing the Atlantic at the same time when help is always near should the need for it arise. This was shown during ARC 87 when the daily VHF, SSB and amateur radio nets again proved their worth. Many participants stated that they would not have crossed the Atlantic without the ARC, as it gave them both the courage and the impetus to take on the challenge of an Atlantic crossing. This was particularly true for many of the wives and mothers who would not have crossed with their partners if it had not been for the support the ARC framework gives. Others join the ARC for the chance to pit their skills against other sailors in similar yachts. They may subscribe to the rally philosophy when they join, but once the starting gun is fired in Las Palmas they do their utmost to win.

One of the most stringent regulations of the ARC is that the owner must be on board for the rally, so as to maintain the amateur nature of the event by excluding professional crews. This ruling has tempted several owners into accomplishing a transatlantic passage instead of having their boat delivered to the Caribbean by a delivery crew. There are also those whom the ARC is helping fulfil a dream. As 76 year old Paavo Lassila, skipper of *Monsoon III*, put it, 'It is my last chance to sail across the Atlantic. I crossed sixty years ago as a boy on a sailing ship and it is something I have always dreamed of doing again.'

Not only was Paavo Lassila the oldest ARC skipper at 76, but he was also the fastest among the 15 skippers over 60. The oldest participant was 78 year old Allen Skarne of *Three Generations* who solved his family's worries about his health by taking his doctor along for the crossing. As an afterthought he also shipped an orthopaedic surgeon in case he had troubles with his two knee caps which had been patched up after a ski-ing accident when he was in his late sixties. There were six over seventy year olds sailing in ARC 87, each of whom received a special award from the Barbados Board of Tourism. They certainly demonstrated that sailing is a sport where age is no impediment to either performance or enjoyment.

In an attempt to make everyone happy, the sailors who had raced hard across the Atlantic and put in good performances were awarded prizes either on speed or on handicap. For those who took their time there were plenty of other prizes, such as the Kellner family, who received a prize for the most helpful crew, as they organized the collection for the crew of *Bamaca* and raised several thousand Barbados dollars. There were prizes for the youngest, oldest, slowest, most polite and even for the most troublesome skipper, on his own suggestion. As the previous year at the prize-giving ceremony, honoured by the presence of the Prime Minister of Barbados, the Hon. Erskine Sandiford, the ARC came together into a whole. The Prime Minister in his speech summed the atmosphere up in saying that the politicians of the world had much to learn from the unity of so many people from so many nationalities joined together in a common pursuit.

As the yachts started leaving Barbados for their myriad destinations, the feeling of being part of the ARC family had won over, the blue and yellow pennant continuing to decorate many a halyard as a way of recognizing fellow participants. For many cruising skippers there was the satisfaction of knowing that they had sailed their yachts well in one of the pleasantest ways to cross the Atlantic Ocean.

INTO THE ARC, TWO BY TWO

In a rally where the boats are as varied as a Folkboat and a Jongert 2200, it is not surprising that the skippers and crews are just as distinctive as their boats. A true cross section of society in respect of age, profession or income is represented in the ARC, a reflection of the cruising population as a whole.

The changes that have taken place in the modern world have also changed the people who go cruising. Improved communications, mobile office facilities, telex and facsimile transmission are all available, which has allowed some businessmen to be able to run their affairs from a yacht almost as well as from an office. Tim Aitken, former chairman of TV-AM and a businessman of long standing in the City of London, described ocean sailing as more challenging than setting up a business deal. Taking part in both ARC 86 and ARC 87, Tim rose to the challenge and brought his *Airwave* into Barbados among the first boats each year.

Nowadays sailing offshore does not necessarily mean being out of reach, it is a question of choice. There are still plenty of sailors who choose to sail offshore because they like to be out of reach. Taking a sabbatical year or a longer gap between appointments is no longer frowned upon by society. Another factor which has changed the composition of the cruising population is the trend towards earlier retirement. In my earlier surveys there was always a sprinkling of retired Service personnel, who had used their gratuities to buy boats, but by the time the ARC took place this phenomenon had spread to many other professions as well. On the other hand the young skipper of *Laga* had just finished his univesity studies and was taking a few months off to cruise in the Caribbean before taking up his first job. He had told his prospective employers what he wanted to do and they were prepared to hold the job for him.

Improved air links and comparatively cheaper fares has also meant that people can cruise in stages, leave their boat in a marina somewhere and fly home to work and return to cruise for another month or two later on. Some people have obviously arranged their lives very carefully so as to gain the maximum enjoyment. Notable were the Bowra brothers, who co-own *Odins Pleasure*, winner of the 1987 Prime Minister's trophy on handicap. The brothers also run a group of companies in England in the construction and engineering business. While one brother is sailing, the other runs the family business and vice versa. So it was Chris Bowra who brought *Odins Pleasure* across in the ARC, while Tony Bowra sailed her back in the TRANSARC from Miami to Gibraltar and managed to win the Rock of Gibraltar trophy for the overall winner on handicap.

Family cruising is obviously a distinctive feature of the present scene. In ARC 86 exactly one quarter of the boats were crewed by a couple on their own and quite a lot more by couples with their children, young or grown up, or other family or friends sailing with them. In ARC 87 there was a slightly smaller proportion of couples sailing on their own, mainly as a result of the insurance companies making a new ruling that they will not insure boats for a transocean passage unless there is a minimum crew of three experienced persons.

The excellent performances and times put in by some of these shorthanded crews surprised a lot of people, especially some of the younger skippers sailing with large crews. It was no surprise to me however, as I knew only too well the toughness and endurance of most long distance cruising people, as well as the teamwork that comes with experience of the same boat or the same crew.

ALBATROS

No better example of these qualities could be given than by Vera Schmidt and Manfred Kerstan who sailed their elegant 61 ft Swan *Albatros* to Barbados in 14 days 16 hours, being the third boat across the line. In the Mount Gay Regatta *Albatros* showed her paces and friends crewing on her from other boats wondered how a couple on their own could manage a boat of that size so easily. In fact with all sails furling hydraulically, petite Vera found it easier than their previous *Albatros*, a Swan 48. Manfred owned the first *Albatros* for twelve years, during which time he and Vera spent five years on a circumnavigation. They had taken the same route to Barbados in 1979, but spent 19 days making that passage, so they were very pleased to have clipped five days off their previous time.

A car dealer from Berlin, Manfred leaves his business in the hands of his son for most of the year, although usually returning for several months every year as a break from cruising and to allow his son to take a holiday. Having sold their house in Germany, *Albatros* is Manfred and Vera's only home and because of that they decided to move up in size from 48 to 61 to provide more home comforts.

Basically a standard production boat, *Albatros* does have a few special features, such as being the first Swan to have a built-in sauna. There was little time to use it, however, during the ARC.

Determined from the start to put in a fast passage, Vera and Manfred were deeply disappointed the first day out of Las Palmas when they lost their spinnaker, a loss they calculated cost them at least a half day overall. Not deterred, they got the best out of *Albatros* by handsteering almost all the 2700 miles.

Manfred did admit that they made more effort because of the ARC. He pointed out that normally they would have reefed that little bit sooner or not paid such close attention to their various instruments if they had been cruising. It is not always a lack of sociability that dictates the absence of additional crew on these boats, but sometimes a question of efficiency. Almost as soon as they arrived in Barbados, Vera and Manfred had friends join them to cruise in the Caribbean. However on passage they rarely take crew, as Vera says she always ends up spending more time looking after the crew than sailing the boat, which is what she really enjoys.

Bouncing Czechs

While Vera and Manfred cruise in style, others do not have the same resources at their disposal. Yet some people cruise equally successfully at the other end of the scale. At the ARC 86 prizegiving ceremony, some of the loudest cheers were heard when a special prize for the most popular crew was awarded to Anna Smidova and Pavel Strasil of *Lyra*. Many of the ARC participants had met this small boat flying the Czech flag as she made her way through the Mediterranean towards the Canaries. Arriving in Las Palmas with only 11 dollars left, Anna and Pavel managed to replenish the kitty by sewing Barbados courtesy flags for other yachts. After provisioning the boat for the transatlantic voyage, there was no money left to buy the compulsory EPIRB. This fact was disclosed at the skippers briefing held before the start and immediately two skippers offered to give *Lyra* their spare EPIRBs. It was a gesture that brought tears to Anna and Pavel's eyes, who had already been overwhelmed by the generosity and warmth of their fellow sailors.

Their popularity among other competitors stemmed not only from their good humour and constant smiles, but from their courage and determination to achieve what they did on so few resources. Never once did they ask for any special consideration because they had less money than anyone else. They showed that anything is possible if one really wants to do it. It was not difficult to imagine Pavel and Anna in twenty years time sailing a yacht like Manfred's, who himself had similarly fled from East to West Berlin to start a new life a generation earlier.

'Cruising is what freedom is all about,' declared Pavel on the eve of the start. 'So much has been said about the *free world* but only those who sail the high seas and taste this kind of life really understand the true concept of freedom.'

For Pavel and Anna, who were both in their early twenties, freedom became a reality the moment they launched *Lyra* in Yugoslavia and pointed the bows of their 24 footer west. It had taken them several years of patient waiting to obtain permission from the Czechoslovak authorities to take the boat they had built themselves for a three week holiday to Yugoslavia. Once the permission was received they loaded *Lyra* on an ancient truck and made a beeline for the Adriatic. Immediately after launching *Lyra* on the sea, they turned their backs on the Yugoslav coast and headed straight for Italy and the Western Mediterranean, picking up casual work whenever they could, for as refugees they had left everything behind and were penniless. In Spain they heard about the ARC and decided to join as they were already planning to attempt a transatlantic voyage. The further west they sailed, the more confidence they gained. In the Canaries, Pavel confided that they had decided to use the ARC as a first leg of a voyage to the USA, as they had just secured an American entry visa.

An arc of hope brought Anna and Pavel of Lyra *across the Atlantic from behind the Iron Curtain.*

By the time *Lyra* reached Barbados, which she did in a very creditable 24 days for a small home built boat, Anna and Pavel were talking of a voyage around the world.

Yet as they set off from Barbados to cruise in the Caribbean, a little something intervened to change their plans. Anna discovered that unbeknown to her she had been carrying a third person across the Atlantic, the first ARC baby. So following a distinctly nautical wedding aboard a friend's trimaran, where even the priest came barefoot, Anna and Pavel settled in St Thomas in the US Virgin Islands, started an upholstery business and sold *Lyra*, which was obviously going to be too small for three people to live on.

Even though their boat had been only 24 feet, they had still brought all their skiing equipment with them across the Atlantic, so after several months in the Virgins and following the birth of their son, they were on the move again, this time to Montana. They had found a life of tropical sunshine too difficult to bear without any change of seasons and without any snow, keen skiers that they are. Whatever they decide to do in the future, and the dream of a bigger boat is still lurking in their minds, they are the kind of enterprising and hard working young people who are bound to succeed.

SCHUSSBOOMER

As the name of the boat implies, the skipper of *Schussboomer* also has another great passion besides sailing, that of skiing. Chuck Hoffman was able to pursue both his favourite activities from his home at Lake Arrowhead, a mountain resort only a couple of hours drive from the Californian coast. Tennis should also be included; as a keen tennis player, he had organized many tournaments, particularly in Palm Springs, where he coached several Hollywood stars. All these sporting activities, however, were in his spare time from his career as headmaster of the Lake Arrowhead Elementary School. Some measure of the esteem he was held in, but which he is reluctant to mention, was that on his retirement the school was renamed the Charles Hoffman Elementary School.

A competitive sportsman, who has brought his four sons up in the same way and whose home is adorned with trophies and plaques, he failed to win anything in the ARC to add to this collection, but instead ran off with one of the most important prizes, that for the most helpful skipper.

Sailing has always played a major part in Chuck's life and on his previous boat, a 36 footer, he would cruise most summers with his family down the Californian coast to Mexico. As a young man he had even worked in Mexico salvaging wrecks and his Spanish was fluent, which was of use to him in Las Palmas during the ARC. With retirement, like for so many people, he had more time on his hands to pursue his dreams, one of which was to cruise in the Mediterranean. The logistics of getting his own boat there were too complicated, so he sold it, took advantage of the strong dollar and came to look for a yacht in Europe. He found what he wanted in Mallorca in the shape of a 12 year old Swan 38. He bought her and spent a year happily cruising around the Mediterranean with his wife JoAnn. Although not planning to cross the Atlantic for another year, when the ARC came along, the sportsman in him could not resist the temptation of racing across the Atlantic as a way of getting his boat back home.

Schussboomer was one of the first boats to arrive in Las Palmas after a fast four day passage from Gibraltar, during which the stern gland cracked and water poured into the bilge as fast as the crew could pump it out. The boat had to be slipped immediately on arrival in the Canaries, but in spite of these problems, by the time the ARC office opened, Chuck had *Schussboomer* and his crew well organized and ready to go. His talent for organizing others exercised throughout his teaching and tennis careers had shown through.

With great patience and always with a smile on his face, Chuck helped in many ways to get the first ARC off the ground and onto the ocean, even dipping into his pocket from time to time and refusing to accept recompense. He ran errands, collected forms, chivvied other skippers along, helped make up the packs for the skippers briefing and was always there asking what else he could do to help.

Chuck, like quite a few other skippers, found the Atlantic crossing a little rougher than he had anticipated. Halfway across a broken luff foil, broken boom and ripped sail following a gybe marred any chance he had of winning a place and the rest of the passage was sailed with a small jib. On the other hand, JoAnn, like a few other wives, had opted out of the crossing and flew in to Barbados to resume their cruise. Following a trend among West Coast sailors they eventually trucked *Schussboomer* home from the Atlantic coast of the USA instead of taking the long route through the Panama Canal and against the prevailing winds up the coast to California.

Bounder

While some prizes, like Chuck's for the most helpful skipper, were a surprise to the winner, others were decided even before the fleet left Las Palmas; all the recipient had to do was get to the other side, sometimes with a little help from the rest of the crew. Alex Plummer laid claim to that of youngest competitor when he joined the crew list of *Bounder* in Las Palmas two months before the start and he never had any serious competition. His parents Lyn and Brian Plummer were not at all concerned about sailing in the ARC with such a young baby. In fact they found it easier than on their passage down from Falmouth to the Canaries when Lyn was heavily pregnant and Brian had to virtually singlehand. Pleased with his Freedom 40, Brian commended the boat as being easy to handle on his own and he had clocked up some fast passages.

Lyn and Brian had bought *Bounder* in Falmouth in 1985 with the idea of sailing her back home to their native New Zealand after many years of working all over the world. At last they were realizing a dream for which they had been saving hard, to buy a cruising boat of their own. An electronics engineer, Brian has worked in various countries over the last 13 years, most recently in Italy. He first started sailing as a child in New Zealand's beautiful Hauraki Gulf and kept up his interest by chartering yachts in different parts of the world. Lyn was also a wanderer, having taught English in Iran, Spain and Italy, although she and Brian met up in New Zealand when both of them were on separate visits back home.

Like many participants, the Plummers were incorporating sailing in the ARC into their longer term cruising plans. They intended spending a leisurely two years sailing home, including six months in the Caribbean and then via Venezuela to the Panama Canal, followed by the classic trade wind route across the Pacific.

Alex's arrival on the scene had done little to change his parents' plans. As Brian pointed out. 'A baby is not a good enough reason to deter anyone from doing what you really want to do.' Only one of them at a time was needed to take care of Alex, leaving the other parent to cope with the boat, although they did take on an extra crew member for the Atlantic crossing. As if proving the point that a boat is a perfect cradle, a contented Alex slept through our entire conversation and only with great difficulty was roused for a photo session. The youngest competitor was set to take the Atlantic Ocean in his stride.

The picture was rather different several months after the ARC when Lynn wrote, 'Alex can now pull himself up on the cockpit coaming, grab the winch and be standing before you've lifted your eyes from the compass. Now as well as needing three pairs of hands for sailing, we need another six to look after Alex.'

The Plummers had taken on Peter Lock as crew in Las Palmas to help them on the Atlantic crossing. It was one of the successful arrangements and Peter stayed with *Bounder* throughout their cruise in the Caribbean as far as the Virgin Islands. A retired professor of English Literature, I suspect Peter had a hand in the selection of limericks handed to me in Barbados, which the crew of *Bounder* had composed to while away the long Atlantic crossing. The LimerARCs sum up the spirit of the ARC and its people and a selection from them are a fitting end to the chapter.

ARC is precisely what made us
Set out in a fleet for Barbados
  The race is for fun,
  The best line is rhumb
With the spirit of Mount Gay to aid us.

Columbus had entered the *Pinta*,
She wasn't exactly a sprinter.
  But Jimmy said 'No,
  You're *sponsored*, and so
You must go on your own, and next winter.

Another to enter was Noah
His ARK was considered a goer.
  But the animals mating
  Diminished his rating
And the ARK and his chances sank lower.

Christian Fletcher entered with Bligh,
And *Bounty*, like *Bounder* could fly;
  But with the men that you start
  You must finish the ARC —
Half crew in a dinghy don't qualify.

Captain Cook in the good ship *Endeavour*
Didn't pay enough heed to the weather.
  His speed was terrific,
  He crossed the Pacific
Missing ARC and Barbados forever.

Captain Ahab and friend *Moby Dick*
Knew they'd get there exceptionally quick.
With a whale them to tow
To Barbados they'd go.
Hoping no-one discovered their trick.

The racers in sloop, ketch and schooner
Will certainly get there much sooner.
But 4 knots is a winner
For catching your dinner
Of bonito, dorado and tuna.

Mark Bromhead and Maureen Boyd of Silent Running, *overall winners of ARC 87.*

INDEX